Per Ardua Ad Astra

*To the memory of my brother-in-law
Flight Lieutenant David Jackson and a good
friend Flight Lieutenant Alastair Gillan.*

Per Ardua Ad Astra

A HANDBOOK OF THE ROYAL AIR FORCE

Philip Congdon

Airlife

ENGLAND

Copyright © Philip Congdon 1987

First published 1987
by Airlife Publishing Ltd.

Congdon, Philip
    Per ardua ad astra : a handbook of the Royal Air Force.
    1. Great Britain.   *Royal Air Force*
    I. Title
    358.4'00941   UG635.G7

    ISBN 0-906393-89-2 Hardback
    ISBN 0-906393-98-1 Paperback

Parts of this book have previously been published under the title Behind the Hangar
Doors — Sonik Books 1985.

Printed in England by Livesey Ltd., Shrewsbury.

Airlife Publishing Ltd.

7 St. John's Hill, Shrewsbury, England.

Contents

Acknowledgements

I am indebted to the following personalities for their support and encouragement in preparing the second edition. Mrs Jean Buckberry, College Librarian, RAF College, Cranwell; Wing Commander Menzies Paterson, RAF (Ret'd); Wing Commander J. Sheldon, BSc RAF, OC Training Wing, RAF Swinderby; Wing Commander T. Cohu, RAF, Wing Commander Training, RAF College, Cranwell; Wing Commander J. Young, BSc Dip PEd, OC Administration Wing, RAF Shawbury; Colonel M. K. Kee, CD, Defence Liaison Staff Canadian High Commission, London; Brigadier D. F. Ryan, OBE, Royal Artillery Institution, Woolwich; Squadron Leader P. Charlton, MC, RAF, HQ East Midlands Wing, Air Training Corps; Squadron Leader P. Giles, RAF VR(T), HQ East Midlands Wing Air Training Corps; Squadron Leader V. Walker, WRAF, RAF College, Cranwell; Squadron Leader D. N. Wiklund, RNZAF, Air Staff HQ, Wellington, New Zealand; Flight Lieutenant J. F. Barter, RAF, OC Recruit Grand Defence Training, RAF Swinderby; Flight Lieutenant L. O'Dea, RAF, Department of Initial Officer Training, RAF College, Cranwell; Flight Lieutenant I. Smith, RAF, OC Military Field Training, RAF Swinderby; Observer Lieutenant Commander (W) J. L. Major, BA, HQ Royal Observer Corps, Bentley Priory; Warrant Officer Brian Carmody, Royal Australian Air Force, Canberra, Australia; The Staff of the National Defence HQ, Ottawa, Canada; The Air Historical Branch Royal New Zealand Air Force, Wellington, New Zealand; C. H. Munday Ltd. of Oxford; Corporal Battye and SACW Gooding (photographic help), RAF Swinderby; Mr Michael De Rose (line drawings) of Bardney, Lincolnshire; Mrs J. L. M. Smith of RAF Swinderby for the historical photographs from her late father Wing Commander L. R. Robinson's collection, and Flight Lieutenant A. Thompson, RAF VR(T), for his personal collection of Air Training Corps photographs. Finally this book would never have been completed without the support of my wife who painstakingly proof read the text.

Ministry of Defence   July 1987.

Preface

As a result of the success of *Behind the Hangar Doors,* Airlife Publishing Limited have undertaken the production of this second, much enlarged and revised edition.

Every chapter has been fully revised in the light of new information and where possible there are fully updated drawings and new photographs. In addition and at the request of the Ministry of Defence (Air) chapters have been added which provide an insight into commissioned and non-commissioned service in today's Royal Air Force. Lest we should forget I have also included a new chapter entitled 'The Other Royal Air Forces' which is dedicated to the memory of former members of the Commonwealth Air Forces who have supported the Royal Air Force throughout its brief history to date and whose sacrifice in war gave us victory.

I hope to further revise and update this book in the years to come and if any of my readers feel that they have something to offer, to shed new light on the facts that have been recorded, I would be more than delighted to hear from them. To those who wrote to me following publication of the first edition I thank you for your constructive comment which was fully taken into consideration before typesetting this edition. To those contemplating a career or short service engagement in the Royal Air Force, I would say that there is no better profession and your aspirations will be amply rewarded.

PSMC

Chapter 1
Birth of a Service

Throughout history man has had flirtations with flying. All too often the dull, resounding thud of man impacting with ground, was a salutary reminder that he was perhaps attempting the impossible. Eventually, technology and enterprise, coupled with a great deal of daring and courage, turned the impossibilities of yesterday into the reality of an infernal contraption that enabled man to fly.

This brief introduction to the Royal Air Force takes up the story of military aviation after the spadework of actually getting machines into the air, albeit briefly, had been achieved. In 1880, the British Army first began to show an interest in balloons as a result of the military use of balloons for observation in both the American Civil War (1860-65) and the Franco-Prussian war of 1870-71. During both wars, balloons, tethered from a windlass, hoisted artillery spotters aloft, who were then able to see into enemy territory to direct a bombardment onto hitherto unseen areas. Whether, because of the unsporting nature of such activities, British reticence, or the belief that 'if soldiers were to fly God would have provided them with wings', the War Office was slow to latch on to the idea. But by 1880, what was good for the Continentals was good for the British Army. A balloon school comprising men of the Royal Engineers (RE) was opened at Chatham, to be followed in 1882 by the opening of a balloon factory at Aldershot. Progress in ballooning skills was slow but steady, and their value came to be recognized during training exercises. The first successful use of British military balloons was recorded during the Boer War.

The advent of a reasonably reliable internal combustion engine at the turn of the century provided the technological know-how to move military aviation a further step forward. An engine could turn conjoined paddles, or propellers, to move a balloon forward. But the added weight of an engine required greater surface area of balloon for lift. For aerodynamic reasons and following much head scratching, the shape of the balloon changed from that of an orange to that of a sausage and greatly increased in size. The description of the vehicle also changed from balloon to airship.

The first military airship was the *Nulli Secundus*. She was 120ft long and 30ft in diameter, and was powered by a 40hp engine with a top speed of 16 mph. Most important of all, she could be steered and directed. Her first successful flight was on a bright autumn day in October 1907. Military flying was now on the move.

At Farnborough, where the balloon school was located, the achievements of the Wright

Nulli Secundus at Farnborough in 1907 heralding powered, directional and controlled flight

brothers in the United States inspired Colonel S. F. Cody to achieve sustained powered flight. Cody was later joined by Colonel J. E. Capper of the RE, with Lieutenant J. W. Dunne of the Wiltshire Regiment soon to join the team. In concert with the civilian designer Alliott Verdan-Roe, members of the team pooled ideas and resources and developed a number of aeroplanes. The centre of their activity was the motor racing track at Brooklands in Surrey. The air-minded men of the Royal Navy, on the other hand, had got together at Eastchurch and by 1909 had begun training pilots. At Larkhill on Salisbury Plain the British Aeroplane Company had established a civil aviation school.

At first, flying machines were treated by the military with some hostility, for the threat they posed to the established ways of Army life. Many regarded flying simply as a sport — few saw its military potential. For all naval and military aviators of that time, flying and the upkeep of airfields and facilities was a private expense. But, War Office recognition was soon to come.

On 28 February 1911, a special Army order was issued announcing the formation of an air battalion of the Royal Engineers with effect from 1 April. Flying was no longer to be treated as an 'officers' sport' but rather as a military skill. Two RE companies, one concerned with airships and one with aircraft, formed the battalion establishment under the command of Major Sir Alexander Bannerman. The headquarters of this new unit was at South Farnborough. Not to be outdone, the Royal Navy was soon to follow the Army's lead and in December 1911 formed the first Naval Flying School at Eastchurch.

Arising from these two key developments, a sub-committee of the Committee of Imperial Defence sat to consider the future of the two air services. The committee recommended the formation of a single Flying Corps, comprising a Naval and Military Wing but with a central flying school. Finally, a permanent Air Committee was to deal with all matters concerning aviation in the two services. The recommendations were accepted and on 13 April 1912 a Royal Warrant proclaimed the formation of the Royal Flying Corps (RFC). The Naval Wing carried out flying training and experiments with seaplanes, airships and land planes, while the Military Wing concentrated on land planes. At first, it was arranged that officers for the Military Wing of the RFC would be appointed from any branch of the Army. The non-commissioned ranks of the Military Wing were provided from the two companies of Royal Engineers that formed the Air Battalion in 1911. Pilots for the new Corps came almost exclusively from the commissioned ranks, as it was considered most unlikely that men of the right quality could be found among the rank and file. A riding background was considered a distinct advantage for potential pilots, as the practical skills necessary to control a horse were deemed not unlike those necessary to fly an aircraft.

The first task confronting the new Corps was to train sufficient pilots, as in January 1912 a quick tally had revealed only eight qualified Navy pilots and eleven Army pilots. There was no shortage of applicants for the RFC and training rapidly progressed. The political intention of the new Corps was that it should be a separate branch of the armed forces, but of equal status to both the Army and Navy. The Senior Service did not readily accept such an arrangement and to make its views known established the headquarters of the Naval Wing of the RFC at Eastchurch, with the commander of the base assuming overall authority. Moreover, the Navy soon bypassed the Central Flying School to do all its pilot training at Eastchurch. Such action ultimately led to divided loyalties within the Corps. By 1913 there appeared to be little in common between the methods of training of the Naval and the Military Wing, and by late 1913 the Admiralty dropped the Corps official description and began the unofficial use of the title 'Royal Naval Air Service' (RNAS). This situation was formalized on 1 July 1914. The Royal Naval Air Service came into its own and the Military Wing sub-title was dropped simply to become the Royal Flying Corps, but now to be considered by many as a corps of the British Army.

At the outbreak of war on 4 August 1914 Britain entered the fray with two separate air services. It was felt that the division of the air services would benefit military and naval aviation, but the reverse was more often true. Each Service would argue its own case for the limited supply of aircraft and supporting equipment, with frequent squabbles in the resulting disharmony. It is not surprising that at the outbreak of the First World War British aircraft were totally devoid of defensive armament. As an interim measure, both pilots and observers (when carried) were issued with pistols; some also took rifles and a daring few even carried hand grenades to drop over the enemy trenches. By early 1915 machine-guns first became available for aircraft armament, but their effective use presented many difficulties. Arranging for the gun to fire forward through the propeller without shooting the propeller off, and dealing with the spent cartridges blown back into the cockpit, were just two of the problems faced by those pioneers. These and many other problems were gradually overcome, and the RFC and RNAS grew in stature and strength, performing magnificently throughout the Great War.

Both Services had expanded to meet the global commitment of world war, and each was establishing its own tradition; however, at government level all was far from well. Politicians were concerned by the friction and chaos that resulted in attempting to co-ordinate and maintain the two air services. In July 1917, depressed by the situation, Lloyd George appointed a special committee to examine the air services situation. The chairman of the committee was the South African statesman General Smuts. Five weeks after its appointment, the Smuts Committee made its recommendations, which included the formation of an Air Ministry to control air power matters, and the formal amalgamation of the two air services. The Government then appointed the Air Organization Committee to act upon the recommendations of the Smuts Committee. On 29 November 1917, King George V gave his assent to the Air Force Bill. All that was now left to do was to dot the i's and cross the t's in the plan to form a new Air Force. On 2 January 1918 the Air Ministry came into being. The following day Viscount Rothermere was appointed as Secretary for the Air Force and President of the Air Council. From the ranks of the Royal Flying Corps Major General Sir Hugh Trenchard was appointed Chief of the Air Staff. On 1 April 1918 the Royal Air Force was formally constituted as the third fighting service of Great Britain.

Any history of the Royal Air Force should strictly begin six months before the Armistice and the ending of the First World War. The fighting history of the service has been more than amply recorded. The history of the RAF from that time to the present day is contained in this book. This history follows the evolution of the RAF through the medium of the customs and traditions, the airfields and the subordinate organizations that have arisen since that grey morning in April in the fifth year of the Great War.

Chapter 2
The Construction Miracle

Among the achievements of air power in this country little has been said or written about the gargantuan task of constructing military airfields. Like many other architectural landmarks, military airfields are now taken for granted as part of our landscape. The reason why they have been so readily accepted and accommodated into our way of life is a tribute to the civil engineers who designed them. Those who have served in the Royal Air Force will know of the high quality of personal comfort that station accommodation provides. The careful use of standardised building designs meant that no matter what station an individual was posted to, the chances were he would already be familiar with the layout of the building and thus soon settle down to his work. But the greater distinction must go to the construction workers, who in ten years between 1935 and 1945 constructed five hundred and forty permanent airfields in the United Kingdom. If the temporary airfields constructed solely for D-day are also included, the total figure swells to six hundred and eighty four. The vast majority of these airfields (75%) were constructed the length of our eastern and southern shoreline. For the United States Air Forces alone facilities had to be constructed to host sixty heavy bomber groups flying B17 Fortress and B24 Liberator aircraft, fifteen groups of medium bombers and twenty five fighter groups. The airfield construction programme is said to have been the biggest civil engineering programme ever undertaken in our nation's history. No book about the RAF would be complete without recording and acknowledging the contribution made by the civil engineers, who in providing the airfields made possible the feats achieved by the RAF and allied air forces.

Some early airfields have disappeared for ever, such as Marske airfield south-east of Redcar, which first opened for civil flying in 1910 and remained in operation until 1919; and Seaton Carew, which opened in late 1914 and closed in 1919. Other stations, such as Central Flying School at Upavon (which opened in 1913), Catterick (1914) and Duxford (1919), survived the First World War and were subsequently developed and enlarged to become the monuments to aviation that we know today. The construction of military airfields before and during the early stages of the First World War took place on an entirely *ad hoc* basis. Flat ground with a firm surface and good drainage were obvious prerequisites, as was site isolation

Between the World Wars design. The Georgian look barrack block (1931), RAF Old Sarum.

The 1935 standard power house design.

to reduce the risk of aircraft crashing on houses. In 1914 the Secretary of State for War, Lord Kitchener, became responsible for the requisition of land and the siting of airfields. Whether as a legacy of the Army's preoccupation with horses, or just by coincidence, racecourses were often chosen as likely airfields. Racing over the sticks, therefore, took on a new meaning at Doncaster, Beverley, Redcar, Thirsk, Lincoln, Ripon and a host of other racecourses. In policy terms, airfield construction for the Royal Flying Corps (RFC) was dealt with under two headings: permanent and temporary. Permanent stations were purpose-built, such as Netheravon and Eastchurch. Temporary airfields were built using canvas 'Bessoneaux hangars' for aircraft and wooden 'Armstrong huts' for personnel. One of the early brick First World War hangars, constructed in 1916, can still be seen at Helperby, south of Thirsk in Yorkshire. The bowed wooden roof of this hangar is a fine example of the carpenter's art. Helperby closed in 1918; it was used only for storage between 1939 and 1945. At Royal Air Force Andover, Catterick, Cranwell, Duxford and also the RAF Museum at Hendon, further examples in the evolution of hangar design can be seen. One of the most successful designs was the 1917 brick style buttressed hangar given the name 'Belfast Type', because of the Belfast roof trusses. An example of this type of hangar can be seen at Bracebridge Heath (now a 'cash and carry' store) near Lincoln.

The construction of the first military airfields was not just a result of the need to train pilots, though training stations were undoubtedly

required. The sleepy empire that had rested its defence on mastery of the sea was to have a rude awakening. On 16 December 1914, battle cruisers approached the north-east coast of England under cover of a dense sea mist. The flotilla's target was the port of Hartlepool, with its surrounding industrial complex. An intensive thirty-five minute ship to shore bombardment took place which resulted in one hundred and fifteen dead, untold lighter casualties and considerable damage to the dock facilities. The next target was Whitby's coastguard station, followed by the barracks at Burniston and then Scarborough. Pandemonium broke out in the War Office and the Admiralty, and after some furious paper shuffling Royal Flying Corps (Naval Wing) airship sub-stations were hurriedly opened along the east coast. Their task was to provide both early warning and aerial defence. Indeed, for a brief period the aerial defence of Great Britain was placed in the Naval Wing's hands. However, if the enemy were to continue to use fog and mist as cover, it would be unlikely that the Navy's airships would see anything; always presuming that the weather allowed airships to be launched! The situation did not improve and the enemy attack broadened. On 19 January 1915, Zeppelin airships attacked Yarmouth and Kings Lynn. By 20 June 1915, a further seventeen raids had taken place against targets along the east coast, reaching as far south as Dover. Moreover, the South of England targets had been subjected to aircraft attack as well. The Royal Flying Corps was swift to react, forming many new squadrons as 'Home Defence Units'. These new units in turn required airfields from which to operate and a major airfield construction and expansion

The 1935 type design sick quarters.

The 1935 design watch tower typifing the flat roof, porthole and ocean liner influence of 1930s style architecture. RAF Swinderby.

programme was set in motion the length of the east and south coasts.

But still the initiative remained with the enemy and on 2-3 May 1916 a Zeppelin airship bombed the city of York. Industrial towns and conurbations now became targets; the war had been brought to the heart of England. It became obvious that airfields would now need to be sited to provide the air defence of industrial centres as well as the coasts. The east coast airfield construction programme was duly extended, and the proliferation of airfields continued. By 1917 a total of seventy-three airfields were available in the UK, the majority being of temporary design. At the end of the First World War a national network of airfields had been established for the aerial defence of Great

Blast proof steel doors, the 1935 plan design.

Britain and placed in the hands of the Royal Air Force.

During the early post-war years most of the temporary landing grounds and airfields were sold off and reverted back to agricultural use, with a few remaining in the hands of civil flying clubs. A nucleus of the permanent bases was retained by the RAF as training depots, or for the east and south coast defence of Great Britain. A good example of a First World War airfield can be seen at RAF Catterick, though the original 1914 hangars have been modified for the station's present task as the RAF Regiment Depot.

The 1920s were relatively quiet years for the RAF. Notably however, and thanks to Trenchard, the RAF presence was increased overseas, particularly in the Near and Middle East. The overseas bases were modelled on home

The 1935 design medical centre with hospital bed facilities, RAF Swinderby.

base facilities, but building design, hangar design and airfield layout were still considered individually, with no broad plan or standardisation in view. A classic example of individual styling occurs at Cardington in Bedfordshire, famed for its balloon sheds as well as its distinctive Officers' Mess. By the 1930s, however, pressure groups in Parliament were demanding improvements to support the RAF. Dramatic changes had occurred in European politics as well as in aviation and it was clear that in any future war, domination of the air would have to be achieved to ensure our defence. Following considerable prompting from Churchill, Trenchard and Sir Samuel Hoare, politicians were forced to look carefully at the RAF in comparison with the German Luftwaffe. If the nation was to survive a future war, it was essential to expand and modernise the Royal Air Force on a scale hitherto seen only in war. At the same time, the government was well aware of the additional employment such a programme would generate. The RAF expansion scheme was presented as not only a military necessity but politically very desirable!

The expansion of the RAF from 1935 to 1939 provided the Air Ministry Works Directorate with its first real opportunity to design and construct permanent buildings of character and uniformity. The first task of the Directorate was to produce standard building designs for both airfield and domestic facilities. The second task was to investigate possible airfield sites, including the preparation of plans to modify existing airfields. In all the architectural plans for permanent buildings, the elevation treatment was to be subjected to approval by the Royal Fine Arts Commission. Similarly this body, and also the Society for the Preservation of Rural

The 1935 design decontamination and cleansing station.

Balloon sheds, RAF Cardington

England, had an interest in the disposition of buildings in relation to the countryside. In the planning of barrack block, Mess and married quarter buildings a 'Georgian' influence can be seen in the architects' attempts to provide dignified, restful lines that would blend in with their surroundings but remain in keeping with the character and purpose of the building. At the same time the quality of accommodation and of the facilities provided was much improved.

The first list of new stations to be constructed contained Marham, Feltwell, Cranfield, Harwell, Stradishall, Ternhill, Waddington and Church Fenton. These were all begun in 1935. It was never intended that there should be a standardised station layout, but all buildings were to be erected to a standardised design with common plans for sick quarters, armoury or whatever, hence the similarity from station to station. The only slight differences in building

design were as a result either of size or of specific building purpose. For example, training bases required larger Messes, supply buildings and the like; bomber bases required larger hangars and more technical accommodation: coastal command seaplane bases required slipways and much taller hangars. Of particular interest are stations like Thorney Island, which included specially designed buildings for torpedo development work, and Pembroke Dock, with its huge hangars and slipways specifically designed for Sunderland aircraft.

In late 1935 a start was made to alter and update existing bases such as Catterick, Cranwell, Halton, Hornchurch, Leuchars, North Weald, Sealand, Tangmere, Turnhouse and Wittering, and it is on these stations that a whole variety of architectural designs can be seen that span the RAF's history. As a matter of

1935 design for the airmen's mess, almost art deco in style.

The 1935 design C type hangar, RAF Cranwell.

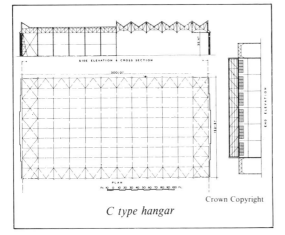

Crown Copyright

C type hangar

interest, the cost of modifications to each of these stations at 1935 prices was between £30,000 and £35,000.

Hangar design and construction provided many headaches. Before the expansion period, the largest general service hangar was the 'A' type, which had a clear span of 120ft and a length of 250ft, with doors at both ends 120ft wide and 25ft high. By 1935 the RAF anticipated a need for housing much larger aircraft. A new design for a hangar of span 150ft and length 300ft, also providing doors at both ends, was prepared and agreed. These were to be known as 'C' type hangars, of which between two and six were built at each of the expansion programme airfields, depending upon the station's role. In 1936 a start was made on the construction of Aircraft Storage Units (ASUs), some to be sited independently, as at Kemble and Aston Down in

Gloucestershire, others located alongside operational bases as at Shawbury and Ternhill. New hangar designs for the ASUs included the type 'E' hangar, which was of bowed shape without visible side walls and constructed of concrete; and a similiar type 'D' hangar, again of reinforced concrete, but with evident side walls. In some cases the roof area of the 'E' hangar was covered with soil and turf to aid camouflage as well as to give protection against blast. Aircraft Repair Depots (ARDs) with engine repair workshops were constructed at St Athan and Sealand in 1937. Because of the distinctive tasks of these stations, buildings of specialist design had to be constructed. Of interest at both stations are the extended 'C' type hangars, of 400ft in length and 200ft wide. Similarly, balloon depots were a further innovation, of which perhaps the best example is Cardington. Balloon barrage was considered a wholly viable means of air defence, and many small balloon depots manned by the Auxiliary Air Force were constructed throughout the country. Balloon stations are easily recognised by their characteristically compact, high-sided corrugated steel hangars. An excellent remaining example of such a station, complete with its hangars, can be seen at Rollestone Camp near Larkhill on Salisbury Plain, although now under the control of the Army.

The airfield construction and expansion programme was just one facet of the 1935 plan. In the same year, work began on building a network of 'Radar Stations Home' along our east and south coasts. In 1937 a huge training

D type hangar, RAF Syreston.

station at RAF Cosford for 4000 personnel was started, and in 1938 the foundations were laid for a 330-bed hospital at Ely. New stores depots were constructed at Quedgeley, Heywood, Carlisle and Warrington, and a Command Headquarters was built at High Wycombe for Bomber Command. While the pre-war expansion programme was going ahead at home, similiar plans were being prepared for our overseas bases in Africa, the Near, Middle and Far East — indeed, a considerable amount of work was started at twenty-seven overseas bases before the outbreak of war in 1939. In the UK, by the outbreak of the Second World War ninety-six permanent RAF stations, four hospitals, sixteen balloon barrage stations and nineteen Volunteer Reserve Training Centres were either under construction or completed. Such was the hive of activity that surrounded the expansion programme in the four years 1935-9; but it was nothing compared with what was to come.

The war years saw the development of the RAF airfield from grass landing grounds to the more complex centres of aviation that we recognise today. Between 1939 and 1945, 684 airfields were constructed in the UK, at a cost of over £200 million (excluding buildings). During the peak year of 1942, new airfields were appearing within our national landscape at a rate of one every three days. In the same year sixty-three major extensions to existing stations were underway where overall 127,000 building and civil engineering workers were employed on Air Ministry works. To bring this figure into perspective, the total constructional labour force

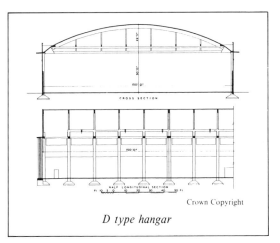

Crown Copyright

D type hangar

available to the nation at this time was 393,400 workers; the Air Ministry Works Directorate was, therefore, using nearly one-third of the total national labour force on RAF works. In 1939, only nine airfields had paved runways, and these were of a maximum length of 1000 yards and fifty yards' width. During the war years over 175 million square ft of concrete, tarmacadam or other hard surfacing was laid in paved runways and connecting track, the equivalent of something like 5000 miles of three-lane motorway. By the end of the war, many of the bomber stations had 3000-yard runways, 100ft wide and to a depth of 12in of high-grade concrete. In terms of material, the runway building programme alone consumed 45 million tons of sand, ballast and crushed stone, and $6\frac{1}{2}$ million tons of cement. Much of the hardcore used in runway construction came by rail from

'T' type transportable shed.

blitzed cities. Of the fifty new airfields occupied by the US Army Air Force (USAAF) in 1942, thirty-six were constructed by the Air Ministry; the remaining fourteen were constructed by the US Army Engineers. The construction of an 'A' class station alone, covering 1000 acres, involved 175,000 cubic yards of high grade concrete, 32,000 square yards of tarmac, 400,000 cubic yards of excavated soil, twenty miles of drain, ten miles of conduit, six miles of water main, four miles of sewer, ten miles of roadway and $4\frac{1}{2}$ million bricks. The average cost of an 'A' class station was £2 million at 1942 prices. The average completion time for runway construction, from foundations down to receiving the first aircraft, was between five to seven months, though it would take an average of one thousand labourers up to eighteen months to complete the construction of all facilities for an 'A' class airfield. Broadly, there were three classifications for airfield construction: A, B and C. 'A' represented the heavy bomber station, 'B' the medium bomber station and the 'C' classification was built for fighter aircraft. In addition plans were available for 'T' or temporary airfields such as those constructed along the south coast to be used for the D-day offensive only and in essence simply a temporary runway facility.

Rapid construction brought a utilitarian, no frills look to buildings. Many designs involved pre-fabrication for ease and speed of erection. Nissen and Romney hutting were perhaps the most common prefabricated buildings. Their construction involved laying corrugated steel sheets between curved steel support frames, of which a number of different sizes were available.

Examples of Hangar Design:

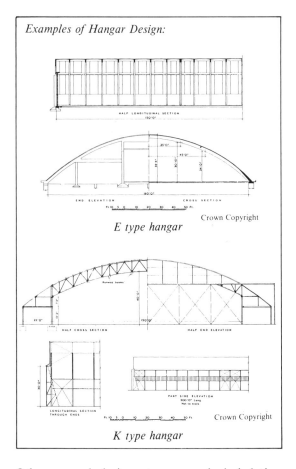

Crown Copyright

E type hangar

Crown Copyright

K type hangar

Other named designs to appear included the concrete pier and beam Orlit hut, the light timber Hall hut and the wood and asbestos Seco hut. All these were designed to be temporary, but they have withstood the test of time, and many of all types of building remain and are in use today. One of the best examples of utilitarian temporary design can be seen at the RAF Hospital Nocton Hall, originally constructed for

The Belfast hangar, RAF Old Sarum.

The distinctive high sided balloon hangars, RAF Rollestone, Wiltshire.

The 'H' shaped flat roofed barrack block 1935 design, RAF Swinderby.

Between the wars design – guard room, RAF Old Sarum, the 1932 design.

D-Day casualties and only closed in 1983. Prefabrication was also ingeniously used in the preparation of runways constructed by the RAF Airfield Construction Branch and the Royal Engineers. Chevron grid, developed in 1938-9, was the earliest form of prefabrication using steel bars, but later in the war, this was replaced by Pierced Steel Plank (PSP), an American invention. PSP was cheap and effective, reducing runway construction time simply to a matter of days. The last form of prefabricated runway was the Prefabricated Bituminous Surfacing (PBS) developed by the Royal Canadian Engineers and used extensively in this country.

Necessity for rapid airfield construction soon became the mother of invention. Improvisation, ingenuity and initiative produced new designs in plant equipment and more efficient methods of construction. Hangars in particular benefited: by late 1938 the 'K' type hangar design of bowed roof constructed on a steel framework had replaced the brick 'C' type hangar. During the early war years the square-shaped Bellman hangars came into use. Although these hangars were prefabricated they were costly to produce and time-consuming to erect. As a result the Air Ministry, in collaboration with Teeside Bridge and Engineering Works, developed a new 'transportable shed'. This type 'T' shed was of unit-welded and bolted steel construction

The ubiquitous Nissen hut. RAF Swinderby.

The temporary 1941 design Secco hut. RAF Old Sarum.

The Orlit hut (concrete beam). RAF Bracebridge Heath.

covered with corrugated steel sheeting, similar to the Bellman hangar but much more practical. It was found suitable and economical for mass production and throughout the remainder of the war was used as the standard hangar. In all, some 906 'T' type hangars were constructed on RAF stations at home and abroad. Many still remain in operational use today. The final type of prefabricated hangar to be produced was the blister hangar; a small, arched construction of wooden frame covered with corrugated iron and sufficient to accommodate one fighter aircraft. Regrettably, few examples remain today despite the fact that some 3000 were constructed.

The layout of RAF and USAAF stations changed dramatically as the war progressed. The results of enemy attacks on airfields in 1940 and 1941 proved the vulnerability of the pre-war airfield layout with the centralised location of hangar and support facilities. Experience now dictated the need to disperse aircraft and buildings over a much greater area than before. There was also an urgent need to camouflage wherever possible. On the pre-war expansion programme airfields nothing could be done in terms of building dispersal, so steps were taken to camouflage by painting and 'toning down'.

This involved painting buildings and runways to blend with the natural surroundings, and it proved very effective. In addition, dispersal points for aircraft were added to perimeter tracks, first in the form of a 'frying pan', and then in loops or 'spectacles'. To assist in camouflage, aircraft dispersal points were often

The temporary brick building. RAF Metheringham.

The 1939-45 'watch tower', RAF Bracebridge Heath.

located in wooded areas on tracks up to two miles from the base. RAF Honington is one station where this can still be seen. On the airfields constructed from 1941 onwards, building dispersal received much greater attention, with perhaps five or six sub-sites being constructed for accommodation and storage between two and five miles away from the main site.

The rapid construction techniques born of the airfield construction programme had their application in other areas after the war. The Blitz had consumed thousand of homes and factories in Britain's cities. In 1945, Aneurin Bevan assessed the extent of the rebuilding task as five million homes. The prefabricated houses, or

Layout for a typical dispersed airfield – RAF Metheringham, Lincolnshire (1941-44).

'prefabs' as they became known, provided an interim measure that stemmed from the lessons learned in the airfield construction programme. Prefab production during 1945-6 was to peak at a rate of 600 units per week — but that's another story. Similarly, the techniques of improved design were applied in the factory rebuilding programme, where large hangar-like constructions were required. The prefabricated design programme also meant that many of the redundant post-war airfield buildings could be dismantled and moved to provide facilities for local authorities.

At the end of the Second World War the Air Ministry prepared plans to close and sell off the majority of the 684 wartime airfields. As the years have gone by, many airfields have been dismantled, including the tearing up of runways and taxiways. The exhumed concrete and tarmac has been used by the motorways builders as hardcore, becoming part of another construction programme. Other airfields, like Ringway, Heathrow and Gatwick, have been developed to become some of the most advanced civil airfields in the world; others, such as Callie, Kenley, Hendon and Croydon, are just aeronautical names from the past.

Since the Second World War considerable improvements have been made to the permanent stations retained by the RAF. Although some married quarters were built before the war, many more were built during the 1950s and 1960s; this task was followed by the construction of the Thor missile sites. For a brief period during the heyday of the Thor and Blue Steel deterrent the number of RAF stations actually

All that remains of the Thor missile era (1958-64) (Sea Vixen foreground), RAF North Luffenham.

The barrack block of the 1980s, RAF Swinderby.

increased, but this lasted less than a decade: in 1969 the nuclear deterrent was placed in the hands of the Royal Navy's Polaris submarines.

The 1980s herald a new era, with new airfields under construction in the Hebrides and Falklands. Dozens of hardened aircraft shelters have already been built to protect aircraft from the fringe effects of nuclear weapons which are inclusive of air and ground crew survival facilities. These mausoleum-like buildings, constructed of steel and stressed concrete, represent the same to the RAF today as the buildings of the expansion programme airfields did between 1935 and 1939 — simply bringing the Service up to date. In time something else will no doubt replace hardened aircraft shelters, and as aviation evolves, these shelters will become monuments to Jaguar and Tornado aircraft and the aspirations of the 1980s.

Chapter 3
The RAF College, Cranwell

In 1915 the Admiralty requisitioned 3000 acres of farmland west of Cranwell village in Lincolnshire for use as a Royal Naval Air Service training station. Construction of a hutted camp and aircraft hangars began almost immediately, and the station was formally opened on 1 April 1916. The greater part of the requisitioned land came from the Earl of Bristol's estate and was chosen for its openness, good drainage and reasonably even surface, all of which made it suitable for landing the new-fangled flying machines. The base became known as HMS *Daedalus* and trained Naval officers to fly aircraft, airships and observer kite balloons. In classical mythology, Daedalus and his son Icarus were the first men to fly, using birds' wings attached to their arms with wax. Daedalus was the teacher; the fact that Icarus later came a nasty cropper is best forgotten. Part of Cranwell's early life is celebrated in the road names that now criss-cross the station. For example, 'Lighter than Air' road passes through the original ballooning area.

The first Commandant of the station in 1916 was Commodore Godfrey Paine, who had previously been the Commandant of the first Central Flying School at Upavon in Wiltshire. But flying was only one aspect of the new station's role. Soon after Paine's arrival a 'Boys' Wing' was established to train Naval ratings as air mechanics and riggers. During the period 1916-18 the embryo Naval Air Service grew steadily stronger; it deliberately segregated itself from any attachment to the Royal Flying Corps, and as a result the flying training task at Cranwell became specialised and totally committed to naval aviation.

The amalgamation of the RNAS and RFC on 1 April 1918 brought new ownership to Cranwell, which was placed in the hands of the Royal Air Force. The former Naval base title was dropped and replaced by the designation RAF Station Cranwell. Training continued much as before, and both the Boys' Wing and the Flying Training School were expanded to meet the demands of the new Service. In addition, a wireless operators' training school was opened in mid-1918. A significant member of the College staff at this time, and a man who was an encouraging influence during the Service's later development, was Prince Albert, second son of King George V and Queen Mary, later Duke of York and then King George VI. He had transferred from the Royal Navy to the RNAS at his own request, and in January 1918 was posted to Cranwell to command No.4 Squadron of the Boys' Wing. He remained with the Boys' Wing until August 1918, and himself adopted RAF uniform after 1 April that year. He was the first member of the Royal family to have a formal association with the RAF.

Immediately after the First World War, the future of the RAF and of RAF Cranwell was by no means certain. Sir Hugh Trenchard, as the first Chief of the Air Staff, knew that the Royal Air Force's position as a single, independent Service had to be consolidated. These views were also shared by the young Winston Churchill. There followed the Churchill-Trenchard memorandum, submitted to Parliament in 1919, which set out various proposals for the future.

The former 1914 railway station, now main guard room, RAF College, Cranwell.

High on the list of proposals was the recommendation to establish a cadet college at Cranwell, to provide basic officer and flying training resources. The recommendation was accepted by Parliament, and the first course of flight cadets began training on 5 February 1920 — a date now acknowledged as Founders' Day. The first RAF Commandant was the distinguished aviator, Air Commodore C. A. H. Longcroft (later to become Air Vice-Marshal Sir Charles Longcroft).

The far-sighted and enterprising Trenchard was also acutely aware of the importance of providing airmen with the skills and expertise necessary not simply to keep the new Service going, but also to develop the potential of air power. As a result of his efforts, an Apprentice School was formed, replacing the Boys' Wing, with No. 1 Entry which started training on the same date as the RAF College opened. The Apprentice School remained at Cranwell until 1927, when RAF Halton assumed responsibility for all apprentice training. During the same period the wireless school blossomed; it later became the Electrical and Wireless School and later still No. 1 Radio School. This school

First World War (RNAS Daedalus) hangars, RAF College, Cranwell.

remained until 1952 when it moved to its present home at RAF Locking, Somerset. At first the College was organised into two schools — flying school and ground school. The student flight cadets were organised into two independent squadrons each pursuing a progressive two-year programme. Flying training started during the first term and it was expected that a solo

Station Headquarters, RAF Cranwell (1933).

Pre-war (1933) cottage design airman's married quarters, RAF Cranwell.

standard could be achieved after ten hours of dual instruction. Flying accidents were frequent, though generally minor. An early Air Publication summarised the requirements for a flight cadet thus: 'It is a fact that the sole conditions of successful flying are physical and mental fitness and the correct temperament . . . For the rest, no finer career could be chosen for an alert and healthy boy. Individuality, resource and rapid judgement are qualities which must find ready appreciation in such a Service.' Like his modern counterpart, the flight cadet also received general service, officer and academic instruction.

The 1920s were a busy period for the College. A notable addition to the station during this period was 338171 A. C. Shaw — in real life the enigmatic Lieutenant-Colonel T. E. Lawrence. He was attempting to seek anonymity by serving as an air mechanic. Records are unclear about what he did and how long he stayed at the station, though it is believed that it was through Churchill's influence the charade was allowed. Today, Lawrence's brief stay at Cranwell is formally acknowledged in the 'Lawrence Room' next to the library in College Hall Officers' Mess, where some interesting letters and memorabilia are permanently on display. Another famous personality of the time was Flight Cadet Frank Whittle, who in 1928 submitted a thesis entitled *Future Developments in Aircraft Design.* It was not until 15 May 1941 that Whittle saw the fruits of his work, but appropriately enough it was at RAF Cranwell that the Gloster-Whittle E28/9 took to the air, ushering in the jet age for the RAF.

By 1929, three hundred and seventy flight cadets had graduated from the College, accumulating between them 32,000 flying hours. (Sadly, there had been seven fatalities.) The late 1920s and early 1930s also saw Cranwell broadening its horizons and becoming closely associated with long-distance flights. The first non-stop flight to India was made in 1929, followed in 1933 by a further non-stop flight to south-west Africa. The College was growing fast and gaining a high reputation as the first Air training college in the world. What it lacked was a college building on a par with Sandhurst and Dartmouth, to add to its credibility. As early as 1922 plans were laid for a new purpose-built college building to replace the original Naval huts, but it was not until the late 1920s that anything either promising or positive was on the cards. Enter Sir Samuel Hoare, Prime Minister Stanley Baldwin's Secretary of State for Air and an energetic supporter of the Royal Air Force. In the face of considerable Cabinet opposition he argued for funds to build a college, and in 1929 obtained approval for an architect's plan to be prepared by the Ministry of Works. He was not pleased with the drawings presented by the Ministry, and consulted the civil architect James West. Sir Samuel took West to Wren's Royal Hospital at Chelsea and togther they amended the Ministry's drawing to the design we know today, which so gracefully reflects the best of Wren's ideas. Time was, however, running out for Baldwin's government, which was facing a general election. To make sure that the College building programme went ahead, and in collusion with Trenchard, the official laying of the foundation stone was arranged for 26 April 1929, with Lady Hoare performing the ceremony. At this stage no expenditure had been authorised for anything more than a plan! As Sir Samuel Hoare said at the time, 'Ours, therefore, was frankly an act of bluff, but it was also an act of faith'.

The new College was completed in September 1933 and provided accommodation and training facilities for 150 cadets. In the best traditions of Wren the whole structure was surmounted by a 130ft tower, which included an internal dome and external clock. To complete the tower design, and with Trinity House agreement, a flashing beacon was finally added, which makes Cranwell the United Kingdom's most inland lighthouse! The official opening of the Royal Air Force College was performed by the Prince of

No. 2 Mess, RAF College, Cranwell (1934).

Wales on 11 October 1934. To coincide with the Royal opening, and as a particularly thoughtful gesture, Sir Samuel and Lady Hoare presented lime trees which today line two avenues leading to the front of the College. The new College building added prestige to the Service and an air of distinction to the campus.

It is worth pausing briefly to describe the life of the Cranwell Flight Cadet during the mid 1930s. The majority of cadets were ex-public school boys whose parents paid fees for them to attend the College. Each cadet was paid 6s 6d a day pocket money, of which 3s 6d a day was accounted for in Mess charges. Sporting and social activities were paid for out of the student's purse and had to be self-supporting. The claims on a cadet's leisure time were demanding and he was expected to meet a hectic work and social calendar. For example, cadets had to dine formally in the Mess on at least three evenings each week, church parade was obligatory every Sunday and a great deal of time was devoted to individual and team sports, quite apart from the flying and ground school training programme. By September 1939, forty-four entries, totalling over a thousand officers, had graduated into the RAF.

At the outbreak of war, on 3 September 1939, flight cadet training ceased and the College closed, to be reopened immediately as the Royal Air Force College Flying Training School. The unit's task was to provide students from

elementary flying training schools with advanced flying training to prepare them for operational training. The course was scheduled to last six months, but the demands of war soon reduced this training time to three months. Students were drawn from throughout the Dominions and European Allies and large contingents also came from neutral Turkey. Although the expansion programme of 1935-9 had added many new buildings at Cranwell, the existing accommodation was soon to be found insufficient. As a result, a rash of temporary wooden huts appeared and satellite airfields were constructed at Fulbeck, Wellingore, Coleby Grange and Spitalgate to support the flying training task. At the beginning of the war,

The pleasing 1935 'Georgian' design senior RAF officers residence, RAF Cranwell.

Trenchard Hall, RAF College, Cranwell, 1966.

931 Cranwell graduates were on the active list; by the end of the war, more than 400 of them had lost their lives. Of the original 931, six hundred were to be decorated, the honours including one Victoria Cross, two George Crosses, eighty-two Distinguished Service Orders and two hundred and sixty-nine Distinguished Flying Crosses.

During the war years RAF Cranwell expanded to meet the operational and training needs of the Service as a whole. In addition to

The Royal Air Force College opened by HRH Prince of Wales on 11 October 1934.

flying training, No. 3 Coastal Command Operational Training Unit (OTU) moved in from August 1941 to June 1943. Headquarters 21 Group, which had arrived in December 1938, expanded and remained until July 1944. In ground support tasks, the School of Clerks Accounting was accommodated from May 1939 to January 1941, while the Equipment Training School, which had opened in December 1936, remained until November 1949. For a brief period from January to June 1944, the Beam Approach School took up residence, and between March and August 1944 No. 314 Supply and Transport Column trained in preparation for the D-Day landings. Finally, between July 1942 and November 1943 RAF Cranwell housed No. 2806 Squadron RAF Regiment, which supported RAF units ashore from the D-Day landings. But the war years were largely uneventful in terms of enemy activity at RAF Cranwell. The first recorded raid was on 6 June 1940, when an unknown number of enemy aircraft dropped bombs near the south airfield. The bombs were dropped short in the outlying field, thanks to the dummy airfield system that had already been constructed. In October 1940 enemy raids became more frequent and as a result night flying training was temporarily curtailed. In February 1941 an unspecified

hostile aircraft again attacked a night flying training sortie, but luckily there was only slight damage to the aircraft and no casualties. In March 1941 an Oxford aircraft was attacked during a daylight training sortie and in August an incendiary bomb hit the College, causing one roof tile to crack. Sadly, however, on 18 March 1942, a Whitley Bomber from the Coastal Command OTU hit the tower between A and B Wing of the College building, causing extensive damage. The aircraft fuel tanks were full and there was extensive fire and smoke damage. The crew of two, Pilot Officers Strachen and Balfour, were on a training night flying sortie. Fog had rolled in that night and instead of going inland to let a master searchlight beam them to a flare path, they tried to land at Cranwell.

Peace in 1945 coincided with Cranwell's Silver Jubilee year, and on 13 June George VI visited the College. The College formally reopened in 1946, and in the years that followed, training expanded to include supply and secretarial officers, navigators and RAF Regiment officers. These changes were also accompanied by a new building programme to replace the wartime huts. A notable gift of a peal of bells was made to the College in 1952 by the Shell Group of Companies. These bells, which are housed in the clock tower, chime not only the hours but also The Retreat at Colour lowering. The house flag (Royal College) is lowered on the chime of the hour and the Ensign on the chiming of the Retreat. This gift was made as a tribute to the bravery of former Cranwell cadets who lost their lives during the Second World War. A fourth wing was added to College Hall in 1959, and the new Anglican Church of St Michael and All Angels was completed in June 1962. In October of the same year Sir Frank Whittle returned to open the newly constructed academic studies building, Whittle Hall. By the end of the year a new swimming pool and gymnasium were also provided. In 1954, the decision was made to introduce jet flying training. As a result extended runways were constructed on the south airfield and at Barkston Heath to accommodate the Meteor and Vampire training aircraft. Flying training was to become all jet by 1961 with the now familiar Jet Provost, the world's first jet powered basic training aircraft.

The post-war years have seen many changes at Cranwell. Some have been brought about for economic reasons, others simply as a result of the need to centralise and to use the RAF's training resources more efficiently. The College's motto, *Superna Petimus* — We Strive for Higher Things — sums up the ethos behind all the changes that have been made. Uppermost has always been a total commitment to training for professional excellence. The first of the major changes came in 1965 when the RAF Technical College Henlow merged with the RAF College Cranwell to become the College's Department of Engineering and more recently the Department of Specialist Ground Training. To coincide with this move, a complex of new training facilities and accommodation was built and given the title Trenchard Hall. The new buildings were opened by Lord Trenchard's son, Viscount Trenchard, on 17 May 1966. In 1970 a further major change occurred when the Graduate Entry Scheme was introduced. This scheme, which replaced the Flight Cadet system, provided university graduates with a short initial officer training course, followed by initial specialist training. HRH The Prince of Wales completed his pilot training with No. 1 Graduate Entry, passing out from the College in 1971. In the same year Cranwell assumed control of the University Air Squadrons, and in 1974 the College of Air Warfare joined the campus to become the Department of Air Warfare. The most recent change came in 1980 when the Service's other officer training unit, located at Henlow, joined the College to become the Department of Initial Officer Training, which at the same time replaced the Graduate Entry Scheme. Cranwell has since become the single gate of entry for all officers entering the RAF.

On the twenty-fifth anniversary of the formation of the RAF, King George VI announced his intention to award Sovereign's Colours to the Service. The first Colour to be presented was for the RAF College Cranwell on 6 July 1948. The Colour is made of silk with a silver leaf, hand-embroidered edge on a light blue background, with the College crest embroidered in the centre. It is paraded on ceremonial occasions. In further recognition of the Service's loyalty to the Crown, Her Majesty Queen Elizabeth II consented to become Cranwell's Commandant in Chief on 25 July 1960. This was also the date when her father's Sovereign's Colour was paraded for the last time before being laid up in the College Chapel. On the same occasion she presented the College with a new Colour, which was renewed by Her Majesty on 30 May 1975.

Chapter 4
The Queen's Commission

The extensive membership of the RAF Club, RAF Association (RAFA) and squadron associations testify that former RAF service is to be remembered, not forgotten. The reason for this may be found in the esprit de corps, comradeship or just plain friendship that all enjoyed whilst serving in the RAF. These values, the spirit, the brotherhood, the loyalty have got to be based on something; perhaps it was personal fulfilment, pride or just the satisfaction of knowing that what they did was worthwhile. But there again, it would be wrong to suggest that former RAF Servicemen or women who do not belong to ex-Service associations do not share the same feelings. The contrary is more often true. It is a striking facet, common to ex-RAF Servicemen and women, that with few exceptions they are proud of their past service and hold many fond memories of time spent in the Royal Air Force. The theme of this chapter is

College gates, RAF College, Cranwell.

the commitment of a commission. For those who have served as officers, much of what is recounted will be familiar. For those outside the Service, or those thinking of a Service career, this chapter is aimed at providing an insight into the commitment that is The Queen's Commission.

The RAF of today is proud of its history, traditions and achievements whether in war, international confrontations or national emergency. But most of all, the RAF is proud of its Servicemen. The standards, the efficiency and the effectiveness of the RAF are a reflection of the Officer Corps, for there 'the buck stops'! The RAF prides itself in its officer selection procedures which in the past have served it well. There is no reason why this should not also be true for the future. But in the first instance, the will, motivation and determination must be within the would-be RAF officer. Most of all, the individual must be prepared for the personal commitment that a commission in the RAF demands, a commitment not only to pursue professional excellence, but also to maintain high personal standards. This accepted, the rewards will be many. But it is worth remembering the old adage that 'many may be called, few are chosen'.

On completion of the Initial Officer Training Course (IOTC) at the RAF College, Cranwell, officer cadets will receive their commission. The process of gaining this honour will have started many months before. The initial application form to join the RAF is first carefully scrutinised by the Service's own recruiting organisation. If found acceptable, the applicant will be invited to attend the Officer and Aircrew Selection Centre (OASC) at RAF Biggin Hill. There, over a period of three days, the first stage in the officer selection process will take place. Aptitude tests will be followed by in-depth interviews so that as much as possible can be learnt about the candidate in the time available. If the candidate is successful at this first hurdle, he or she will be invited to stay at OASC to take part in group activities which aim to identify leadership

Command management and leadership training, an early phase of the RAF College, Cranwell, course.

potential. By the time this second stage begins, the number of candidates who originally started will have been reduced by between forty and fifty per cent. Once the group activities are over, this figure may have been further eroded. Only a mere five to ten per cent of those who apply to be RAF officers will be successful at the OASC and be offered a place at the RAF College, Cranwell.

All Initial Officer Training (IOT) for the RAF is centralised at the RAF College, Cranwell. Every six weeks a new intake begins the eighteen week-long commissioning course. No exemptions are given for past non-commissioned service, or university education. Rather, a common bond is struck between all who strive for the honour to hold The Queen's Commission. The only exceptions to attendance on this course are former commissioned officers, who seek re-entry to the Service, doctors, dentists, and members of the clergy. For these candidates there is a Special Entrant and Re-Entrant Course (SERE). Both the IOT and

SERE courses aim to prepare RAF student officers (those with a degree), and officer cadets (ex-Service airmen or airwomen and non-degree direct entrants from civilian life) for the basic responsibility of being an RAF officer. Flying, engineering, or other branch specialised training is not undertaken until such time as the individual has proved his worth by successfuly completing IOT.

Although only eighteen weeks in length, the IOT course is intensive, being both physically and mentally demanding. Inevitably some will fall by the wayside. The course standards are high, the pace is exacting. If the individual does not have the motivation, drive and determination to succeed as an officer in the RAF, the IOT course will soon find him out. But the majority do not fail and in the case of borderline students, the college authorities may consider that an individual will benefit from further training. These students will be offered a recourse in the hope that they will improve their overall performance. The student need feel no stigma at being recoursed.

Those who successfully pass the IOT course will be commissioned into the RAF, but this is by no means the end of officer training — more realistically, it is the end of the beginning of officer training. But it will be a memorable day; the commissioning parade, the church dedication, lunch and graduation ball with family or friends in attendance. Officer training never ends — who can say he or she knows it all? There will still be something to learn in officer training the day retirement eventually comes.

The award of The Queen's Commission is formally recognised by the Commissioning Scroll. This is the authority to command and a reminder also to obey those of more senior rank. Whatever leadership may or may not be (and there is no authoritative definition), the literal statement 'leadership by example' cannot be misunderstood. Much time is spent during the IOT course discussing the merit and need for high personal standards. Such words as integrity, loyalty, honesty, trust, courage, determination and judgement are frequently used in lectures and presentations to awaken awareness and to stimulate thought. In classroom discussions, analogies will be drawn with everyday life, to alert officer cadets to the different values expected of a commissioned officer. Where there are wide differences in accepted levels of social behaviour between

Camp Two exercises – A 10-day arduous leadership training camp.

Service and civilian life — such as the homosexual movement, drug taking and membership of extremist groups — it is made clear that these activities are incompatible with commissioned, or for that matter, non-commissioned service. Part and parcel of accepting The Queen's Commission is also acceptance of Queen's Regulations and Air Force Law, to which all RAF personnel are subject. Not surprisingly, therefore, social misconduct, financial irresponsibility, extra-marital relationships, drunkenness and the like can hardly to considered as commensurate with service as an officer or as a fitting example for others! If leadership is to be by example, the example must be exemplary. To quote Her Majesty Queen Elizabeth II, 'Remember that the best form of leadership is example: that "Come on" is a much better command than "Go on".' To serve in the Royal Air Force is an honour. It is also an unequivocal commitment to duty; to a duty that is shared by all ranks, whether

commissioned or not. The rank structure is an inherited tradition from the Army and Royal Navy which has many centuries worth of proven record. It is based absolutely on mutual respect. A commissioned officer is tasked to uphold these traditions by ensuring, above all, a respect for senior and subordinate alike. The NCO cadre represents the foundations on which the service is built. The officers represent the architects who design and build the Service's infra-structure and are ultimately responsible for its strength and operational effectiveness. The airmen represent the resource with which to fashion and power the Service with the latest techniques in modern warfare. Each has his part to play and without a mutual understanding and respect of the other, the structure will fail. There is no class distinction, and no particular rank, commissioned or not, has the monopoly of virture, or any other attribute for that matter; how foolish it would be to suggest so. All commissioned officers are bound by a code of conduct and personal commitment to ensure the integrity of the non-commissioned ranks, which is itself a reflection of mutual respect. There are no short cuts to this code; time and experience have shown this.

Leadership

Leadership potential would seem an obvious pre-requisite for an RAF commission. It is the function of the OASC, at RAF Biggin Hill, to identify its presence. However, if all leaders were born fully-fledged, OASC and the RAF College would soon be out of business. In reality the candidate may possess certain qualities which if recognised, tutored, and strengthened through training, may enable him to realise his full potential as a leader. These qualities have to be

Camp One – tactical leadership camp – 8 days of intensive combatant training.

Graduation parade, RAF College, Cranwell.

naturally present, it is true, so to describe a list would be pointless. On the other hand, the reader would find it relatively easy to draw up a list of desirable leadership traits. His list might show some similarity to the leadership requirements of OASC. However, no two people will ever produce identical characteristics and an examination of the qualities in a well-known leader will not include all the listed traits put forward! But, there will always be easily discernible common factors. One view is that leadership is a personal quality, or rather a combination of personal characteristics. This leads to an examination of the qualities of successful commanders. The problem with this approach is that except for a high level of motivation, successful leaders seem to differ widely in their characteristics; the difference between Attila the Hun and Gandhi for example. There is no single set of abilities, or inborn traits which characterises all successful leaders and it would not be fruitful to consider leadership as a universal pattern of characteristics possessed by certain people. It is more useful to recognise that there are skills, attitudes and actions which can be taught to individuals who differ widely in their inborn

traits and abilities, and who can be fashioned and tempered into what the Service requires, providing their spirit is willing.

The RAF College Cranwell aims to develop leadership in the individual through practical exercises, discussion and tuition. Thus, there is much that can be done for the under-confident cadet. 'Knowledge dispels fear' to quote a well-known RAF motto; the knowledge will be provided, but it is the positive response from the individual that will dispel the fear. Cranwell is not the end of leadership training. Command and staff training, as it is termed, is a continual process that never ceases. The following quotations all refer to leadership where each points to a conclusion; they are provided for mind-provoking thought, rather than as definitive statements.

'At the top there are great simplifications. An accepted leader has only to be sure of what it is best to do, or at least have his mind made up about it. The loyalties which centre upon Number One are enormous. If he sleeps, he must not be wantonly disturbed. If he is no good he must be pole-axed.' W. C. Churchill, *Their Finest Hour.*

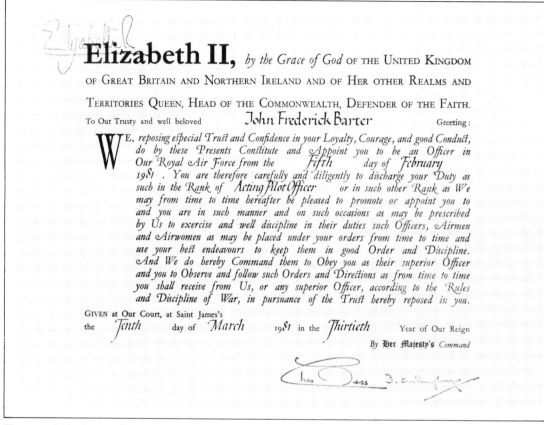

Elizabeth II, *by the Grace of God* OF THE UNITED KINGDOM of GREAT BRITAIN AND NORTHERN IRELAND AND OF HER OTHER REALMS AND TERRITORIES QUEEN, HEAD OF THE COMMONWEALTH, DEFENDER OF THE FAITH.

To Our Trusty and well beloved *John Frederick Barter* Greeting:

WE, *reposing especial Trust and Confidence in your Loyalty, Courage, and good Conduct, do by these Presents Constitute and Appoint you to be an Officer in Our Royal Air Force from the* **Fifth** *day of* **February** *19 81 . You are therefore carefully and diligently to discharge your Duty as such in the Rank of* **Acting Pilot Officer** *or in such other Rank as We may from time to time hereafter be pleased to promote or appoint you to and you are in such manner and on such occasions as may be prescribed by Us to exercise and well discipline in their duties such Officers, Airmen and Airwomen as may be placed under your orders from time to time and use your best endeavours to keep them in good Order and Discipline. And We do hereby Command them to Obey you as their superior Officer and you to Observe and follow such Orders and Directions as from time to time you shall receive from Us, or any superior Officer, according to the Rules and Discipline of War, in pursuance of the Trust hereby reposed in you.*

GIVEN at Our Court, at Saint James's the **Tenth** day of **March** 19 81 in the **Thirtieth** Year of Our Reign

By Her Majesty's Command

The commissioning scroll.

'Our army would be invincible if it could be properly organised and officered. There were never such men in an Army before. They will go anywhere and do anything. But there is the difficulty — proper commanders.' General Robert E. Lee (to Lieutenant General T. J. 'Stonewall' Jackson).

'The military commander is the fate of the nation.' Helmuth von Moltke ('Moltke the Elder'), 1800-1891.

'The Commander must know how to get his men their rations and every other kind of stores needed for war. He must have imagination to originate plans, practical sense and energy to carry them through. He must be observant, untiring, shrewd; kindly and cruel; simple and crafty; a watchman and a robber; lavish and miserly; generous and stingy; rash and conservative. All these and many other qualities, natural and acquired, he must have. He should also, as a matter of course, know his tactics; for a disorderly mob is no more an army than a heap of building materials is a house.' Socrates, 469-399 BC.

'Leadership is a psychological force that has nothing to do with morals or good character, or even intelligence: nothing to do with ideals or idealism. It is a matter of relative will power, a basic connection between one animal and the rest of the herd. Leadership is a process by which a single aim and unified action are imparted to the herd. Not surprisingly, it is most in evidence in time or circumstances of danger or challenge. Leadership is not imposed like authority. It is actually welcomed and wanted by the led.' Correlli Barnet.

'The kind of leadership available to an organisation is a principal factor in its operation. So far as the RAF is concerned the quality of leadership determines its success: indeed, it may determine its survival.' Anon.

It is the aim of leadership training to develop individual command abilities to meet the challenge of air warfare in all its enormity.

Chapter 5
Airman and Airwoman Service

Airman and Airwoman Service, like Commissioned service, is a personal commitment: a commitment in time and endeavour to military aviation. The airmen and airwomen are the bedrock of the Service who will finally dictate the RAF's effectiveness in combat. The forerunners of today's airmen were the Royal Engineer sappers and Royal Naval Air Service ratings of the past who laid down the standards for today's serving personnel.

The airmen and airwomen of today are distinguished individuals adept at many skills and dedicated to their craft; they have to be to deal with the complexities of modern aircraft, whether airframe, armament, engine or avionics, or, as non-commissioned aircrew, to be an integral member of the flying elite. But such a description would not wholly describe the variety and opportunity in airman and airwoman service. As the teeth arms of the Army are supported by their Corps, so similar support is given by the ground branches of the Royal Air Force to ensure the Service's flying capability. There are a total of 78 different ground trades which are listed at the end of this chapter inclusive of entry qualifications. For convenience and to provide a structure, the trades are described as either 'list 1' or 'list 2'. List 1 includes the technical trades and introduces two special and additional ranks over and above the list 2 trades: Junior Technician (Jnr Tech) and Chief Technician (Chf Tech). (See Chapter 7) Pay is also different within the two lists as financial recognition is given for the technical skills and expertise acquired. List 2 represents the non-technical trades. However, it is fair to point out that whether List 1 or List 2 trade, progress and advancement in the RAF has nothing to do with the list number, but everything to do with performance on duty; thus both lists offer equal opportunities.

The control and management of the 78 different ground trades lies within the Service's branch structure each of which has a directorate at Ministry of Defence level to look after it. The main branches may be summarised as follows: Administration, Engineering, Security, Supply, Air Traffic Control, Medical and Dental and Music. No one branch or trade looks down upon the other; each has its part to play. It is, in other words, a matter of teamwork.

Selection for airman and airwoman service begins at the Career Information Office (CIO) where those interested in RAF Service can gain first-hand information about the opportunities available. The next step will be to match aptitudes and preferences with a trade to form the basis of a written application. A completed written application will be viewed by the officer commanding the CIO who will then interview the applicant to learn as much about him or her as he can to determine overall suitability for Regular Service. The RAF is proud of its track record and, as this book records the would be RAF recruit has a lot to live up to. Those who continue in the path of the pioneers of aviation must be determined, and resolute with a strong personal belief in the RAF — this will be important when the going gets tough as it does during Station training for war exercises, or more realistically, as it did during the Falkland Islands' Campaign. It is worth remembering that the exploits and achievements of RAF aviators from the past to the present day are as a result of teamwork: the pressures on the ground staff can be equal to those who fly.

Assuming that the initial application has been successful, all airman and airwoman training is conducted at No 1 School of Recruit Training at RAF Swinderby in Lincolnshire. The training course lasts six weeks. Its aim is to accustom the recruits to Service life and to teach them the basic skills and knowledge so that they may proceed to the next phase of Service training as well-disciplined airmen and airwomen who have developed a sense of pride in, and responsibility to, the RAF. Those lucky enough to have been selected for RAF apprenticeships will also have to complete the recruit training course at RAF Swinderby before starting their apprenticeships at the world famous apprentice schools at RAF Halton, Cosford and Locking. (Apprentice schools were an original idea of Sir Hugh Trenchard as an investment for the future. They have served the RAF well and provided many of its most senior officers. There is no reason why future trends should change this.)

As Mark Twain commented, 'Training is everything, a cauliflower is a cabbage with a college education!' The recruit training course is based on pre-selected objectives. Every recruit is expected to reach the objectives through the comprehensive training programme. The course is carefully controlled to enable everyone to gain steadily in confidence and expertise. Drill is important to establish teamwork, discipline and personal pride. General Service knowledge is taught to ensure an understanding of the Service, its administration and how it functions on a day-to-day basis.

Development of the mind is complemented by development of physical fitness — these two facets are related. There is every encouragement and opportunity to take part in a variety of sports. But the physical fitness objective itself is to be able to complete a 1.5 mile course in eleven minutes or less. For some this is a real test of determination and effort, for others it is quite easy. For sure, it is well within a recruit's capability to achieve given the training. Similarly, the WRAF must reach an objective time of $14\frac{1}{2}$ minutes for the same distance. A major proportion of the recruit training course is devoted to ground defence and military field

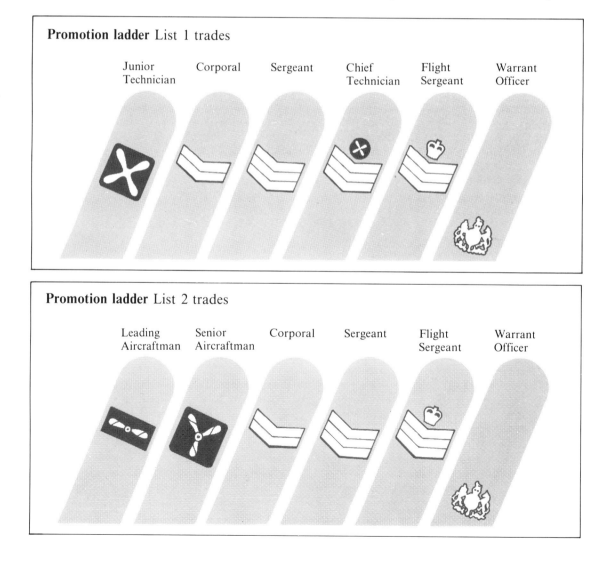

Promotion ladder List 1 trades

| Junior Technician | Corporal | Sergeant | Chief Technician | Flight Sergeant | Warrant Officer |

Promotion ladder List 2 trades

| Leading Aircraftman | Senior Aircraftman | Corporal | Sergeant | Flight Sergeant | Warrant Officer |

Graduation parade, RAF School of Recruit Training – RAF Swinderby.

training which also includes a 48-hour battle camp spent living under canvas practising combatant skills. This is arduous training which has no regard for weather — it serves as an introduction to the operational air force and is a test of the skills and knowledge taught during the course. It is also a test of the individual's motivation and determination to succeed. As with passing the physical fitness test, passing the military field training objective will give the recruit a feeling of pride and achievement; it will tell the RAF that they may safely rely on this person when the going gets tough.

On completion of recruit training there will be a formal graduation parade (Wednesday morning) where parents and friends may look on with due pride as a full military parade with arms (rifles) is undertaken. A reviewing officer of rank Group Captain or above will inspect the parade and take the salute at a full "March Past" which will be accompanied by one of the RAF bands (normally the Band of the Royal Air Force College, Cranwell). In addition there will be a fly past given by operational aircraft to herald the recruits entry into service. Following the graduation parade festivities continue at an informal luncheon before the recruits leave to begin trade training at one of the many and varied trade training stations such as Hereford, Cosford or Catterick. On satisfactory completion of trade training the recruit will be promoted to the rank of Leading Aircraftman (or aircraftwoman) and be posted to an operational station. Thereafter, advancement is entirely up to the individual by passing promotion exams and having good reports. The current non-commissioned ranks for list 1 and list 2 trades are shown on page 28.

Airman and airwoman career management is viewed each year through the meduim of an annual confidential report (officers are subject to similar reporting action). Personal qualities and trade performance are numerically assessed on a 1-9 scale (airmen with a 9 rating walk on water!) In addition, at least three different officers will each provide an accompanying narrative report. However, before the report leaves the station to be recorded on the airman's file, he or she will have been 'debriefed' (counselled) on both strengths and weaknesses and advised how best to improve his or her performance, particularly with regard to promotion. By such reporting the Service will identify potential non-commissioned officers and streamline future training requirements. It also aids the longer term development of the under confident to ensure that his or her needs are not overlooked in career management. Every opportunity is given to the airmen and airwomen of today to succeed.

RAF Swinderby has been involved with recruit training for over twenty years. Each year some five to six thousand recruits pass through its gates. The staff are hand-picked for their ability and every encouragement is given to the recruit to succeed. Of those who do not succeed first time there are opportunities for extra or re-flight training. There is no stigma attached to this re-flight training, the training staff simply believe that he or she will benefit from additional training. But in the first place, the motivation and the determination must be present for the recruit to want to succeed and be a member of the Royal Air Force.

There are a variety of engagements on offer to airmen and airwomen inclusive of pensionable service. For those who join the RAF and select the short length engagements there will be ample opportunities to apply for re-engagement or extension of service. Details of airman and airwoman careers can be obtained from RAF Career Information offices, the address of which can be found in a local telephone directory.

	No. of O-levels or GCE equivalents required	Minimum age RAF	Minimum age WRAF	List
Aircraft Engineering Technician (Propulsion/Airframe)§	4	16	-	1
Aircraft Technician (Airframe)	2	16½	17	1
Aircraft Mechanic (Airframe)	-	16½	17	1
Aircraft Technician (Propulsion)	2	16½	17	1
Aircraft Mechanic (Propulsion)	-	16½	17	1
Aircraft Technician (Weapons)	2	16½	17	1
Aircraft Mechanic (Weapons)	-	16½	17	1
Aircraft Technician (Electrical)	2	16½	17	1
Aircraft Mechanic (Electrical)	-	16½	17	1
Electronics Engineering Technician (Air Communications/Air Radar)§	4	16	-	1
Electronics Technician (Air Communications)	2	16½	17	1
Electronics Mechanic (Air Communications)	-	16½	17	1
Electronics Technician (Air Radar)	2	16½	17	1
Electronics Mechanic (Air Radar)	-	16½	17	1
Electronics Engineering Technician (Flight Systems)§	4	16	-	1
Electronics Technician (Flight Systems)	2	16½	17	1
Electronics Mechanic (Flight Systems)	-	16½	17	1
Electronics Technician (Synthetic Trainer)	2	16½	17	1
Electronics Technician (Air Defence)	2	16½	17	1
Electronics Mechanic (Air Defence)	-	16½	17	1
Electronics Technician (Airfield)	2	16½	17	1
Electronics Mechanic (Airfield)	-	16½	17	1
Electronics Technician (Telecommunications)	2	16½	17	1
Electronics Mechanic (Telecommunications)	-	16½	17	1
General Technician (Electrical)	2	16½	17	1
General Mechanic (Electrical)	-	16½	17	1
General Technician (Ground Support Equipment)	2	16½	17	1
General Mechanic (Ground Support Equipment)	-	16½	17	1
General Technician (Workshops)	2	16½	17	1
General Mechanic (Workshops)	-	16½	17	1
Aerial Erector	-	16½	-	2
Carpenter	-	16½	17	2
Medical Transport Technician	2	16½	17	1
Mechanical Transport Mechanic	-	16½	17	2
Mechanical Transport Driver	-	17	17	2
RAF Police	-	17½	18½	2
Kennelmaid	-	-	17	2
RAF Regiment Gunner	-	17	-	2
Fireman	-	17½	-	2
Assistant Air Traffic Controller	-	16½	17	2

	No. of O-levels or GCE equivalents required	Minimum age RAF	Minimum age WRAF	List
Physical Training Instructor	-	17½	18½	2
RAF Administrative	-	18	18	2
RAF General Duties	-	16½	17	2
Telecommunications Operator	-	16½	17	2
Telephonist	-	16½	17	2
Radio Operator (Voice)	-	18	18	2
Special Telegraphist	-	18	18	2
Aerospace Systems Operator	-	16½	17	2
Painter and Finisher	-	16½	17	2
Survival Equipment Fitter	-	16½	17	2
Air Photography Processor 2	-	16½	17	2
Photographer Ground	-	18	18	2
Air Cartographer	-	16½	17	2
Plotter Air Photography	-	16½	17	2
Administrative Clerk	-	16½	17	2
Data Analyst	-	16½	17	2
WRAF Shorthand Typist (Qualified)	-	-	17	2
WRAF Typist (Qualified)	-	-	17	2
Musician	-	16½	-	1
Enrolled Nurse (General)	-	20	20	2
Pupil Nurse (General)	2	17¾	17¾	2
Laboratory Technician	5	16½	17	1
Physiotherapist (Qualified)	-	21	21	1
Mental Nurse	4	18	18	1
Medical Assistant	-	16½	17	2
Environmental Health Technician	3	17½	17½	1
Operating Theatre Technician	2	16½	17	1
Electrophysiological Technician	5	16½	17	1
Pharmacy Technician	5	16½	17	1
Radiographer	3+1'A'	18	18	1
Dental Hygienist	2	17	17	2
Dental Surgery Assistant	-	16½	17	2
Dental Technician	4	16½	17	1
Supplier	-	16½	17	2
Movements Operator	-	16½	-	2
Cook†	-	16½	17	2
Catering Clerk	-	16½	17	2
Steward/Stewardess†	-	16½	17	2

CORRECT AT TIME OF PRINTING

Chapter 6
The History of RAF Uniform

On 13 April 1912 a Royal Warrant created the Royal Flying Corps. One month later Army Order 13/1912 decreed that the headquarters of the Corps was to be at Netheravon on Salisbury Plain. In order to join the Corps officers had to be medically fit and had to have attained the Royal Aero Club Aviation Certificate standard of flying. Furthermore, no officer was to hold executive rank unless he had qualified as an expert flyer. What the Corps now lacked was its own distinctive uniform. Although Army Dress Regulations had been amended in 1911 to take account of the Air Battalion of the Royal Engineers, a more comprehensive revision took place in 1913 and the first dress regulations for the RFC were published under Army Order 378 of that year.

In essence, the new Corps' uniform was to be of standard Army style but with new designs for badges and buttons. The RFC cap badge was based on the Royal Engineers' cap badge, where the Royal Cypher is replaced by RFC (to be replaced in 1918 by the letters RAF — see also Chapter 5 RAF Badges and Brevets). Buttons were similarly modelled. The first distinctive RFC uniform, which appeared in late 1913, was a double-breasted jacket with no visible buttons and made of a drab khaki serge (sometimes referred to as a maternity jacket). It was worn

The RFC Cap badge based on the Royal Engineers Cap badge where the Royal Cypher has been replaced by the letters RFC.

with khaki breeches, puttees and ankle boots. Full dress or 'Blue' uniform, on the other hand consisted of a dark blue tunic buttoned to the neck, dark blue overall trousers with a red stripe down the sides, and a forage cap. Similarly, Mess dress consisted of a dark blue jacket with scarlet cloth roll collar worn with matching blue trousers. Despite the introduction of an RFC uniform many officers, who had been seconded to the Corps, continued to wear their own regimental dress, changing badges and buttons to suit. This unofficial practice remained until the introduction of the first Royal Air Force uniform in 1918. The Royal Navy Air Wing (the other half of the Corps) made only minor changes to its uniform. Although the Naval wing of the RFC had been in existence since 13 May 1912, the first formal institution of a flying element or 'Naval Air Wing' in the RN did not materialise until the publishing of Admiralty Circular Letter No. 22 on 11 July 1912. By the time the Royal Naval Air Service was formed two years later, in July 1914, the Air Wing had

The Distinctive maternity jacket style khaki uniform worn by all RFC ranks from 1912-18

RNAS officer's cap badge circa 1915 (Notice the presentation of the eagle)

produced separate dress regulations that introduced the wearing of a small gilt eagle in the RNAS officer's cap badge, and a similar red silk embroidered eagle arm badge for ratings. The Navy was determined to go its own way, and in July 1914 formally announced its separation from the RFC through Admiralty Circular Letter EW 13964. Thereafter, the RNAS was to be considered as a branch of the Royal Navy and, therefore, subject to Naval regulations.

British Army (RFC) cuff rank titles circa 1915

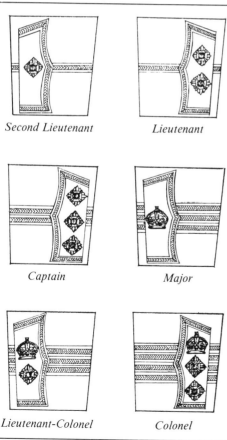

Second Lieutenant   Lieutenant

Captain   Major

Lieutenant-Colonel   Colonel

Royal Flying Corps badges of rank

With the departure of the Naval Wing, the RFC fell entirely under the authority of the War Office. Commissioned officer rank titles and badges were the same as for the Army, as were the non-commissioned ranks. The first new addition to the non-commissioned officer (NCO) rank badges came in late 1913, with the introduction of a four-bladed propeller badge to be worn above chevrons to denote that the NCO was a member of the RFC. In 1916, Army Order 322 introduced the two-bladed propeller badge to be worn as a trade badge by air mechanics. The badge itself originates from the propeller-swinging task undertaken by mechanics and NCOs to start aircraft engines. The first distinctive rank title for NCOs came with the introduction of the Flight Sergeant rank. Here the term 'flight' described a body of men equivalent to a platoon or troop in the Army. The illustrated NCO rank titles shown below remained in use until the formation of the RAF in 1918.

NCO rank badges for the RFC.

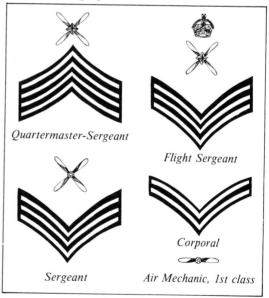

Quartermaster-Sergeant   Flight Sergeant

Sergeant   Corporal

Air Mechanic, 1st class

Early RAF officers' uniforms

One of the tasks of the Smuts Committee, which had recommended the formation of the RAF, was to recommend a suitable rank structure for the Service with outline proposals for a style of dress. Smuts could not have failed to be aware of animosity that existed between the two former air factions, and his task of welding a single

Early RAF uniform (circa 1919) made in khaki colour with light khaki lace rank braid topped by a gilt eagle with crown

Service was a difficult one. Nevertheless, he did it with style and panache, basing many of his recommendations on the great British compromise — and that in essence is what RAF uniform is; a compromise in dress and insignia based on early RNAS and RFC styles. Initially, the committee recommended that the method of showing rank distinction should be based on Naval lace, but in khaki material. Moreover, a gilded metal eagle, also borrowed from the RNAS, should be ensigned by a crown and worn above the rank lace as a common distinguishing badge for all officers. Finally rank titles were to follow the Army form from Lieutenant to General. In due course, the first khaki RAF uniform appeared. But in late 1918, a mysterious light blue uniform also appeared for RAF officers. The idea of a blue uniform had been mooted in Air Force memorandum No. 2 in March 1918, but nothing formal appeared, so how the light blue uniform arrived is something of a mystery. Apparently the Tsar's government ordered vast quantities of light Ruritanian blue material in 1915 to clothe a Cossack cavalry regiment. By 1917 the order had been completed and was ready for shipment, but the abdication of the Tsar in 1917 left the material on the textile

manufacturer's hands. What was he to do with this cloth? It proved impossible to dye. Then, in 1918, the sudden announcement of the formation of a Royal Air Force seemed a heaven-sent opportunity to get rid of the now surplus cloth in the manufacture of new uniforms! Fact or fiction? The records are unclear. Part and parcel of the light blue uniform were gold wire badges and brevets. Legend attributes this innovation to a Lily Elsie, who thought it rather dashing and suggested it to one of the senior members of the Air Council. However, the serving officers of the time did not share either the textile manufacturer's or Lily Elsie's enthusiasm for the light blue uniform and in due course it was abandoned under Air Ministry Order (AMO) 617 published in July 1918. Instead, a more sober blue-grey material was selected, sanctioned as the official uniform colour and authorised as such in AMO 1049 published on 15 September 1919. The present RAF blue-grey colour dates from that time. A further important change was made on 27 August 1919 when the Army rank titles for RAF officers were abolished, to be replaced by more descriptive ranks that have remained in use. A little later, in October 1919, the gilt eagle and crown worn on the sleeve above rank braid was withdrawn and the khaki lace itself was replaced by a blue equivalent. Since those early days there has been remarkably little change to the RAF officers' No. 1 uniform in basic style and design. The cut of the uniform is Army based on a cavalry officer's tunic, the method of portraying rank Navy. The eagle insignia is RNAS, the brown gloves a legacy from the RFC.

Early uniforms – Other Ranks
The first distinctive uniform was the double-breasted 'maternity jacket', worn with breeches, puttees and brown ankle boots, introduced in 1913. In addition, shoulder titles bearing the inscription 'Royal Flying Corps', or brass epaulette studs denoting RFC were worn to distinguish members of the Corps from other branches of the Army. While in 1918 officers were given the option of the light blue uniform, other ranks were not. Instead, khaki dress continued to be worn even after the formation of the RAF until the new blue-grey uniform was introduced in 1919. The new uniform was restyled to include a five-button serge tunic with matching breeches and puttees worn with black ankle boots. At the same time the shoulder titles

The RAF eagle arm badge worn by all airmen from 1919 to 1973 – from the RNAS distinguishing arm badge

were replaced by an eagle arm badge of embroidered light blue silk worn at the top of each sleeve so that the head of the eagle faced to the rear. This was taken from RNAS dress. The origin of this badge dates back to Admiralty weekly order No. 2 dated 23 June 1914. It was on Winston Churchill's instructions that the order was issued as a means of distinguishing naval airmen from seamen. The eagle arm badge remained in use for fifty-nine years as a distinguishing sleeve badge for all airmen's uniforms; it was withdrawn on the introduction of a 'restyled' uniform in 1973.

RAF uniform between the wars and after

The first RAF officers' blue-grey uniforms proved a great success. They were worn with a blue or silver grey shirt, black tie, blue-grey slacks or breeches, with matching puttees and black ankle boots. Squadron Leaders were allowed the option of wearing field boots, which became optional wear for all officers in 1920. By late 1920 the colour of shirt changed to white and at the same time the fad of officers' white cane walking sticks first appeared. The origin of this tradition is obscure, but it was generally taken as the RAF's equivalent of the Army's swagger stick. White walking sticks continued in fashion for the next twelve years and were carried on ceremonial occasion. There is even reference to officers' cane-drill in early drill manuals.

Nothing in the RAF is sacred, and the service's curious preoccupation with shirts and their colour reared its head in 1936 when the official white shirt was replaced by one of blue-grey. The blue-grey version remained in use until the 1970s, when all sorts of different shades of blue were tried out until the current shade of wedgwood blue was adopted in 1973. The first major change to airmen's uniform design came in 1936 with the introduction of an open-neck tailored tunic worn with blue-grey shirt and black tie. This was a far more comfortable dress than the high-neck tunic and proved very popular.

The onset of the Second World war in 1939 brought a full review of RAF dress. First to go were the breeches and puttees, which were replaced by slacks for all ranks. At the same time, a second working dress, termed 'battle dress' and modelled on the Army equivalent, was introduced for general wear to replace dungarees. The Air Force pattern was the same as that of the Army, but it was worn unbuttoned at the neck to display collar and tie. After the war this style was refined to include tailored lapels and was accepted as No. 2 Home Service Dress until it was formally replaced in 1973 by a restyled jacket and trousers. With the exception of the introduction of 'battle dress', RAF Service Dress remained undisturbed until the end of the Second World War. Then in 1946, the Committee on Post War Dress published its findings on the subject of 'Home Pattern Dress for the RAF'. The aim of the committee was to recommend a smarter and neater Service dress. The changes suggested for the officers' tunic were striking and included abolishing the two side pockets and the bottom button, and introducing two side vent slits to replace the single slit. Furthermore, silk thread flying badges were to be replaced by gold wire badges. Fortunately this style was never made compulsory, and the old pattern was restored in 1951. Not all the committee's recommendations were rejected: a proposal to replace the rough serge of airmen's dress with barathea was well received. The first barathea uniforms for serving airmen were introduced in 1952, in time for the Coronation. This design remained in service until the introduction of the current airmen's No 1 uniform in 1973.

RAF Full Dress

Full Dress, as it was described at the time, was first introduced in April 1920 and authorised in Air Ministry Weekly Order No. 332. The dress consisted of a high buttoned tunic of blue Venetian cloth with seven buttons down the front, and a skirt to the jacket with three pleats at the back and two buttons at the top of the pleats. Rank was displayed on the collar using oak leaves and acorns in gold embroidery — the size and number of oak leaves indicated the wearer's rank. The tunic had blue shoulder straps with an eagle and crown embroidered in gold on each and was worn with matching trousers and ankle boots until 1928, when under Air Ministry Weekly Order 538 ankle boots were replaced by

RAF Full Dress circa 1921

high-waist trousers (overalls) and wellington boots. The original headwear for Full Dress was the standard service dress cap but this was replaced by the busby in June 1921. The RAF Full Dress was prohibitively expensive for young officers and unpopular among senior officers as it was uncomfortable to wear. Legend also has it that King George VI particularly disliked the head-dress. Full Dress, to the relief of many, was not reintroduced after the Second World War, although in the late 1970s a similar style of uniform, including a busby, was introduced for RAF musicians to carry forward the Full Dress tradition.

RAF Officers' Mess Dress

The design and style of RAF Mess Kit closely resembles that of both the Army and the Navy's equivalent dress. It was first introduced by the Army. In pre-Crimean War days it was customary for officers to dine together in Full Dress — a dress that was heavy, uncomfortable and cumbersome. As a result of the long hot summers experienced during the Crimean campaign of the 1850s, the Royal Artillery introduced a lightweight 'walking out dress' termed Stable Jacket, which consisted of a short, cutaway, Eton-style jacket worn with overalls. It became a very popular form of dress, finally evolving into Mess Dress by the latter part of the 19th century. RAF Mess Dress was simply modelled on the equivalent Army wear. It was first authorised on 25 March 1920, under Air Ministry Order No. 291. An Eton-style jacket of blue Venetian cloth was adopted, displaying gold rank braid around the sleeve cuffs. In addition, miniature gold-embroidered brevets were permitted, to be worn attached to the left lapel facing. The jacket was worn with white, stiff-fronted shirt, wing collar, black bow tie, white waistcoat and blue slacks. In 1928, the slacks were exchanged for overalls with gold wire lace side seams, and patent leather wellington boots were introduced as standard

foot wear. Mess Dress was not worn during the Second World War but was reintroduced in 1947, with some changes. A blue, Venetian cloth waistcoat was introduced, in addition to a white waistcoat for selective wear, and the gold stripe down the side seam of the trousers was abolished. Finally, black shoes were accepted instead of wellingtons. Today, the stiff shirt, wing collar and white waistcoat (No. 5A Dress) is reserved for Royal or Court occasions, being replaced by a soft-fronted shirt with turned down collar (No. 5B Dress) for Mess dinner nights. This style of dress is not unlike the 'mess undress' that enjoyed a brief span in the late 1930s.

Modern RAF Dress

The RAF uniform of today still proudly bears the distinguishing features of its origins as dress for the Naval and military wings of the RFC. Sadly, few are aware of the uniform's pedigree. No. 1 Home Service Dress is now only worn on ceremonial occasions, while No. 2 Dress is for everyday wear. A total of eleven different dresses are available to the Service for wear throughout the world, including on operational duty. At the time of publication (1987) a further review of RAF dress is in progress.

RAF and WRAF Mess Dress 1985

Chapter 7
RAF Badges and Brevets

The first recognition by the British War Office of the military potential of aviation is attributed to the period 1878-82, when the Royal Engineers were experimenting with balloons and kites. The Royal Engineers, therefore, paved the way for British military aviation. Appropriately, when on 13 April 1912 a Royal warrant created the Royal Flying Corps, the design for the Corps' badge was purposely taken from the Royal Engineers' badge. The RFC badge consisted of the monogram RFC 'ensigned' by a crown that breaks the surrounding laurel wreath. On the formation of the Royal Air Force on 1 April 1918, the only change needed was to replace the monogram RFC with the letters RAF. This badge is now titled the airman's cap badge, and it is worn by all airmen up to and including the rank of Flight Sergeant.

The RFC cap badge (all ranks) and RAF cap badge (non-commissioned ranks)

Officers' cap badges for the Royal Flying Corps and Royal Air Force
Before 1 April 1918 officers seconded to the RFC wore their regimental cap badge while RFC officers wore the same design cap badge as that of the soldiers. The first distinctive officers' cap badge appeared on the formation of the RAF. The origin of the design is unclear, but it closely resembles the 1914 design of the RNAS officer cap badge and may well have been a compromise design when the RNAS and RFC formally merged to form the RAF in 1918. There is no doubting the adoption of the gilt eagle from the Naval Air Service badge. The RAF officers' cap badge is worn by all officers up to and including

the rank of Group Captain on the Service dress cap. A miniature version of this badge is worn on the beret, but a simplified gilt eagle surmounted by a crown is worn on the forage or field service cap. Before 10 July 1918, RFC officers of the rank of General and above wore a cap badge similar in design to the 1918 pattern officers' cap badge. The present air rank officers' cap badge which includes a lion above the Crown, dates from late 1918 and has remained unchanged. The last distinctive officers' cap badge is that worn by chaplains. In their badge the gilt eagle and large laurel wreath has been exchanged for a 'black cross paty with wings'; the cross is surmounted by a small laurel wreath encircling the letter RAF ensigned by a crown. This badge too, was introduced in 1918.

RNAS – RAF cap badges

RNAS officer

RAF officer below air rank

Officer's cap badge (field service)

Air Officer's cap badge

Chaplain's cap badge (King's Crown pre-1953)

Warrant officer's cap and sleeve badge
The early rank structure of the RAF described two distinct ranks for Warrant Officer — Class 1 and Class 2. This titling was a direct copy of the Army form, where a Warrant Officer Class 1 was Regimental Sergeant Major, and the Class 2 the Company Sergeant Major. The Royal coat of arms as worn by Warrant Officers today was the badge for the Class 1 and a simple crown in light blue worsted embroidery was displayed by the Warrant Officer Class 2. Both classes of rank badge were worn on the cuffs. The usage of the term 'Sergeant Major' lasted in the RAF until the early days of the Second World War, when the Class 2 Warrant Officer rank was abandoned along with the term Sergeant Major. Instead, the straightforward titling of 'Warrant Officer' became the accepted description. This title remains to the present day for all ground branch Warrant Officers. The distinctive hat badge for Warrant Officers dates from the early days of the RAF and is modelled on the officers' cap badge. The formation of the laurel wreath is slightly different and the badge is made of metal, as opposed to the officers' embroidered badge. The Warrant Officer's cap badge is worn by aircrew and ground branch Warrant Officers alike; only the cuff rank badges differ.

In July 1946 a new rank badge scheme recommended by the post-war committee on dress came into effect for non-commissioned aircrew. The general idea was that the flying branch of the service should be segregated and given separate title badges. In effect the NCO ranks from Warrant Officer to Sergeant disappeared, to be replaced by five new ranks from Aircrew 1 to 4, with a new rank corresponding to Warrant Officer, entitled 'Master Aircrew'. The insignia on these new badges was embroidered in blue silk on the traditional blue-grey background, and the badge was worn on both jacket sleeve cuffs. Note the symbolic use of the RNAS eagle in the badge design once again. The new style of aircrew badge was generally unpopular, and was cynically known as the 'star and garter badge'. Air Ministry policy bowed to popular expression, and in August 1950 the aircrew ranks 1-4 were abolished, to be replaced by the former Flight Sergeant and Sergeant titles. However, the Master Aircrew badge and rank was retained as aircrew equivalent to ground branch Warrant Officer, and has lasted to the present day. Master Aircrew are normally referred to by their aircrew category — Master Pilot, Loadmaster and so on.

Warrant Officer cap and sleeve badges

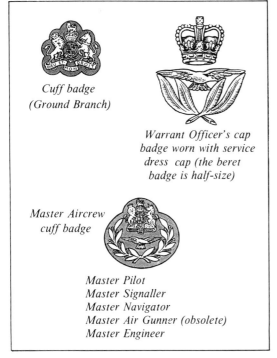

*Cuff badge
(Ground Branch)*

Warrant Officer's cap badge worn with service dress cap (the beret badge is half-size)

Master Aircrew cuff badge

*Master Pilot
Master Signaller
Master Navigator
Master Air Gunner (obsolete)
Master Engineer*

Revised aircrew NCO badges 1946-50

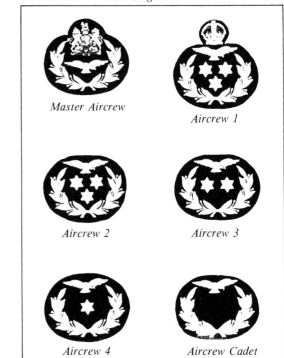

Master Aircrew

Aircrew 1

Aircrew 2

Aircrew 3

Aircrew 4

Aircrew Cadet

The Royal Air Force badge

The RAF badge as we know it today was sanctioned in 1949 and described in Air Ministry Order A666 as 'In front of a circle inscribed with the motto *"Per Ardua Ad Astra"*, and ensigned with the Imperial Crown, and eagle volant and affronte, the head lowered and to the sinister'. The original RAF badge, which dates from 1918, was different having the motto borne on a garter circlet. This misuse of heraldic devices was corrected by the College of Arms in 1922 by the substitution of a plain circlet, and the revised badge was duly registered on 26 January 1923, though not sanctioned until 1949. The identity of the designer of the badge is regrettably unknown, though one suggestion is that it was a clerk belonging to Gieves the tailors.

The Royal Air Force badge

The Motto 'Per Ardua ad Astra'

The origin of the RAF's motto is said to be associated with the RFC's first commanding officer, Colonel F. Sykes (later General Sir Frederick Sykes). During the early days of the Corps he invited his officers to suggest a motto which would encourage *esprit de corps*. Group Captain Stradling in his book *Customs of the Service,* tells of two officers walking from the Officers' Mess to Cody's Shed at Farnborough discussing the problem. Lieutenant J. S. Yule suggested the Virgilian 'Sic ictur ad Astra' (Journey to the Stars) as a possible contender, but this idea was rejected and the Drummond family's motto of 'Ad Astra Per Ardua' was presented as an alternative. This too was rejected and 'Per Ardua Ad Astra' was finally chosen, to be translated as 'Through Struggle to the Stars' (though the College of Arms said at the time that

no authoritative translation was possible). Other sources suggest the arms of the Mulvany family from Ireland, which bears the same inscription.

The Royal Air Force roundel

The first RFC aircraft to land in France in August 1914 (A BE2B of 2 Squadron) bore no marking other than an aircraft number painted on the rudder. Clearly some form of aircraft identification was required, and towards the end of August 1914, instructions were issued to mark under wing surfaces with a Union flag. This made the identification of aircraft at low level easy, but at high level the colours of the flag were not clearly discernible and appeared to merge into the shape of a cross. This cross was frequently confused with the Maltese Cross adopted by the Germans and led to Allied 'Archie' gunners (anti-aircraft) firing on friendly aircraft! The French had adopted the idea of displaying their national colours in the form of concentric circles. The device was adopted by the RFC in October 1914, but the colours were reversed to avoid confusion with French aircraft. At the same time, the Union flag was retained in miniature form, painted between the roundels and the wing tip, and on the rudder. In May 1915, the Union flag on the rudder was replaced by red, white and blue stripes and additional roundels were painted on each side of the fuselage. At the same time, the Union flag was removed from the wings.

The RAF Roundel

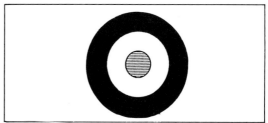

The Pilot's wings

The original pilot's brevet was designed by General Sir Frederick Sykes and General Sir David Henderson (the first senior officers of the RFC) and approved by King George V in February 1913 under Army Order 40/13. It consisted of the wings of a swift (not an eagle or albatross) in white silk embroidery, bearing the monogram RFC encircled by a laurel wreath of brown silk. The monogram was surmounted by a crown, and the background material was drab

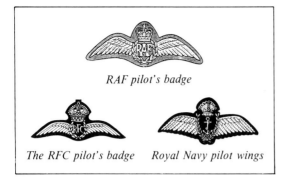

RAF pilot's badge

The RFC pilot's badge   *Royal Navy pilot wings*

blue cloth. Today this badge is proudly worn by all pilots of the RAF above the left breast pocket of dress uniform, though the monogram RFC has been replaced by the letters RAF and the crown design has changed. (On change of monarch the crown design may change from that of a King's crown to a Queen's crown.) The design of this flying badge, the first in the world, has been used as the prototype for pilot's badges of many other nations. RAF pilots' wings differ from the naval equivalent in that Naval wings represent an albatross and the monogram is replaced by an anchor; they also differ in that they are worn on the left cuff of Naval uniforms above rank braid.

The Observer's badge

The observer's badge was the second specialist flying badge to be adopted by the RFC. The badge was introduced in September 1915, authorised by Army Order No. 327. At first, the observer's badge was restricted to officers, but in November 1915 the spectrum was widened to include Warrant Officers and NCOs 'who are in the qualified list of observers'. The idea of a second flying badge dates back to the early days of the First World War, when a second crew member was required to assist the pilot with a multitude of tasks from navigation to aerial gunnery. Not unnaturally, the second crew member, or 'observer', believed that he deserved some recognition. A case for an observer's badge was forwarded to the War Office, and in due course the half wing observer's badge was authorised. In later years, the design of the observer's badge formed the foundation for the air gunner's badge although the observer's badge remains unique amongst RAF badges (see also other aircrew flying badges). The observer's badge was worn in the same manner as the pilot's wings, and was of white embroidered silk on a

drab blue cloth where the half wing protrudes from the letter O; a subtle difference from the later air gunner's design where the half wing is attached to the laurel wreath.

The Observer's badge

The Air Gunner's badge

By the end of the First World War, considerable progress had been made in aircraft design, including the introduction of the first twin-engined long-range bomber aircraft. These aircraft were considerably more sophisticated than earlier models and required additional crew to assist with navigational, defence and signalling tasks. After the First World War armament tradesmen were carried in multi-engined aircraft as unrecognised air gunners until this matter was given serious consideration by the Air Council in 1922. The result was that in 1923 the trade skill of 'air gunner' was established and authorised in Air Ministry Order (AMO) 204/23. This order also introduced a trade badge consisting of a winged bullet made of brass, worn on the right sleeve. The winged bullet continued in use until the last month of 1939 when a new half wing brevet, similar to the observer's brevet, was introduced.

A suggested design for the new air gunner's brevet was forwarded to the Air Ministry for approval in early 1938. Marshal of the RAF Sir Cyril Newall examined the design carefully and noticed that it had thirteen feathers embroidered in the half wing. Superstition or not, Sir Cyril did not like it and decreed, 'either stick another feather on, or cut one off!' Accepting the wartime principle of economy, a feather was cut

Air Gunner's badges

Pre-1939   *Post-1939*

off — and today all half wing brevets have twelve feathers. The other major difference in design from the observer's badge was the inclusion of a laurel wreath around the letters AG, where the half wing is attached to the laurel wreath. Buffs will note that the observer's badge has the half wing directly attached to the 'O'. The reasoning behind this change dates from the pilot's wings, where the monogram RAF was surrounded by a laurel wreath, with the wing's roots attached at the wreath — a means, perhaps, of standardisation in design. On 21 December 1939, AMO 547 was duly published authorising the half wing air gunner's brevet. This brevet was to become the model design for a succession of other aircrew brevets.

Pilot's, Observer's and Air Gunner's badges

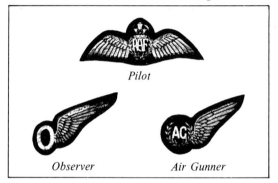

Pilot

Observer   *Air Gunner*

Other aircrew flying brevets
Soon after the outbreak of the Second World War, a new policy was introduced with regard to rank within qualified aircrews. Broadly speaking the policy said that all aircrew should hold either commissioned, warrant, or non-commissioned rank; moreover, the lowest rank of qualified aircrew (pilot, observer or air gunner) was to be Sergeant. Thus, all non-commissioned aircrew became known by their rank and aircrew category 'Sergeant Pilot', 'Flight Sergeant Observer' — and so on. However, the number of defined aircrew categories was soon found to be insufficient as more sophisticated, and much larger, multi-engined aircraft came off the drawing board. Significant advances had been made in air navigation techniques, including radio and radar navigation aids, and the observer now found his time entirely devoted to manning and operating this equipment. The all-embracing observer became the specialist navigator, and a new brevet, modelled on the air gunner's brevet, but containing the letter 'N',

was authorised accordingly in AMO 1019 published in September 1942. The introduction of the new 'N' brevet was not popular among those who had already qualified as observers, who, quite reasonably, jealously coveted their distinctive badge. The Air Ministry was not unsympathetic, and in due course regulations were issued entitling observers to continue wearing their badge provided that they had qualified for it before 3 September 1939. At the same time as the introduction of the navigator's brevet, two further aircrew categories were introduced; that of bomb aimer (B) and engineer (E). During the Second World War came the introduction of further later aircrew categories for radio observer (RO) (also known as observers radio), meteorological observer (M), and signaller (S). All of these brevets were again modelled on the twelve-feather air gunner's badge. By the end of the war there was a total of eleven different aircrew categories.

In 1945, the post-war committee on dress discussed the future of aircrew badges, and their recommendations resulted in the previous aircrew categories being reduced to five: pilot, navigator, signaller, engineer and air gunner. (It was at this time, too, that the 'star and garter'

Aircrew half wing badges 1939-45

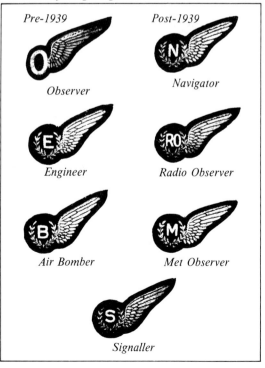

Pre-1939   *Post-1939*

Observer   *Navigator*

Engineer   *Radio Observer*

Air Bomber   *Met Observer*

Signaller

badges were introduced.) Since the Second World War the air gunner has become obsolete and the badge is no longer awarded but three new aircrew categories have been introduced. In February 1956, and as a result of the sophisticated avionics incorporated in the 'V' Bombers (Victor, Vulcan and Valiant), a new skill of air electronics operator (if NCO) or officer (if commissioned) was recognised. The monogram of the brevet was AE, and in due course it replaced the signaller's (S) badge. The expansion of the air transport fleet, first to tackle the Berlin Airlift and in the 1950s to support British Forces overseas, required a new aircrew category responsible for the safe loading, unloading and in-flight custody of freight and passengers. The title given to this aircrewman was 'air quartermaster', and the brevet carried the letters 'QM'. By the mid 1970s the quartermaster's role on aircraft had gone well beyond that of freight and passenger handling.

Post-war flying badges

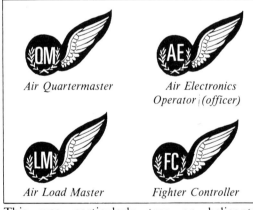

Air Quartermaster　　　*Air Electronics Operator (officer)*

Air Load Master　　　*Fighter Controller*

This was particularly true on helicopter squadrons, where he became sometimes navigator, radio operator, air gunner and winch man, as well as, perhaps, the 'emergency' second pilot. In view of these multifarious tasks, the quartermaster on helicopters was given the subtitle crewman. In 1972, the title quartermaster was dropped in favour of a new description, loadmaster, with a corresponding new brevet incorporating the letter 'LM'. In the early 1980s plans were announced to introduce a new airborne early warning system based on the Nimrod aircraft and to include the new aircrew category of airborne fighter controller. At the time of publishing Nimrod has been abandoned in favour of the Boeing AWACs aircraft which is likely to enter service in the early 1990s.

Nevertheless a half wing flying badge, was introduced in 1983, recognised by the letters FC. It was the first for eleven years and is reserved for fighter controllers employed on airborne early warning duties.

The Parachute Jumping Instructor's badge
There is one half wing badge that displays an emblem rather than capitals — the badge awarded to parachute jumping instructors (PJIs) which contains the inflated parachute design. This badge dates from the Second World War and was worn at first as a light blue armlet by

Parachute Jumping Instructor's badge　　　*Early armlet badge for parachute instructors*

volunteer parachute jumping instructors recruited from the RAF's physical education branch specifically to train airborne forces. Later, they also acted as paratroop despatchers during the various airborne offensives. As a result of the courage and tenacity shown by these military parachuting pioneers, they were awarded the distinction of wearing the full half wing badge under AMO A 1079, published in 1945, with the additional status of 'honorary aircrew'.

Preliminary flying badges
In addition to the substantive flying badge awarded for satisfactorily completing flying

The five preliminary flying badges

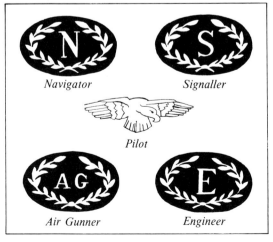

Navigator　　　*Signaller*

Pilot

Air Gunner　　　*Engineer*

training in one of the named categories, there were also preliminary flying badges. Five of these type badges were authorised under AMO A/631 on 8 September 1949 for pilot, navigator, signaller, air gunner and engineer. These badges were embroidered in blue drab on a dark oval patch, worn as for the full badge and awarded on successful completion of basic aircrew training. Today, only the preliminary flying badge for pilot remains and this badge is worn by University Air Squadron cadets who have completed the requisite training.

The symbolic eagle – Pathfinder's badge

Over the years there have been many queries, sometimes resulting in arguments, as to the origin of the eagle portrayed in many of the RAF badges. The eagle contained in the RAF badge is described heraldically as 'an eagle volant and affronte, the head lowered to the sinister'. However, the Navy claimed for many years that it was not an eagle at all but an albatross, despite the fact that the bird did not have webbed feet! In the best traditions of compromise there were even those who suggested an albatreagle or eagletross! The truth can be found in early RNAS records. Admiralty weekly Order No. 2 dated 23 June 1914 states, 'The badge of an eagle

Early RNAS designs based on the eagle badge

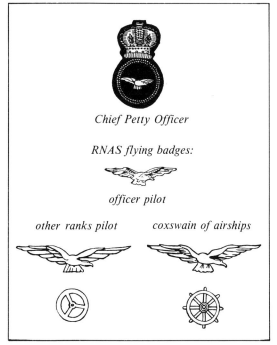

Chief Petty Officer

RNAS flying badges:

officer pilot

other ranks pilot   *coxswain of airships*

Pathfinder's badge

will be worn by members of the RNAS at the top of the left sleeve' — to distinguish naval airmen from naval seamen. As already mentioned, it was an idea of Winston Churchill, who wanted the badge for the RNAS. However, it was Admiral Murray Sueter who was given the task of finding a suitable design. An artist produced a design like a goose but Mrs Sueter was not impressed. She had a gold eagle brooch of French Imperial design purchased in Paris and much preferred that as did the Admiral. The Admiral took this brooch to the Admiralty to show to Mr Churchill and Admiral Prince Louis of Battenberg. Both preferred the eagle brooch to the goose design, and agreed that it should be adopted. It became the basis for many other early RNAS flying badges. Strange that the Royal Navy should later adopt the albatross as representative in Naval Pilots' wings? Again, the RAF adopted the swift's wings for the Pilot's badge! As embroidered eagle badges and brooches disappeared from Naval uniform, so in April 1918 they began to appear on the new uniform for the RAF, becoming the basis for many of the designs. During the Second World War the gilt eagle worn on the left breast pocket flap below medal ribbons became a treasured and highly respected emblem synonymous with bravery and outstanding devotion to duty. This emblem was the pathfinder's badge.

The Pathfinder force came into being on 15 August 1942 at the behest of Air Chief Marshal Sir Arthur Harris, the Air Officer Commanding-in-Chief of Bomber Command. The Pathfinder squadrons were manned by experienced crews skilled in navigation and bomb aiming techniques, and Sir Arthur proposed that as a reward for their outstanding devotion to duty, Pathfinders should receive quick promotion and wear some sort of distinguishing badge. For obvious reasons it was never worn on operations. After the war the Pathfinder force was disbanded and an attempt was made to ban the wearing of this badge. Fortunately, and after representations from the Pathfinders Association, any such idea was overruled. In the most recent past, the gilt eagle has reappeared on RAF dress uniform above chevrons to denote non-commissioned officer aircrew ranks and more recently still it was introduced at the RAF College Cranwell in 1982 as part of the epaulette slide badge for the senior duty officer cadet.

NCO air crew badge

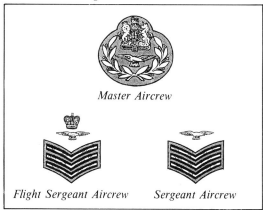

Master Aircrew

Flight Sergeant Aircrew   *Sergeant Aircrew*

The Wireless Operator's/telecommunications trade badge

The embroidered badge displaying a clenched fist grasping six forks of lightning is one of the oldest airman's arm badges, first introduced under AMO 1066 on 19 September 1918. At first it was confined to those who qualified as wireless operators and was worn on both sleeves below the eagle arm badge. At the end of the First World War it became obsolete, but was reintroduced in 1920 as an incentive for airmen to qualify in an advanced skill, and became known affectionately as the 'sparks' badge. Despite the recommendation to abolish this badge in 1949, it survived and in 1951 AMO No. A 380 authorised the badge to be worn by airmen and airwomen of all ground signalling and radio engineering trade groups. Today this badge is worn by all airmen involved with telecommunications. It is not worn by officers or warrant officers.

The 'Sparks' badge

The Works and Building badge

The works and building badge was authorised by AMO/825 on 20 October 1921 to be worn by airmen employed within the service building trades. The badge was made of metal to a design of a mason's square with a 'W' and 'B' ensigned by the now familiar eagle and crown. This badge was worn on the cap, with quarter-size badges on the tunic collar, but was abolished in 1929.

The Works and Building badge

The Physical Training Instructor's (PTI) badge

Another of the early airman qualifying badges was the physical training instructor's badge. The first PTI arm badge design, of three arms bent, each bearing an Indian club, joined at the centre by a hub and displaying the initials PTI, was introduced in 1923. Curiously, AMO 747 of August 1918 had previously introduced a PTI badge of crossed swords surmounted by an eagle and ensigned by a crown. This badge appears to have fallen out of use soon after the First World War, but when the three-arm badge was reviewed in 1949 it was decided to reintroduce the 1918 style of badge, embroidered onto a light blue cloth background. This badge was again sanctioned in October 1949 and remains to the present day. It is worn as a sleeve badge below chevrons on dress uniforms and in the centre of a white PT vest; the badge is not displayed on an officer's uniform.

The Physical Training Instructor's badge

Pre-1948   *Post-1948 (1918)*

The Apprentice and Boy Entrant badge
From the earliest days of the RAF boy apprentices played a significant part in the operational effectiveness of the Service. This factor was recognised in 1919, when AMO 500, published on 17 April of that year, authorised a special badge for boy apprentices. The badge was made in gilded metal and consisted of a four-bladed propeller contained within a circlet and was worn on the left arm sleeve only. Between the wars and as a result of Lord Trenchard's endeavours, apprentice and boy entrant training stations were opened to train technical tradesmen to service and repair aircraft and equipment. The most famous of these training units is Number 1 School of Technical Training at RAF Halton. Apprentice rank was first displayed as miniature chevrons worn below the circlet badge, but in 1973 the system of distinction changed to that of wearing coloured lanyards. Other distinguishing insignia included various coloured cap bands, which were later replaced by coloured discs worn behind the beret badge.

Apprentice and Boy Entrant badges (obsolete)

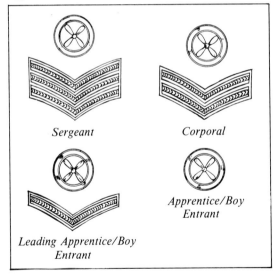

Sergeant

Corporal

Apprentice/Boy Entrant

Leading Apprentice/Boy Entrant

Badges of the RAF Regiment
On 6 January 1942, King George VI signed a warrant declaring the RAF Regiment to be a Corps formed as an integral part of the RAF. On 1 February 1942 the RAF Regiment came into being under the command of Major-General Liardet, tasked with aerodrome defence. Members of the Corps wear the RAF Regiment

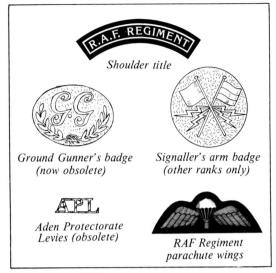

Shoulder title

Ground Gunner's badge (now obsolete)

Signaller's arm badge (other ranks only)

Aden Protectorate Levies (obsolete)

RAF Regiment parachute wings

RAF Regiment badges

shoulder title on all dress uniforms, which was introduced by AMO/466 published in early 1942 and abolished the previous 'ground gunner's sleeve badge. The RAF Regiment has had a distinguished career, with the responsibility for locally enlisted overseas forces including the RAF Regiment Malaya, Aden Protectorate Levies, and the Iraq Levies. On 9 March 1944, AMO/207 authorised qualified wireless operators and signallers to wear the arm badge bearing two signalling flags with four forks of lightning. The badge was worn by airmen on their battledress uniform sleeves. The RAF Regiment has one parachute squadron (No. 2 Squadron), where qualified parachutists wear the arm badge parachute with wings underneath the shoulder titles on the right arm sleeve. A brief history of the RAF Regiment has been recorded at Chapter 15. This badge may also be worn by other RAF personnel who have served with airborne units.

The Education Officer's badge
On 22 February 1940 AMO/116 introduced badges for officers of the RAF Volunteer Reserve (VR) employed as education officers. The badge was made in gilt metal and consisted of a design of crossed flambeaux and an eagle with outstretched wings. The badge was worn on the service dress jacket collar, with the VR device placed centrally above. This badge was abolished by AMO 368 dated 14 June 1948. There is no specific badge for the education branch today.

RAF Education Officer's badge

Air Sea Rescue service badge

During the early part of the Second World War a marine branch was added to the RAF with the task of rescuing aircrew who had 'ditched' into the sea. In recognition of their services, AMO 17 of 1943 authorised the introduction of a badge composed of a high-speed launch breaking through a choppy sea, bearing between its masts the letters 'ASR'. This was a cloth embroidered badge worn on the right sleeve of service dress, below the eagle arm badge but above chevrons. A further, but rarely seen badge, was that of the outstretched pilots' wings attached to a life belt containing the letters HSL (High Speed Launch). The origin of this second badge is unclear. Both badges were abolished by AMO 368 published on 1 June 1948, and today there is no distinguishing badge for the RAF Marine Branch. Sadly, at the time of publication (1987) the branch has disbanded.

Marine Branch badges

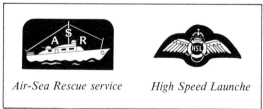

Air-Sea Rescue service   *High Speed Launche*

The Marksman's badge

The crossed rifle marksman badge was introduced by AMO 570 in 1949 to encourage small-arms proficiency amongst airmen. The badge is worn only by airmen, on their No. 2

The Marksman's badge

service dress at the bottom of the left cuff. This badge requires annual qualification for retention.

The Bomb Disposal badge

The bomb disposal badge was an early wartime design introduced by AMO 69, published on 23 January 1941. The embroidered badge consisted of a bomb in the descent, flanked by the letter 'BD' encircled by a laurel wreath. The badge was worn only by airmen on the right sleeve dress above chevrons. This badge was one of the many to be abolished by AMO 368 published on 1 June 1948. However, it has since reappeared, and is currently worn as an arm brassard by armament tradesmen employed on explosive ordnance disposal tasks within the RAF.

The Bomb Disposal Badge

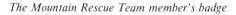

The Mountain Rescue Team member's badge

On 23 February 1959, the mountain rescue team member's badge was introduced, authorised by AMO 38 of that year. This embroidered badge recognised the contribution made by volunteer mountain rescue teams in support of both military and civil rescue teams. The badge consists of two ice axes surmounting a coil of rope, with the words Mountain Rescue forming an upper and lower arc and is worn on the lower edge of the right sleeve of No. 2 Home Service Dress.

The Mountain Rescue Team member's badge

Propeller badges

The badge of the two-bladed propeller worn by Leading Aircraftmen was introduced in 1938. However, all the propeller badges date in origin from the early days of the RFC, in particular the two-bladed propeller worn by the air mechanic first class, authorised in October 1916. The four-bladed propeller is derived from the similar badge worn above Sergeant chevrons by RFC non-commissioned officers (see previous chapter). The origin of the three-bladed propeller is unclear, though its logic is obvious. It was introduced on 1 January 1951. The present-day usage of these three badges is to represent Leading Aircraftman (LAC), Senior Aircraftman (SAC), and Junior Technician (Jnr. Tech.). The Junior Technician four-bladed propeller is only worn by technical tradesmen or musicians, and is a rank midway between Senior Aircraftman and Corporal. The propeller badges are worn on both upper arm sleeves on all dress uniforms.

The two, three and four bladed propeller badges

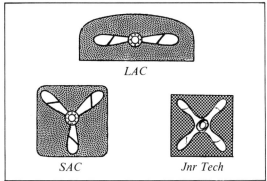

LAC

SAC   Jnr Tech

RAF Bandsmen's badges

The first RAF School of Music opened on 1 July 1918. The school was disbanded in early 1920 to be replaced by a Central Band on 1 April of that year. A year later the RAF College Band was established. During the war years many other command bands were created, of which several included famous personalities conscripted into the RAF for the duration of hostilities. Since the war, and despite the establishment of regional bands in 1949, musicians have been the subject of several of the post-war defence cuts. Today, the Service maintains only five established bands — the Western Band, the RAF Central Band, the Band of the RAF Regiment, the RAF College Band and the RAF Germany Band — though

volunteer bands are still encouraged. The traditional bandsman's badge is the gold-embroidered lyre, which was first introduced on 23 March 1933. Other bandsmen's badges are shown below. Musicians are not confined to wind instruments. The RAF Central Band includes a salon orchestra.

The RAF has a distinguished and well-deserved reputation for its musicianship. During the war years many famous musicians were conscripted into the Service including personalities like Steve Race, George Chisholm and Geraldo. Apart from providing their own concerts, accompanying morale-building radio programmes such as 'ITMA' and 'Much Binding in The Marsh', perhaps the most famous of all the RAF wartime bands was the 'Squadronaires'. This was a self-styled swing dance band that toured wherever the RAF were present to provide morale-raising concerts for the 'erks' as well as providing radio concerts. In January 1987 the decision was made to re-form a 'Squadronaires' band from within the RAF Central Band, at RAF Uxbridge. At an opening concert in front of former wartime 'Squadronaires', the new band gave its first offering which was acclaimed as a huge success and in keeping with high standards set by their predecessors. Thus the tradition of the Squadronaires will continue, albeit after a break of 42 years.

RAF Bandsmen's badges

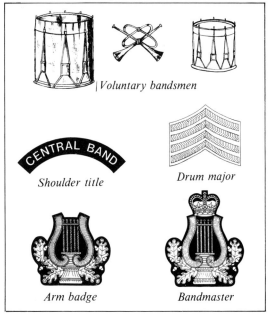

| *Voluntary bandsmen*

CENTRAL BAND
Shoulder title

Drum major

Arm badge   *Bandmaster*

RAF Medical Branch badges

There have been many changes and additions to the RAF medical branch badges since the branch evolved from the Army's Royal Army Medical Corps in 1918. In May 1918 AMO 162 authorised all medical officers to wear the gilt collar badge, composed of the rod of Mercury with one entwined serpent. Later, in October 1918, AMO 1217 added some further distinctive dress changes, including a maroon band around the medical officer's Service dress cap. The same AMO also prescribed that Warrant Officer and Sergeant medical attendants were to add the rod of Mercury badge to their uniform, and all ranks, Warrant Officer and below, were to include the Geneva Cross badge worn on both sleeves of dress jackets. In 1920 AMO 571 abolished the maroon cap band and introduced a restyled rod of Mercury collar badge, which included a winged rod ensigned by a crown and two serpents entwined around the staff. This badge remains to the present day as the standard

collar insignia for all members of the Service's medical branch. Apart from abolishing the Geneva Red Cross arm badge in February 1924, there were no further changes to the branch's insignia until after the Second World War. In 1960, a non-commissioned element was introduced to Princess Mary's Royal Air Force Nursing Service (PMRAFNS), composed of student nurses undergoing a three-year training course. The shoulder title PMRAFNS was introduced in 1960 for dress uniforms, followed by a ward uniform badge based on the winged rod of Mercury, and a metal training school badge. The branch's involvement with flying, and more particularly with casualty evacuation from overseas, has been acknowledged by the introduction of two new badges. The first is the light blue silk embroidered flight medical officer's sleeve badge and the second is the similar in-flight nursing attendant's badge based on the Geneva Cross. A variety of medical branch badges spanning the Service's history is shown at on page 48, and a brief history of the PMRAFNS is included at Chapter 13.

RAF Medical branch badges

PMRAFNS shoulder title and ward uniform badge

The Air Steward's badge

On 14 June 1967, Defence Council Instructions (DCI) S 119 (which had by then replaced Air Ministry Orders) authorised an air steward's badge. It is similar in design to the flight nursing attendant's badge, and is likewise worn on the upper right sleeve below the shoulder seam of uniform jackets. The badge, which is embroidered in light blue silk surrounded by a light blue laurel wreath, bears the letters AS. Air Stewards are volunteers drawn from the catering branch of the Service.

Air Steward's badge

The Chaplain's badges

The emblem of the black cross paty and gold wings previously seen in the chaplain's cap badge may also be seen ensigned by a crown embroidered on a chaplain's stole. In addition, honorary chaplains to the Queen wear a special gilt badge consisting of the Royal cypher and crown within a laurel wreath, which is worn below medal ribbons on the left hand side of the clerical stole. When Jewish chaplains served in the RAF, the cross paty was replaced by the Star of David.

Chaplain's badge

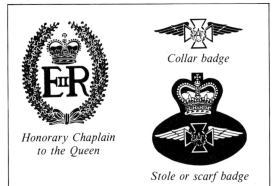

Collar badge

Honorary Chaplain
to the Queen

Stole or scarf badge

Emblem of the Judge Advocate General

A rarely seen badge is the emblem of the Judge Advocate General which was authorised by AMO 804 on 21 December 1950. This badge was worn as a shoulder flash by the Judge Advocate General's staff when under active Service conditions. It is one of the few badges to have been given a full heraldic description: 'Per fesse gules and azure a fess sable fimbriated and charged with letters JAG or between in chief 2 swords in saltire, points upwards, and in base an eagle displayed volant affronte gold. The shield ensigned with a Royal Crown proper surrounded with a wreath of laurels or, At the base 2 Lord Chancellors Maces Gold.'

Emblem of the Judge Advocate General

Brass collar letter studs

There are three types of miniature brass letter stud that may be worn affixed to the RAF uniform collar: A, VR and finally VR(T); all relate to RAF reserve personnel. The letter 'A' is applicable to the Royal Auxiliary Air Force (R Aux AF); the letters VR are worn by members of the RAF Volunteer Reserve; and the letters VR(T), where the 'VR' appears above the letter 'T', are worn by members of the RAF Volunteer Reserve (Training) branch. Airmen of the R Aux AF wear an embroidered 'A' on both upper sleeves of uniform dress. There are no airmen ranks in the RAFVR. In the RAFVR(T) Warrant Officers wear brass letter studs displaying 'ATC', which refer to the Air Training Corps cadet formation. A brief history of the Auxiliary Air Force Volunteer Reserve and Air Training Corps is recorded at Chapter 17.

The inverted chevron badges

In 1951 a new trade structure was introduced in the RAF which sought more readily to identify technician non-commissioned ranks, firstly by describing four new technical ranks, and secondly by displaying the rank badges using inverted chevrons. For the first time also, the single inverted chevron was introduced. This system lasted for thirteen years but was again revised in mid-1963. The result of the revision was that technician ranks were to be acknowledged, but shown in a different way. The Junior Technician's single chevron was replaced by an embroidered four-bladed propeller in light blue silk, and all other chevron rank badges were to revert to the upright

The inverted chevron badges (now obsolete)

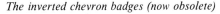
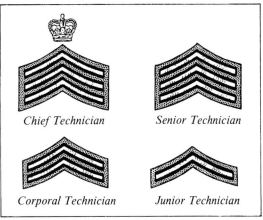

Chief Technician   Senior Technician

Corporal Technician   Junior Technician

position. The Senior Technician was redescribed as Sergeant, and a new rank of Chief Technician was created between Sergeant and Flight Sergeant, and recognised by an embroidered four-bladed propeller on a circular dark blue cloth background worn above three chevrons. The Flight Sergeant rank was retained, and marked by the traditional crown worn above chevrons. The 1963 system remains in use to the present day.

The symbolic use of the chevron dates from Roman times, and its design is taken from the battlefield formation of the inverted V. Soldiers selected to lead a formation wore an inverted V arm badge to distinguish themselves from the rank and file. This insignia has been carried through the ages and was adopted by the British Army in 1802 to denote non-commissioned rank.

Flight Sergeant and Chief Technician
Modern badges

| Flight Sergeant | Chief Technician |

Miscellaneous badges

War Service
A red bar printed on cloth was worn above the cuff of the left sleeve to indicate length of service since 3 September 1939. This became obsolete at the end of World War II.

Wounds
Again during the Second World War a gold bar badge was worn above the cuff of the left sleeve to indicate that the wearer had been wounded. This badge was abolished in 1945.

Good Conduct badges
This badge — an inverted single stripe for each occasion when awarded — was worn above the left cuff. One stripe signified three years' service and two stripes eight years' service. Since, before World War II they carried an emolument of 3d per day and were much sought after. They were worn only by AC2, AC1 and LAC ranks and were discontinued in 1941.

Aiguillettes and epaulettes
Aiguillettes are the plaited cord shoulder distinctions worn on ceremonial occasions by air officers, equerries and aides-de-camp. The word aiguillette has a French origin and a history that extends to medieval times. The original purpose of the aiguillette was to provide needle-ended points or tags that would secure pieces of armour to the leather undergarment worn by knights. When armour ceased to be worn during the Elizabethan era, knights continued to adorn their dress with tags, or aglets, as a sign of chivalry. The aglet fell in and out of fashion until they reappeared on dress in Charles II's court. By King George I's reign, aglets were used as a symbolic distinction to identify aides-de-camp and latterly general officers of the Army. Soon after this time, the aiguillette was formally reintroduced in its revised form as a shoulder cord adornment as part of full dress. The present RAF custom is, therefore, taken directly from the Army's interpretation pertaining to chivalry.

Aiguillettes

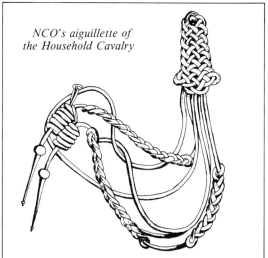

NCO's aiguillette of the Household Cavalry

The epaulette, despite its distinguished French origin, has a much less colourful history. It was simply an additional uniform shoulder strap incorporated as a means of retaining the cross body belt. It was particularly favoured by cavalry soldiers to reduce the chances of the sword belt shaking off when they rode into battle. It was first introduced by the French in 1759, and soon after won favour in this country. Early epaulettes were sometimes known as shoulder knots (not to be confused with aiguillettes) and were later used to display rank badges as they are today. The epaulettes worn with tropical mess dress have the addition of an eagle badge worn above the gold braid — a distinction dating back to the earliest days of the RAF.

The sash and stable belt

The custom of sash wearing in the RAF is an extension of established British Army tradition. The original purpose of a sash was simply as a cross body support that could be used to drag or pull a wounded soldier off the battlefield. However, because sashes were made of a distinctive coloured silk, they also evolved into a means of identifying officers on the battlefield. In about 1687, the custom arose of officers wearing a coloured sash around the waist with one end hanging loose on the left-hand side. This practice soon caught on, to become established custom by the late seventeenth century for all officers and sergeants in horse, foot and dragoon regiments. In 1747 clothing regulations were issued dictating that officers of the foot regiments should wear their sashes over the right shoulder, cavalry officers over the left shoulder, with Sergeants wearing the sash around their waist! By 1845 some further standardisation took place with all multi-coloured sashes being abolished in favour of a single crimson sash for wear by British Army NCOs as a cross body sash, with a waist sash reserved for general officers. This tradition remains today. The RAF has taken its custom from the Army, introducing a blue sash for drill NCOs and Warrant Officers. A distinctive blue and gold hooped silk waist sash, with one end hanging loose on the left-hand side is worn by air officers above the rank of Air Commodore.

Sash.

The stable belt is a further custom borrowed from the Army. The tradition dates back to the heyday of cavalry regiments, when saddle girth belts were often manufactured in a regiment's own distinctive colours. For non-ceremonial duty the cavalry regiments also evolved their own stable dress, which was a relaxed everyday style. What better way to hold up trousers and span the human girth than a belt of the same distinctive colours? The RAF Regiment was the first to adopt the stable belt in the RAF, which soon won popularity throughout the Service. It is worn only with Number 2 dress.

Chapter 8
Heraldry and Insignia

Heraldic devices have been used for centuries as a means of identification; RAF badges and crests perpetuate these traditions. In medieval times the monarch granted coats of arms to knights and lords in recognition of loyalty and support to the crown; subsequent rewards, when additions were sanctioned to existing coats of arms, were know as 'Augmentations of Honour'. Military badges are believed to have originated with the grant of 'Honourable Distinctions', which were the Service counterpart of 'Augmentations of Honour' and granted to military formations to commemorate distinguished service. They were later borne on Regimental Colours dating from the Standing Army of 1661, and now remain part of the British military heritage.

The tradition of heraldry in the RAF is inherited, dating from the Royal Naval Air Service, and Royal Flying Corps. Both the Army and the Royal Navy have a deep and honoured association with heraldry, and it was not long after the formation of the first RFC and RNAS squadrons that unit badges began to appear. At first pilots simply invented their own devices and emblems which they would then have painted on the fuselage of an aircraft, or on shields that were hung in the Mess. Many of these early devices were of a humorous or 'Rabelaisian' nature; all were unofficial. Clearly, something had to be done to rationalise and co-ordinate the selection of squadron and unit badges.

Historically the King's Heralds were tasked to trace pedigrees, and it was Edward III who created the position of Chester Herald with the responsibility of preparing coats of arms to be granted by the College of Arms. It was not until March 1935 that the College of Heralds, in conjunction with the Air Ministry, created the post of Inspector of RAF Badges, who became the heraldic adviser to the Air Council on all matters concerning squadron, unit and formation insignia. The first appointment to this post was appropriately that of the Chester Herald; in more recent years the post has been filled by Clarenceaux King of Arms, but now Surrey Herald of Arms Extraordinary.

The appointment of an Inspector of RAF Badges brought an abrupt end to the use of unofficial emblems and devices and marked the introduction of well defined procedures for units that wished to apply for their own crest. The Chester Herald became responsible for ensuring that meticulous research and scrupulous impartiality was exercised in the consideration of all draft RAF badges. His first measure was to design a standard frame for all badges; later came the introduction of qualifications that a unit must establish before it could be awarded its own badge — for example, a unit had to have a reasonable life expectancy and a status and function that justified the sanction of a badge. Furthermore, if the badge was to be awarded to a station, that station had to have its own separately established headquarters. Finally, each design and application had to receive the Sovereign's approval.

In addition to badges and crests, six Royal Air Force establishments have been granted coats of arms, or armorial bearings as they are termed. These are the Royal Air Force College, Central Flying School, the Royal Air Force Flying College now the College of Air Warfare, the Royal Aircraft Establishment, Farnborough, the Empire Test Pilots School and the Aeroplane and Armament Experimental Establishment. The grants of coats of arms were authorised since all establishments could claim to be permanent institutions with their own buildings.

The Coat of Arms of Royal Air Force College (RAFC) Cranwell
The original College Coat of Arms was approved on 19 December 1929 and further

embellished by the addition of 'supporters' (two eagles) in 1972.

At the top is the figure of Daedalus, the legendary father of flying, to show the connection with the RNAS station of that name built at Cranwell in 1915. Under Daedalus is the helmet which symbolises the military character of the College. This rests on the shield, which contains three cranes to signify association with Cranwell village. According to the 'Domesday Book' the village was named after the de Cranewell family, who included three cranes in their coat of arms. The three lions' heads on the inverted chevron depict the Royal status of the College: that HM King George VI was a flight commander at the College when he was the Duke of York. HM The Queen is the Commandant-in-Chief.

Coat of Arms for the Royal Air Force College Cranwell

The two eagles, with red beaks and legs supporting the shield, associate the College with Lord Trenchard, the principal founder, and they are taken from his family coat of arms. The astral crowns round the necks of the eagles recognise that the RAF College was the first air academy in the world and the Fleur de Lys on the crests of the eagles signify association with Lincolnshire (green border) and with Bedfordshire (red border), whence the RAF Technical College came on transfer to the RAF College in 1966.

The legend *Superna Petimus* means 'We strive for higher things'.

The Arms of Central Flying School (CFS)

Central Flying School, the home of military aviation, was the second RAF establishment to be granted its own coat of arms on 9 December

1931. The pelican which surmounts the bearings was chosen because of its heraldic representation of a seat of learning, and its attitude is a reminder that traditionally this bird will peck at its breast and suckle its young with its own life blood, rather than let them die in time of need. The School's original Naval and Military origin is signified by the Naval Crown around the bird's neck and the military (mural) crown above the

Coat of Arms for the Central Flying School

helmet. The coat of arms consists of a pilot's brevet, a series of wavy lines representing the River Avon, on the banks of which the original school stood, and a Naval anchor crossed with a military sabre. The motto is *Imprimis Praecepta*, which means 'Our teaching is everlasting'.

The Arms of the Royal Air Force Flying College (RAFFC)

The Royal Air Force Flying College was originally situated at Manby in Lincolnshire and was formed to combine certain aspects of the work of the Empire Flying School, the Empire Air Armament School and the Empire Air Navigation School, with a view to integrating more closely their studies and doctrines. The third grant of arms to the RAF was made to the Royal Air Force Flying College on 1 June 1951 and was the first grant after the appointment of an Inspector of Royal Air Force Badges. The devices present include the pelican, representing the seat of learning; Astral and Naval Crown, reminiscent of the close contact between the Navy and the Royal Air Force; a knight's helmet representing officer training, with the cardinal points of the compass against a background of stars contained on a shield, both relating to air and navigation training. The simple motto 'Progress' aptly defined the College's task in providing flying training. Since the original grant of arms, the Flying College has become the department of Air Warfare at the Royal Air Force College, Cranwell.

Coat of Arms for the Royal Air Force Flying College now Department of Air Warfare RAF College, Cranwell

The Arms of Royal Aircraft Establishment (RAE), Farnborough

The history of the RAE starts at Woolwich Arsenal in 1878 with the formation of a specialist headquarters to support the first Royal Engineer balloon flights. After the formation of the Royal Flying Corps, the headquarters was transferred to Farnborough to become the Royal Aircraft Factory. With the formation of the Royal Air Force in 1918 the title again changed to the now familiar Royal Aircraft Establishment. Sponsorship was at first placed in the hands of the Air Ministry and later Ministry of Aircraft Production, until 1946, when it fell under the control of the Ministry of Supply. Today the RAE forms part of the Ministry of Defence Procurement Executive (MODPE).

The Arms symbolise the history and purpose of the Establishment. On the shield (the dominant feature of all Arms), the Golden Key in an azure field denotes the Establishment's search for knowledge in the skies. The Chief Or (or gold) embattled at the upper portion of the shield and the crowns of the three fighting services inset (in seniority order) emphasises the part the Establishment plays in the defence of the country.

Royal Aircraft Establishment, Farnborough

Above the shield is the symbol of chivalry — the helmet and mantle of oak leaves — surmounted by an Astral Crown as a crest coronet and the pterodactyl, indicative of the Establishment's long and proud history of aeronautical research since the early days of flying. Interpreted liberally, the motto *Alis Apta Scientis* means 'Winged Science'.

Arms of the Empire Test Pilots School (ETPS) located at RAF Boscombe Down

The Arms of the Empire Test Pilots School (ETPS)

The Empire Test Pilots School was founded at Farnborough in 1943 to provide specialist pilots for test flying duties at aeronautical research and development establishments. The full grant of armorial bearings was made by King George VI in September 1949. The features of the bearings include an eagle displaying elevated wings rising from the Astral Crown set above a knight's helmet. The inflamed torch of learning is set on a shelf decorated with stars, representing the skies. The Empire Test Pilots School is now situated at the Aeroplane and Armament Experimental Establishment at Boscombe Down in Wiltshire.

The Arms of The Aeroplane and Armament Experimental Establishment, Boscombe Down (A&AEE)

The Grant of Arms to A&AEE was made as part of the celebrations in 1971 of fifty years of aeroplane and armament testing, the focal point of which was a visit by HRH Princess Anne, deputising for Her Majesty The Queen.

The Aeroplane and Armament Experimental establishment RAF Boscombe Down

The Arms incorporate features representing the history of the Establishment and perpetuate the central feature and motto of the unit badge authorised by King George VI in 1939. The background to the shield is of green and white bars from the Arms of the County of Wiltshire, to reflect its origin as part of the Central Flying School at Upavon in 1914, and the location at Boscombe Down since 1939. The central motif is from the unit badge and shows an arrow, representing true flight, between an airman's glove and a mailed gauntlet representing aeroplanes and armament. The birds in the quarters are martlets, or swallows, in heraldic form. They recall the Establishment's time at Martlesham Heath (Martlets Village) in Suffolk from 1917 to 1939.

The dominant feature of the Crest is the great bustard, once Britain's largest native bird, which last roamed wild on Salisbury Plain towards the end of the nineteenth century. It is also present on the Arms of the County of Wiltshire but is shown in a different stance. The Arms also incorporates an heraldic pun. The device on the wing is the *boss* from a horse's bit and the bird is standing in a valley or *combe* in a *down*, the name given to the chalk uplands above or between river valleys.

The bearings are completed by the motto *Probe Probare* meaning 'Properly to Test'.

The Astral Crown

The Astral Crown included in the Flying College's and other arms also appears in many other unit and squadron badges. In the herald's vocabulary there are four representative crowns: the Naval Crown, which consists of the sterns and sails of ships; the Mural Crown, which is used by the Army and resembles the turreted top of a tower; the Eastern Crown, ornamented with triangular spikes; and finally the Celestial Crown, adorned with three spikes terminating in stars. A fifth crown called the Astral Crown has now been added to this list by the Kings of Arms. It consists of alternating wings and stars, was authorised by King George VI and first used for the badge of No. 1 Flying Training School. It can now be granted, with armorial bearings, to distinguished officers in the RAF and to persons or corporations especially connected with military or civil aviation. It appears in many of the Service's more recent badge designs.

The Astral Crown

Squadron and unit badges

Following the appointment of an Inspector of RAF Badges in March 1936, the first seven squadron badges were ready for approval by King Edward VIII in May of the same year. These were the badges of Nos. 2, 15, 18, 19, 22, 216 and 603 Squadrons. There are now more than a thousand such badges for all manner of RAF units, and each is listed and registered at the College of Arms in large albums known as 'The Inspector's ordinary copies'.

Royal Air Force badges normally contain designs that bear some allusion to the units to which they are granted. They may also combine parts of an original unofficial design. The significance of a design, often with a hint of humour, will be found in the unit's history. One of the more amusing designs can be found in the 22 Squadron badge, which includes the Greek letter pi. During the First World War 22 Squadron and 7 Wing were co-located. In the race to the air 'to meet the Hun', 22 Squadron always took off over 7 Wing's lines! Appropriately the symbol pi was selected for their badge — twenty-two over seven. The choice of 40 Bomber Squadron badge involves the distinguished aviator Major Edward Mannock VC. To urge his pilots into the air, he frequently used the expression, 'Sweep the Huns from the skies!'. The broom was, therefore, an appropriate emblem. Other squadrons adopted the type names of aircraft to be represented in their badge — 12 Squadron flew the Fairey Fox and adopted the fox's mask; in 1916 No. 27 Squadron was equipped with the Martinsyde G-100 Scout, but this aircraft was known affectionately as the elephant — and an elephant was duly accepted as the squadron badge design. Similarly the gamecock is featured on 43 Squadron's badge to commemorate flying Gamecock aircraft in 1926. There was certainly plenty of scope for imagination, and 204 Squadron, which flew flying boats, selected a cormorant perched on a buoy, while 58 Squadron, a night fighter squadron, featured an

---

Example RAF Badges

No. 22 Squadron Badge

No. 40 Squadron Badge

No. 12 Squadron Badge

No. 27 Squadron Badge

No. 43 Squadron Badge

No. 58 Squadron Badge

No. 34 Squadron Badge

No. 611 (County of Lancaster Squadron) Royal Auxiliary Air Force

Badge for Royal Air Force Germany

Badge for No. 45 Maintenance Unit

No. 72 Squadron Badge

Squadron Aircraft Markings

No. 25 Squadron

No. 65 Squadron

No. 29 Squadron

No. 56 Squadron

No. 41 Squadron

No. 85 Squadron

No. 43 Squadron

No. 600 Squadron

No. 1 Squadron

No. 601 Squadron

No. 17 Squadron

No. 247 Squadron

owl on its badge. The use of a bird on squadron badges was both obvious and natural. A less obvious badge is that of 34 Squadron, which is composed of a wolf and crescent. This was an adaptation of an old unit badge of a star and crescent which was derived from the badge of the 33rd Punjab Regiment — an officer from this regiment became 34 Squadron's first commanding officer. Other heraldic devices came from squadrons associated with counties and cities, particularly the Auxiliary Air Force Squadrons. The County of Lancaster Squadron, No. 611, adopted the Red Rose, and the County of Warwick Squadron, No. 605, adopted the bear and staff badge taken directly from the arms of Warwick. Station and formation badges again utilised easily recognisable devices on their design. Although heraldically the badge for RAF Germany is described as 'Issuant from Astral Crown, demi lion, winged, and holding in dexter join an olive branch': the lion represents courage and strength, while the olive branch signifies the generous attitude taken by the Royal Air Force in the country of occupation. More difficult to understand is the No. 45 Maintenance Unit badge which displays a sporran.

An example of a squadron badge that did not get past the Inspector was that of 72 Squadron. The prototype design included a shield, bearing in the first quarter a foaming pint tankard, in the second quarter a scroll of 'bumf', in the third quarter a heart pierced by an arrow, and in the fourth quarter five aces, including a joker! The crest was a crashed aircraft with the motto *Altera potatio non nocebit* meaning 'Another little drink won't do us any harm'. Today the badge is of a swift volant with the motto 'Swift'. The earlier badge is, however, greatly treasured by the Squadron. Only a few of the many RAF badges can be described in a book of this size. Those who have the opportunity to delve further in other references will be amply rewarded with tales fraught with danger and adventure and not least humour.

The traditions of squadron markings on aircraft

The idea of marking aircraft with distinctive insignia other than national markings dates back to the early years of the First World War. Distinctive marks were painted in black on the top, bottom and both sides of the fuselage to provide pilots with an individual aircraft and squadron code. The idea was simply to afford a distinguishing mark for recognition purposes. The pattern was laid down by RFC Headquarters, and the designs were based on geometrical figures. Later came the addition of embellishments to produce more colourful and imaginative markings. One of the interesting designs is that of 29 Squadron, which uses the triple X to produce the Roman numeral 30. The story goes that in the early days of the First World War it was decided to paint the squadron number on the rudder of all the squadron aircraft. A rigger was detailed to do the jobs and told to cut away smartly and paint the squadron number in Roman numerals on the rudder of all aircraft. 'Roman numerals, sir?' came the reply. 'Yes, you know — two Xs and one X,' the officer replied. The rigger duly painted two Xs plus one more X instead of the XXIX that represents the number twenty-nine. RFC markings on aircraft were taken over by the RAF in 1918, but were only painted on fighter aircraft. This tradition remains to the present day. During the Second World War it was decided for security reasons to drop squadron markings since they would provide a useful source of information to enemy intelligence. In their place an alphabetic code was used. However, the post-war years have seen a resurgence of squadron markings on fighter aircraft, together with various lettering codes.

Squadron numbering

How RAF squadrons are numbered has been a source of considerable confusion to the uninformed. A sequence of numbers is reserved for particular squadrons but a squadron number does not necessarily relate to its operational task as fighter, bomber or any other role. Rather it is of historical significance. The squadrons numbered 1 to 200 represent regular RAF squadrons, many of which date back to the Royal Flying Corps. Squadrons numbered 201 to 299 are again regular RAF squadrons, but many of them were originally Royal Naval Air Service squadrons before the amalgamation of the Corps on 1 April 1918. The squadrons numbered 300 to 399 date from the Second World War and were mainly allotted to the allies from Poland, Czechoslovakia, Holland, France, Norway, Greece and Belgium who fought and flew with the RAF; but some of the 300 series numbers were used by RAF squadrons operating in India. The 400 to 499 series of numbers were assigned to squadrons of the Royal Canadian, Royal Rhodesian, Royal Australian and Royal New Zealand Air Force who formed part of the Home Air Force during the Second World War. Numbers 500 to 599 were originally intended for special reserve squadrons but many of the numbers were taken up for wartime-only units. Similarly, the 600 to 699 series were originally allotted to the Royal Auxiliary Air Force squadrons but were also later used for specialist squadrons such as Pathfinder squadrons and of course the Dam Buster Squadron 617. The numbers 700 to 899 were allocated to the Fleet Air Arm, where numbers 700 to 799 were given to second line and Catapult squadrons and 800 to 899 to first line Fleet Air Arm squadrons. Finally, the series 900 to 999 was allotted to the Barrage Balloon squadrons.

This arrangement was not, however, rigidly enforced. For example, not all of the numbers were taken up, and Commonwealth squadrons operating outside the UK sometimes reverted to their home country squadron number. Moreover, during both world wars large numbers of Commonwealth personnel served in RAF squadrons and vice versa. Finally, Article 15 of the British Empire Air Training Scheme allowed for the provision of a certain number of squadrons manned by Canadian, Australian and New Zealand personnel to be allocated to RAF Commands. The one exception to Article 15 was the South African Air Force, who throughout the Second World War used their home numbers.

Vehicle star plates

A badge that is frequently displayed above the front and rear bumpers of a staff car is a rectangular plate with up to five stars attached. Star plates are used to identify the occupant of a staff car, who will always be of at least air rank. This form of vehicle marking was advocated by Marshal of the Royal Air Force Lord Tedder and the system came into use on 1 January 1951. The idea had been gained from a similar American system. An Air Commodore's plate carries one star, an Air Vice-Marshal's plate two stars, an Air Marshal's plate three stars, an Air Chief Marshal's plate four stars and a Marshal of

the RAF five stars. This system was later adopted by both the Army and Navy. The background colour of the plate indicates the Service: red for the Army, navy blue for the Navy, and a light-blue for the RAF. Star plates are only displayed if the air officer is present, otherwise the plate will be covered.

Officer flags and pennants

Like many other aspects of the Service, RAF officers' flags and pennants are perhaps the perpetuation of custom and tradition. Heraldically, our modern officer flags and pennants are related to the pennants flown by knights from their lances or more recently to the pennants flown on a pike staff. The pennant's significance was not only for identification but also, and perhaps more usefully, to give some idea of wind speed and direction. During the First World War, the Royal Flying Corps Squadron and flight commanders trailed a coloured streamer from their aircraft for identification purposes. By 1917, the War Office had regularised this practice and authorised the first pennant flag; from then on the idea seems to have mushroomed, finally becoming a standadrised insignia by the Second World War. Examination of Second World War aircraft photographs may indicate officer pennants stencilled underneath the cockpit area.

By 1948 the whole business of officer flags and pennants was discussed by a Standing Committee of the Air Council and many sweeping changes were made. By the early 1950s, and thanks to Air Chief Marshal Sir Dermot Boyle, a standardised collection of officers' flags and vehicle flags evolved, largely based on the earlier designs. Eight masthead distinguishing flags were authorised for the ranks Squadron Leader in command, up to Marshal of the RAF. Today, it is the practice to fly these officer flags at the top of the masthead above the RAF ensign to distinguish the rank of the commanding officer. Similarly, the flags may be flown from mastheads outside wing, squadron, group or command headquarters buildings, or be stencilled on the forward fuselage of aircraft. However, except in the RAF Regiment these officer flags are no longer flown from vehicles. Instead, distinguishing flags of appointment were introduced for cars, to cater for such as the Secretary of State for Air (title now obsolete),

Chief of the Air Staff, members of the Air Force Board of the Defence Council, Air Officers Commanding-in-Chief of RAF Commands, Air Officers Commanding Groups and Air Headquarters, with finally a Station Commander's flag. Thus, star plates will describe the rank of an air officer in a vehicle; if the air officer holds a further executive position it will be described by his appointment flag. The only appointment vehicle flag below air officer status is that for a station commander. Vehicle flags are flown from above the radiator on the centre of a vehicle bonnet.

Vehicle Star Plates

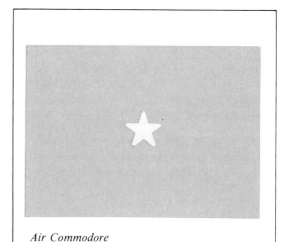

Air Commodore

Rear Admiral

General

Air Marshal

Marshal of the RAF

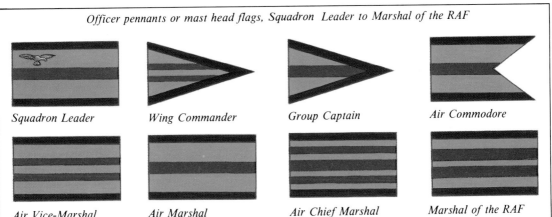

Officer pennants or mast head flags, Squadron Leader to Marshal of the RAF

Squadron Leader

Wing Commander

Group Captain

Air Commodore

Air Vice-Marshal

Air Marshal

Air Chief Marshal

Marshal of the RAF

Distinguishing car appointment flags

Secretary of State for Air (obsolete)

Chief of the Air Staff
Commanders-in-Chief Abroad

Air Officers Commanding
Group Headquarters

Members of the Air Council (except the
Secretary of State for Air and the Chief of
the Air Staff) Inspector-General of the Royal
Air Force (obsolete)

Sector Commanders or
Station Commanders of the rank of
Wing Commander and above

Air Officers Commanding-in-Chief of
Commands at Home

Chapter 9
The Other Royal Air Forces

A visit to any of the Imperial War Grave Commission Cemeteries which lie across the breadth of the world is a salutatory reminder that there were other 'Royal Air Forces' contributing with our own to the overall air battle during the two World Wars. The sacrifice of the Commonwealth air forces was no less than our own and when seen as a percentage of their home population, probably greater than our own. When our need was there, the Commonwealth of Nations arose to meet the enemy of the mother country and gave of its all for us to achieve victory. The customs and traditions of the Commonwealth Royal Air Forces have become intermeshed with our own, in that, perhaps, we became one Royal Air Force. Lest we forget, this chapter is devoted to the Royal Australian, Canadian, Indian, Rhodesian and New Zealand Air Forces whose singular character, individuality and strength of purpose was never lost. Any ideas that they were ever subordinate in their role to the Royal Air Force is a total misunderstanding as well as being untrue. All gave something to the RAF, all are part of its heritage and history. The memory of their sacrifice is enshrined in the RAF of today.

The Royal Australian Air Force
In 1981 the RAAF celebrated its 60th anniversary. From a small fledgling defence Service relying on Great Britain for equipment and know-how, it has developed into a prestigious, effective and innovative air force recognised as being amongst the finest in the world. Their history starts a long time before 1921, going back to the halcyon days of the pre-First World War years.

It is a little-known fact that as early as 1910 Australian air pioneers were inventing and flying their own machines. Lawrence Hargrave was experimenting with boxkites and rotary engines before 1910. In 1910, the brother partnership of John and Reg Duigan flew an aircraft of their own design at Mia Mia in Victoria. Duigan had

never previously seen an aircraft or had a flying lesson! However, the first formal interest in flying by the Government came in 1909 with the offer of a £5000 prize to the inventor of the first military aircraft. The potential in Australian aviation had been realised; it was now a matter of development.

One of the key personalities in early Australian aviation was Senator G. F. Pearce. In 1911 he returned from a visit to England convinced of the need for a National Military Aviation Corps. The Australian government accepted his recommendations and applications were invited for two aviators. The lucky two were Henry Petre and Eric Harrison. Both were commissioned into the Australian Army in 1913.

Senator G. F. Pearce, Minister of Defence in 1911, father of Australian Military Aviation.

RAAF Pilots Wings

Petre's first task was to identify a suitable site for an airfield; this he did at a place called Point Cook in Victoria which offered 734 acres of suitable ground with good access to the sea. Lieutenant Harrison, on the other hand, had been out on a shopping trip to the UK and in April 1913 returned to Australia with five aircraft and two mechanics. The party set-to at Point Cook, designed and built their own hangars and created Australia's first military airfield and flying school. The first course began flying training on 18 August 1914 on a motley selection of two BE 2as, a Bristol Boxkite, and two Deperdussins. The first student to qualify for his 'wings' did so on 12 November 1914 and thus military aviation in Australia became a fact on that date.

Back in Europe, war had been declared and the limited resources of the RFC deployed to France. As ever, there was an immediate shortage of pilots and a request was made for airmen from the Dominions. Such was the generosity that Australia immediately responded, providing air forces for Mesopotamia (Iraq) which eventually merged with RFC personnel already in situ to become No 30 Squadron, RFC. Petre was amongst this first contingent; he later went on to win both the DSO and MC. Overall, however, Australia resisted Britain in her policy to absorb Dominion pilots into the RFC and instead established her own Australian Flying Corps (AFC) — the only Dominion to do so. The policy was that AFC pilots would be partially trained in Australia before completing their flying training in the UK. They were then posted to one of four squadrons serving overseas; No 1 Squadron in Egypt, Nos 2, 3 and 4 in France. Altogether, the AFC mustered eight squadrons. The AFC served with distinction throughout the First World War, gaining a high reputation for its excellence as well as winning many battle honours and personal decorations for gallantry.

At the end of the First World War the AFC returned home and was disbanded. But the end of the war heralded the introduction of civil aviation in Australia when the brothers, Ross and Keith Smith flew their Vickers Vimy from England to Australia in 1919 — their courage earned the honour of knighthood. By 1920 it was clear that Australia needed a permanent air force and Lieutenant Colonel Richard Williams, DSO, the first pilot to gain his 'wings', was placed at the head of an autonomous Australian Air Force. On 15 February 1921 the Air Board recommended to the Air Council that the Australian Air Force be formed with effect from 31 March 1921. Williams had won his cause. In July of the same year, word came of the honour to add the Royal prefix; the Royal Australian Air Force was established.

The between-the-wars years of industrial depression and uncertainty were by no means easy. Although new airfields were opened at Richmond and Laverton, the depression period of the early 1930s saw only a limited growth with no great investment. Some gratis aircraft arrived from the UK and a liaison was maintained with the RAF in London. At this time the decision to adopt RAF style uniform was made, but in a distinctive navy blue colour. With the ending of the depression came a small expansion of the RAAF to include a reserve element and, by 1936, aviation and the RAAF were turning into growth industries. Australia's investment became Britain's gain long before the Second World War. The RAAF found that many of its trained personnel who had completed a short service commission at home departed to the UK to join the RAF. By 1939, 150 former RAAF pilots had been commissioned into the RAF.

RAAF Pacific operations, 1943, with the Boston aircraft.

Royal Australian Air Force Squadron Crests.

Temporary runway construction, Far East War 1944.

That was a bonus for the RAF. Similarly, as the RAF went through an unprecedented expansion in the early pre-war years, so too did the RAAF. In 1938 it was decided to increase the front-line force of the RAAF to eighteen squadrons involving 212 aircraft. At the same time the aircraft industry in Australia was booming, with more new airfields also under construction.

When war was declared against Germany by Great Britain on 3 September 1939, Australia immediately followed suit and began to mobilise. The first unit to come to England was 10 Squadron in 1939 equipped with Sunderland flying boats; it was the first squadron of any Commonwealth country to go into action. In addition there were 450 Australians already serving with the RAF. But this was only the beginning and a mere drop in the ocean of what was to come. At the height of the Second World War the RAAF was to expand to 20,000 officers, 144,000 airmen and 18,000 airwomen. Operational aircraft rose to a total of 3037 with 2808 training aircraft in support. During the early war days further help was offered to Great Britain by the Australian Government with the Empire Air Training Scheme. Overall this scheme provided a staggering 50,000 trained aircrew each year. Australia's contribution was 11,000 trained aircrew who eventually joined the Dominion squadrons under RAF operational control. Under the Empire Air Training Scheme the RAAF formed seventeen squadrons in the UK and Middle East. In all the RAAF trained 27,837 aircrew providing an additional 10,351 aircrew who later completed their training in Canada. The RAAF's record throughout the

Second World War was impressive. Of the thirty Australians who flew in the Battle of Britain, fifteen were killed in action. Australian aircrews flew in every major operation mounted by Bomber Command. Closer to home, however, was the war in the Pacific following Japan's simultaneous attacks on Pearl Harbor and the East Coast of Malaya on 7 December 1941.

Following these attacks, the Australian government immediately approved a plan to expand the RAAF to 72 squadrons. However, the drain on the country's resources was such that in 1943 the Australian war cabinet had to review its manpower to limit the number of personnel who could be recruited into the RAAF. The cabinet emphasised that henceforth the Australian military effort would be concentrated in the Pacific theatre of war. By 1944 the situation was reviewed again. This time, the RAAF was depleted by 15,000 personnel, released to boost the nation's industrial effort. Meanwhile, from the Australian factories came a varied selection of aircraft: Beauforts, Beaufighters, Boomerangs, Wirraways, Mustangs and Mosquitoes.

The war in the Pacific grew to a crescendo in 1944 with over 131,000 RAAF personnel manning 3187 front-line aircraft actively involved in operations against the Japanese. By the end of the war, Australia had paid dearly. Some 15,000 Australians had been involved in the European war. They had flown 31 million operational miles on 65,841 sorties. They had sunk thirty-five ships and damaged over 200 more; they had shot down 109 enemy aircraft and further damaged over 230; they had dropped 65,000 tons of bombs. The cost of victory in Europe was horrific, 6,636 dead; one fifth of the entire Australian war deaths, and twelve per cent alone in Bomber Command. No 460 Squadron, operating Wellington bombers and then

Lincoln bombers of No 1 Squadron RAAF operating in support of British forces during the Malayan Emergency (1950-58).

9 Squadron helicopter operations, South Vietnam, 1972.

Lancasters, suffered 1,019 fatal casualties. In terms of bravery, RAAF personnel gained two VCs, sixty-two DSOs (four with bars), 1880 DFCs (118 with bars), 126 AFCs and 402 DFMs (two with bars).

When peace came in 1945, the RAAF was the fourth largest air force in the world with a firmly established aircraft industry. Demobilisation soon took place to reduce the force to peace time requirements which were assessed in 1948 as a fixed figure of 12,000 men.

The early post-war years saw a wind of political change blow through the Far East inspired by Communist terrorists. During the Malayan Emergency the RAAF operated Lincoln, Dakota, Sabre and Canberra aircraft from their base of Butterworth in Malaya and Tengah on Singapore Island. In all, the Lincoln squadron dropped 16,000 tons of bombs; some 85 per cent of the total tonnage dropped. In Europe during the same year RAAF Dakota crews flew 6000 hours transporting 7264 tons of supplies, and 8000 passengers to Berlin when the Russians blockaded the city. Later during the Korean War of 1950-53, RAAF squadrons flew from Japan and South Korea as part of the United Nations force. By the end of the Korean war in July 1953, the RAAF had flown 18,872 individual sorties at a cost of 42 pilots killed in action. In addition the RAAF reinforced the island garrison of Malta in 1952 to provide additional air power for Britain in the Mediterranean. This commitment lasted for two years.

The most recent conflict in which the RAAF has been involved is the war in Vietnam. The first unit to arrive in the theatre was a Caribou transport Flight in July 1964. By June 1966 the Flight had expanded into a squadron, officially numbered No 35 Squadron and tasked for supply duties for the US Seventh Air Force. Two further RAAF squadrons soon followed flying Iroquois helicopters and Canberra bombers respectively (the Canberra was the only Vietnam-based aircraft with a low-level bombing capability). Later, in 1966 an airfield construction squadron also joined the forces deployed in Vietnam. RAAF squadrons flew many sorties from ground attack to casualty evacuation and RAAF pilots also acted as Forward Air Controllers directing strikes by Allied aircraft. In addition, Hercules aircraft squadrons maintained the air re-supply link with the Australian mainland.

Australia began withdrawing its forces from Vietnam in May 1971, and this was complete by early 1972. In the $4\frac{1}{2}$ years of Australian involvement, transport aircraft had carried 27,000 tons of freight and 337,000 passengers in over 47,000 sorties. Strike aircraft had destroyed 7000 structures, 11,000 san pans, 36 bridges and 10,000 bunkers. The cost to the RAAF was four killed in action. A total of 4443 RAAF personnel served in Vietnam.

Such, then, is the track record of the RAAF; an Air Force second to none and distinguished by its own brand of heroism, professionalism and achievement. The RAAF's spirit of today is enshrined in the past. The RAAF of the 1980s is a modern, well-equipped force respected throughout the world. Links are still maintained with the RAAF with some exchange postings between the two Services.

9 Squadron Iroquois helicopters operating in Vietnam. They also later operated in Sinai as part of the peace keeping force in April 1982.

The Royal New Zealand Air Force

Sir Henry Francis Wigram has been described as the father of New Zealand aviation. As early as 1909 he was urging the Legislative Council to form a flying corps as part of the country's defence. As ever, with new and far-sighted ideas, his colleagues showed little interest. Nevertheless, Wigram was a visionary; he was also a shrewd and determined man with outstanding administrative ability. He died in May 1934, but not before he had created his own aviation establishment — Canterbury Aviation Company — and made generous gifts of land and money to establish the airfield that now proudly bears his name. But the story of the RNZAF can be traced back tenuously to 1913 when the New Zealand Government was forced to express an interest in military flying when some patriotic British businessmen sent a two-seater Bleriot monoplane as a nucleus for a New Zealand air fleet trial. The aircraft arrived in September that year.

RNZAF Pilots Wings

Although progress was slow, with the coming of the First World War, Wigram's voice was heard again encouraging the New Zealand government to get more involved in aviation, to train pilots and create the country's own flying corps. His words fell on deaf ears. The training and organisation for aviation in New Zealand was to be left to private enterprise based at two schools, the New Zealand Flying School at Kohimarama, Auckland, and the already mentioned Canterbury Aviation Company at Sockburn, Christchurch.

Lacking both finance and expertise in aviation, the early New Zealand air pioneers built aircraft and taught themselves how to fly, at more or less the same time. The brothers Leo and Vivian Walsh were the first to get aviation moving at the New Zealand Flying School and from those humble and precarious beginnings manned flight in New Zealand became a reality. Back in Europe the war in the air was hotting up;

more importantly the RFC could not provide sufficient replacement pilots for those lost in action. Motivated by the highest patriotism, the Walsh brothers offered the Imperial Government their services to train pilots. The British government readily accepted this offer of help. Thus, in 1915 the Walsh brothers gave New Zealand the distinction of being the only country where pilots were trained for the RFC through private enterprise! The Flying School at Sockburn, on the other hand, did not open until 1917. Altogether, 982 pilots were trained at Sockburn and 110 pilots at the New Zealand Flying School before the end of the First World War. Of those trained, 158 were later commissioned into the RFC. Of particular note is the fact that the first VC awarded to an RFC pilot went to 2nd Lieutenant W. B. Rhodes-Moorhouse, a New Zealander. Besides those trained at home, several hundred other New Zealanders joined and fought with the RFC and RNAS in the UK, France and Mesopotamia (Iraq). Unlike the Australians, however, New Zealanders were absorbed directly into the British flying services.

When peace settled over Europe in the autumn of 1918 the New Zealand government approached the newly established British Air Ministry requesting assistance in setting up a New Zealand air arm. In response, Colonel A. V. Bettington, DSO, was despatched to New Zealand in 1919 complete with two mechanics and four aircraft. This team was based at Sockburn, and together with three former New

Cessna Golden Eagle light transport RNZAF.

Strikemaster RNZAF.

Zealand pilots who had flown with the RFC, set about planning the formation of an air arm.

Bettington's recommendations included forming an air arm to comprise two each of flying boat, fighter and bomber squadrons supported by one torpedo bomber squadron. He also proposed an aircraft depot and two aircraft parks. However, the New Zealand government considered this plan far 'too ambitious' and asked for it to be amended and reduced. Bettington duly completed revised plans, but this too was unacceptable. The upshot was that Bettington returned home to the UK just a little disappointed, but at least the aircraft remained. All was not lost, however, and the New Zealand government set up an air advisory committee to monitor the situation.

More aircraft were requested from the UK and although not the aircraft specifically requested, a motley collection of Avro 504s, DH4s and Bristol Fighters arrived by early 1920. In the same year, an Air Board was established to advise the New Zealand Defence Department of aviation matters. At last, flying training (albeit under private enterprise) was established and began providing a reservoir of trained aircrew.

The next major breakthrough came in 1923 when the government agreed to the establishment of the New Zealand Permanent Air Force (NZPAF) as part of the Dominion's Military Forces (ie Army). In addition, the New Zealand Air Force (NZAF) was also constituted as part of the territorial forces. To accommodate the 'two' air forces, Sockburn was purchased by the government from the Canterbury Aviation Company. At the same time Wigram gave a generous donation of £10,000 to the new Air Force. For this, and in recognition of Wigram's support of New Zealand aviation, Sockburn was renamed 'Wigram'.

Further progress for the 'two' air forces was slow but steady. In 1925 a new airfield and flying boat base was opened at Hobsonville (Auckland). In 1928 Air Marshal Sir John

Salmond visited New Zealand to advise on air defence. He recommended that the NZPAF should be expanded and at the same time introduced a scheme for short service commissions in both the NZPAF and RAF. Although the depression of the 1930s prevented some of Salmond's proposals proceeding, others went ahead. In particular, in December 1929 RAF ranks and titles were introduced into the NZPAF and in 1931 'blue' uniform was first introduced. However, back in 1930, the NZPAF carried out its first active service operations in Western Samoa with a DH60 floatplane in support of *HMS Dunedin* during a native uprising. The NZPAF was now a well-established, disciplined and professional force. Perhaps it was in recognition of this, that the King in 1934 granted permission to add the Royal prefix; thus the title Royal New Zealand Air Force came into being.

In the remaining years up until the Second World War, the RNZAF continued to expand and re-equip with more modern aircraft. By 1936 it was obvious to all, not least of all in the Dominions, that war clouds were building up in Europe. Early that year the New Zealand government decided to establish the RNZAF as a separate Service and requested further assistance from the UK. Wing Commander The Hon R. A. Cochrane, AFC, RAF, arrived from England later in the year to formulate recommendations for the establishment of this new and independent force. Together with New Zealand's Director of Air Services, Squadron Leader Tom Wilkes, Cochrane set about his mission with gusto and was to have a profound influence on the early development of the RNZAF. (Cochrane was later to go on to become Air Chief Marshal Sir Ralph Cochrane, GBE, KCB, of 5 [Bomber] Group fame.)

Hercules in Pacific Islands. (RNZAF Archives)

Avro 626 – Restored part of the RNZAF Historic Flight.

Cochrane's main recommendation was for the RNZAF to be constituted as a separate Service inclusive of a reserve element. The new organisation was modelled on the British Air Ministry. The recommendations were accepted, the Service was authorised by the Air Force Act of 1937 and Cochrane was, in turn invited to extend his tour of duty to become New Zealand's first Chief of the Air Staff. Cochrane accepted, the UK Air Council agreed and he was promoted Group Captain and assumed his new appointment on 1 April 1937. In the same period new air-fields were placed under construction at Whenuapai (Auckland) and Ohakea, with orders to the UK for thirty Wellington bombers. The expansion programme continued apace, and by the time Cochrane completed his tour in 1939 the RNZAF was becoming a well-equipped and formidable force. When war broke out in Europe on 3 September 1939, over 500 New Zealanders were already serving as aircrew in the RAF. In addition, thirty crews had been despatched from New Zealand to collect the Wellington bombers that had been ordered. However, the NZ government, realising the mother country's needs, agreed that these aircraft and their crews could remain in the UK. As a result No 75 (New Zealand) Squadron, RAF, was constituted in April 1940 flying from RAF Feltwell in Norfolk. Some 1370 New Zealanders flew with this squadron and of those 422 were killed in action, a further 77 were killed after being posted to other squadrons. During its service with the RAF, 75 Squadron flew 8150 sorties dropping 21,630 tons of bombs, 2344 tons of mines, and destroyed at least 45 enemy

RNZAF Squadron Badges

The fleet types. (RNZAF Archives)

fighters. Moreover, the squadron gained one Victoria Cross, six Distinguished Service Orders, eighty-eight Distinguished Flying Crosses (plus four bars), seventeen Distinguished Flying Medals and two Conspicuous Gallantry Medals. At the end of the war, 75 Squadron was disbanded and in 1946 the RAF granted the squadron number permanently to the RNZAF in recognition of its wartime record.

From 1941 onwards New Zealand airmen began arriving in the UK in large numbers. To create full RNZAF squadrons in Britain would have been a difficult task. Under Article 15 of the Empire Air Training Scheme, the UK undertook that 'Pupils of Canada, Australia and New Zealand shall, after their training, be identified with their respective Dominions either by organising Dominion units or formations, or in some other way, such methods to be agreed upon with the respective governments'. It was subsequently agreed   at six RNZAF squadrons should be formed within the RAF, to be designated 'New Zealand Squadrons'. Of the six squadrons so formed, three became fighter squadrons, two Coastal Command squadrons and the other a bomber squadron. They were numbered 485 to 490. These six squadrons, together with 75 Squadron, served with distinction throughout the war operating in West Africa, the European and Mediterranean

theatres. Some of the fighter aircraft used had been purchased from public subscription in New Zealand. It is noteworthy that during the Battle of Britain, perhaps the turning point of the whole Second World War, nearly one fighter pilot in twelve was a New Zealander. Thus, it comes as no surprise to learn that 41,595 New Zealand men and women served in the RNZAF throughout the war; by comparison with the size of New Zealand's population an unequalled contribution of personnel from any Dominion.

During the early stages of the war, the primary thrust of the RNZAF was to train aircrew for the RAF as part of the Empire Air Training Scheme. By the end of the war, the RNZAF had trained upwards of 12,000 aircrew at a rate of over 3000 per year. But the war in Europe and training aircrew was only part of the whole contribution. In December 1941 Japan entered the fray.

With the deteriorating situation in the Pacific, the New Zealand government pressed the British government for more aircraft and resources, eventually getting some requests granted. During the Japanese offensive of 1941-45 a total of 27 RNZAF squadrons were formed and served in the 'Pacific War' in support of the Allies. The RNZAF joined forces with the Americans and carried out operations as far afield as Guadalcanal, Espiritu Santo, New Georgia, Green Island, Los Negros and Bougainville. The squadrons fought hard

75 Squadron standard presented by Sir Richard Bolt, 4 April 1985. (RNZAF Archives)

against a bitter and determined enemy. The airfields from which they operated had been carved out of the jungles and were primitive in the extreme. Under the most appalling conditions, the New Zealanders, with our other Allies, gave of their all, finally achieving a total domination of the air in the Pacific theatre. When peace came in 1945, New Zealand contributed its oldest operational fighter unit, No 14 (Fighter) Squadron, to the British Commonwealth Occupation Forces in Japan.

It was now time to think about a post-war air strategy. Many of the New Zealanders who had flown in Europe had elected to remain with the RAF, and indeed, had risen to key appointments. Others returned home to be 'demobbed'. There was uncertainty about the future of the RNZAF, but one thing was for sure, it had to shrink. The government set up a

committee to look at this and in due course the RNZAF was reshaped into a compact and efficient Service. Some squadrons were stationed overseas, including one squadron serving in Cyprus with the RAF from 1952. During this period, the home squadrons were re-equipped with modern jet aircraft.

By 1955 it was clear that New Zealand's defence priority lay in South-East Asia. The Cyprus-based NZ squadron (No 14) was duly moved to Singapore, re-equipped with Venoms and there took part in the Malayan Emergency and Terrorist campaign, again supporting the RAF. Prior to this date, 41 Squadron, RNZAF, had supported the anti-terrorist campaign flying Dakotas from RAF Tengah, from 1949-51. The squadron re-equipped with the Bristol Freighter in 1955 and returned to Singapore, to remain until 1977. The squadron's links with Singapore remain to the present day where they provide a flight detachment of UHI helicopters. RNZAF squadrons again supported the RAF during the two years of confrontation with Indonesia from 1964-66.

No 14 Squadron, RNZAF, now equipped with Canberras, flew several operational missions in support of land forces. After 'confrontation' had ended the gradual withdrawal of British forces from the Far East began. A key aspect to the defence of this theatre was entrusted to the Australian, New Zealand and United Kingdom treaty, known as the ANZUK treaty. Whilst stability was achieved in Malaya, the melting pot of Vietnam drew the RNZAF in support of the Australian and United States forces engaged in the campaign against the Vietcong terrorists. The RNZAF contribution was to provide Forward Air Controllers for the USAF and helicopter pilots who flew with 9 Squadron, RAAF, on combat operations. Of the thirty pilots who participated, ten received gallantry awards.

The RNZAF of the 1980s is justly proud of its record and professionalism. The force maintains seven operational flying squadrons and is a key element in the defence forces of South-East Asia.

In addition the RNZAF is also actively involved in Antarctic support operations. The RNZAF gave magnificent support to the RAF in two World Wars. We should not forget the sacrifice that the New Zealanders made for freedom in Europe; we should remind ourselves that together with the RAAF and United States forces, they created the victory in the Pacific.

Links between the RNZAF and the RAF are maintained today through a variety of exchange postings in a wide spectrum of aviation skills. Thus, the opportunity remains for RAF officers to serve with this proud and distinguished air force.

The Royal Canadian Air Force

The first successful aeroplane flight in Canada occurred on 23 February 1909, when J. A. D. McCurdy piloted the 'Silver Dart' for a distance of half a mile over the ice-covered surface of Baddeck Bay, Nova Scotia. This flight has been recognised by the Royal Aero Club of the United Kingdom as the first successful powered heavier-than-air flight by a British subject anywhere in the British Empire. In this enterprise McCurdy was assisted by four other air enthusiasts, Casey Baldwin, Glen Curtiss and Lieutenant Selfridge of the US Army; the fourth was Alexander Graham Bell, the inventor of the telephone. Although attempts were made by these pioneers to interest the military at a major demonstration the 'Silver Dart' crashed, which singularly failed to impress the Army audience! Thus, apart from amongst enthusiasts, aviation was slow to gain recognition in Canada.

On 16 September 1914, in response to war in Europe, Colonel Sam Hughes, the Minister of Militia and Defence, authorised a Canadian Aviation Corps (CAC). It originally consisted of two officers, a mechanic and a single Burgess-Dunne biplane. Personnel were Captain E. C. Janney, Lieutenant W. F. N. Sharpe and Staff Sergeant H. A. Farr. The CAC was shipped to England in October 1914 and trucked to Salisbury Plain. The aircraft never flew in England as none of the three CAC members was

qualified as a pilot. The aircraft deteriorated in the English climate and was eventually written off. Nevertheless, a gradual expansion followed and members of the Corps were despatched with the Canadian Expeditionary Force to Britain to continue flying training with the RFC and RNAS. At the same time many volunteers came from within the Canadian Expeditionary Force to join the RFC and RNAS direct. However, the British flying Services would not accept the Canadians unless they had full pilot's certificates. To overcome this hurdle, the Canadian government opened the Curtiss School of Aviation in September 1915 at Long Branch, Ontario. Here, and at flying schools in the United States, many Canadians gained their pilot's certificates. This qualification was immediately recognised by the RNAS and by December 1915 a Canadian RNAS aircrew had claimed their first air victory. However the distinction of the first Canadian airman to see action was to go to Flight Sub-Lieutenant Redford Mulock who had earlier transferred from the Royal Canadian Artillery to the RNAS in 1915.

The flow of trained pilots arriving from Canada to join the RNAS steadily increased as the war progressed. By the summer of 1916, forty Canadian pilots were serving with No 3 (Naval) Wing in France flying the Sopwith 1½ Strutter two-seater aircraft, mainly on bombing missions. The first Canadian ace to emerge during this war was Captain Edward Grange.

The Allied air war did not get off to a good start. By the spring of 1917, the RFC was suffering heavy casualties, so much so that the Corps reserves were almost non-existent. To offset these losses, the RNAS offered its services, changing tack from the defence of coastal installations, to support the RFC on the Western Front. No 3 (Naval) Wing was eventually disbanded and its pilots reassigned to RFC squadrons. Altogether twelve Canadians gained twenty or more victories with the RFC. Of particular merit amongst the 'Aces' was Major 'Billy' Bishop who by August 1917 was the RFC's top scorer. By the end of the war he had achieved 72 victories and was the first Canadian airman to be awarded the Victoria Cross. In all, during the First World War there were 152 Canadian 'Ace' pilots (five victories or more); two other Canadian airmen also received the Victoria Cross: Second Lieutenant A. A. McLeod and Major W. G. (Billy) Barker, with

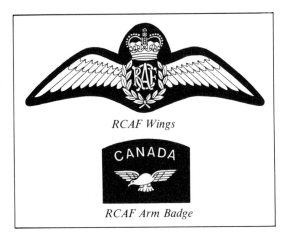

RCAF Wings

RCAF Arm Badge

400 Squadron	402 Squadron	406 Squadron
414 Squadron	417 Squadron	438 Squadron
450 Squadron	General Badge	Canadian Forces Badge

RCAF Squadron Badges

CAF Archives

203 other airmen destined to receive the Distinguished Flying Cross (nine with bars). As a grand total, 800 decorations were awarded to Canadian aviators. This distinguished record was achieved from within 22,000 Canadians who served in the RFC/RAF during the First World War. The price paid by the Dominion was 1563 killed in action.

During the closing years of the First World War the Canadian Government established close ties with the United States Army where Canadians joined Americans in Texas to undergo flying training. The United States provided the land facilities; the Canadians provided the aircraft. At the same time, the embryo of Canada's aircraft industry was born with the Canadian Aeroplane Company. It is a staggering fact to realise that from a cold start of

NIL military pilots in 1914, a training organisation had been set up by August 1918 that had provided 3135 pilots and 137 observers. Some 2539 of these aircrew later served in France. Moreover, thanks to increased 'U' boat activity in the Atlantic, an aviation arm was formally incorporated into the Royal Canadian Navy to become, by 1917, the Royal Canadian Naval Air Service.

Meanwhile, back in Britain, such was the enormity of the Canadian air effort that, in August 1918, the government of Canada decided to form a Canadian Air Force on similar lines to that of the Australian Flying Corps. England provided the training base and the two (Canadian) RAF squadrons that were preparing to form became pure Canadian units. No 81 Squadron, RAF, formed at Upper Heyford with all Canadian personnel in November 1918, just in time for the Armistice. However, the die had been cast and the squadron was later numbered No 1 Squadron, Canadian Air Force; No 2 Squadron was similarly formed from No 123 Squadron, RAF. When peace came on a dull November day, the future of the two squadrons was unsure. In 1919 both units moved to Shoreham to hold there temporarily, but only to disband in February 1920. The Directorate of Air Services, as a branch of the General Staff of the Overseas Military Forces of Canada, of which Lieutenant Colonel W. A. Bishop was the first Commander, was disbanded on 9 August 1920.

As in the other Dominions, the end of the First World War saw a virtual disbandment of Canada's Air Force. However, in 1919 an Air Board was set up by the Canadian government to control what was left of both military and the infant civil flying resources. At the same time, a study group was convened to provide recommendations for the future. The outcome was that a new Canadian Air Force was to be formed, but on a non-permanent basis and composed of auxiliaries. An Air Headquarters was opened in Ottawa and Lieutenant Colonel A. K. Tylee was appointed the first Air Officer Commanding. Camp Borden was selected as the first training centre. By March 1922 the Canadian Air Force had become well established with 550 officers and 1272 airmen under command.

At first the task of the new Air Force was to support the provincial governments with the domestic tasks of aerial survey, fire patrols and communications work. Operating bases were opened at Vancouver, Morley, Winnipeg and Ottawa. As the tasking for the new Air Force gradually increased, so it became apparent that a permanent, not auxiliary, organisation was required. The government listened and on 1 April 1924 The Royal Canadian Air Force came into being, responsible to the Canadian Army General Staff. The RCAF was initially organised at three levels, a permanent Active Air Force, a non-permanent Active Air Force and finally a Reserve Air Force.

Over the next decade the RCAF at all levels gradually expanded, even though ninety per cent of the flying was geared towards civil requirements with non-military tasking. Although the depression years of the 1930s saw cuts being made, by 1933 these had been made up and the RCAF regained its former strength with now dedicated fighter and bomber squadrons. At the same time new airfields were opened at Toronto and Winnipeg to support the enhanced military aviation activities. In 1936, the RCAF was reorganised as a purely military force.

Canadian military and air strategists looked on uneasily as Europe re-armed in the mid-1930s. There had been a quantum leap in aircraft development and the Canadian government realised the need to streamline and modernise its Air Force. In 1937 an expanded military aviation budget was announced which provided several up-to-date new aircraft types including the Blenheim bomber, Stranraer flying boat and the now famous Harvard trainer. At the same time, both the Permanent and Auxiliary squadrons were reorganised and re-numbered, the Auxiliary squadrons adding one hundred to the original squadron number. The RCAF became an independent force on 19 December (vice 19 November) 1938 responsible to the Ministry of National Defence. At this time the head of the RCAF became Chief of the Air Staff. The next step was to form an Air Council with Air Vice-Marshal G. M. Croil as the first Chief of the Air Staff. The RCAF had now been fully constituted and organised into three operational Commands: Western, Eastern and Air Training. In the same year (1938) a British Air Mission arrived in Canada to organise the production of additional aircraft for the RAF. The mission was well received and every support given to it. The outcome was that a new company, Canadian Associated Aircraft Limited, was formed to

Reporting to their section heads, three airmen of the RCAF Bomber Group's "Snowy Owl" squadron tell of blasting an important enemy airfield close to the strategic city of Le Mans in Normandie. CAF Archives

build eighty Hampden bombers. At the same time, the Canadian Car and Foundry Company built Hurricane fighters and Anson trainers under licence, while the National Steel Car Corporation of Toronto built Westland Lysanders. By the spring of 1939, twenty Hurricanes had been shipped to Britain with several more in the pipeline.

When Germany invaded Poland on 1 September 1939, Canada mobilised her armed forces. The peacetime strength of the RCAF stood at 270 aircraft organised into twenty squadrons (out of the twenty-three established), involving 4061 personnel. On 10 September 1939, the Canadian government declared war on Germany. The main thrust of the RCAF at home was to contribute to the Empire Air Training Scheme whilst providing for the nation's air defence. Some 4000 training aircraft were ordered for the Air Training Scheme and during the period 1939-45, 131,553 aircrew were trained. Of these aircrews, eighty per cent were

Canadian nationals. The scheme in Canada involved the establishment of over a 100 flying schools, and nearly 200 ancillary units which saw 10,000 training aircraft of all types in use. At the peak period of 1943 more than 3000 trained aircrews were leaving the training schools each month. The results achieved are astonishing: 72,800 aircrew were trained for the RCAF, 42,100 for the RAF, 9600 for the RAAF and 7000 for the RNZAF.

Meanwhile, the home air force continued improving its air defence and maritime patrol capabilities in support of the Atlantic convoys, later becoming involved with anti-U-boat operations. With the entry of Japan into the war, in December 1941, measures were taken, with the United States, to boost the air defence of the Pacific coastline. To meet this task, new squadrons with new aircraft (Liberators, Hudsons and Catalinas) were formed involving 34 new flying squadrons.

The major contribution by the RCAF to

active operations was in Europe. The first RCAF squadron to reach the UK was 110 Squadron which arrived at Odiham in February 1940, equipped with Lysanders. In June 1940 No 1 Squadron, RCAF, joined the orbat equipped with Hurricanes flying from RAF Middle Wallop. An early RCAF victory came on 15 June when a Dornier 17 was shot down. However, before 1940 the RAF held its own Canadian squadron which was formed in 1939 and numbered 242, flying Hurricanes. This heroic squadron achieved distinction from the first days of the war operating in support of the Dunkirk evacuation (Operation 'Dynamo') and later during the Battle of Britain. The first Canadian victory is attributed to Squadron Leader F. M. Gobeil of 242 Squadron in May 1940. During this time the squadron was under the command of the legendary Squadron Leader (later Group Captain) Douglas Bader. As time passed, and following severe losses, the Canadian 'flavour' of 242 Squadron was steadily diluted with an influx of pilots from the RAF and other Dominion air forces.

In March 1941 three new Canadian squadrons arrived in the UK and to avoid confusion they were re-numbered using the prefix of 400; thus 1 Squadron, RCAF, became 401 Squadron and so forth. In April of the same year the first bomber squadrons began to arrive whilst the RCAF itself undertook a gigantic expansion programme. In all the RCAF contribution to the European war was fifteen bomber squadrons, twenty fighter squadrons, five Coastal Command squadrons and one Transport Command squadron. In addition, RCAF squadrons served within the Desert Air Force in North Africa, on the island of Malta, as well as in Burma, Ceylon and in the Far East campaign against the Japanese.

It is difficult to find words to adequately describe the contribution made by the RCAF in defence of this country. By the end of the war No 6 RCAF Group alone of Bomber Command had flown 40,822 sorties in less than $2\frac{1}{2}$ years. They had dropped 126,122 tons of bombs at a cost of 814 aircraft lost; No 419 Squadron lost 129 aircraft — some five times its normal strength. The reward to the RCAF, if that is the right word, was in excess of 8000 decorations for bravery. In the dark world of the night fighter, RCAF squadrons destroyed 186 enemy aircraft; in total, RCAF fighter squadrons are believed to have destroyed in excess of 1000 enemy aircraft.

By the end of the war the RCAF was the third largest air force in the world. In addition, their home aircraft industry had became well established.

A post-war re-assessment of the RCAF took place in February 1946. The Regular Air Force was reduced to 16,000 men backed up by 4500 auxiliaries organised into fifteen squadrons. The jet age had arrived and the RCAF began to equip with Vampire aircraft from the UK and Canadian-built North Stars. But in 1948, the government announced a programme expansion for all of the armed forces to counter the threat posed by the Iron Curtain descending across Europe. Moreover, Canada was to become a leading contributor to the NATO forces. During the Korean War the RCAF expanded again providing Sabre jet pilots to fly American Sabres of the United Nations Task Force. RCAF North Star transport aircraft also took part in the Korean airlift over the Pacific Ocean. During this same period Canadian squadrons returned to the UK to provide support during the Berlin Airlift crisis as well as providing occupation air forces in Germany. By 1958 the RCAF had reached a peak of 56,000 men supporting over 3000 aircraft, inclusive of 600 jet combat aircraft. The 1960s saw new aircraft and technology brought into the Service which maintained Canada's status as the world's third largest air force. The cost to the taxpayer, on the other hand, made the government think again and from 1965 onwards economies had to be undertaken. The Phantom aircraft, for example, was twenty times the price of a Spitfire by relative pricing. As part of the envisaged economics a major change took place in defence organisation on 1 February 1968. The government decided to combine the three Services into 'The Canadian Armed Forces'. As a result the RCAF uniform disappeared, as did its ranks, to be replaced by a dark green uniform with gold rank braid utilising Army style ranks. However, in September 1986 the Canadian Air Force changed its livery again to one of light blue. Since 1968 the Canadian Armed Forces have continued to provide support to NATO, and the United Nations peace-keeping forces deployed throughout the world. The strength of the Air Component of the Canadian Armed Forces remains at 33 regular and six reserve air squadrons. Exchange postings with the CAF help to maintain links with the RAF.

The Royal Rhodesian Air Force
(formerly the Southern Rhodesian Air Force)
The Royal Rhodesian Air Force is now a matter of history. Its passing went without comment as Macmillan's 'wind of change' blew through the former British colonies of East and West Africa. The colonies are now proud, independent nations striving to succeed in a competitive world. Many of the former colonies maintain their own national Air Forces; in several cases modelled on our own Royal Air Force. But of all the former African Colonies, Rhodesia is perhaps the best known. During the Second World War, Rhodesia became the aviation training school for free Europe under the full title of 'Southern Rhodesia Group of the Empire Air Training Scheme'. Through the gates of its training stations passed tens of thousands of Allied aircrews from the United Kingdom, Greece, Yugoslavia, France, Belgium, Poland, Czechoslovakia, South Africa and, of course, from the homeland of what was then Southern Rhodesia.

As in the other former colonies and Dominions, the perception of aviation as an instrument of peace, as well as one offering obvious military advantages, was realized soon after the First World War. Some Southern Rhodesians had made their way to the UK in 1914 and had joined the RFC or the RNAS. On return home, they struggled to develop aviation, but it was not until 1920 that an aeroplane physically arrived in the colony. The first aircraft to land in Southern Rhodesia was a Vickers Vimy piloted by Lieutenant Colonel Van Ryneveld and Major Brand, who flew it from Croydon, near London, in March 1920. The local effect was dramatic. Here was a means of achieving speedy communication and carrying a limited payload of freight and mail. By April of the same year, an aviation company was registered at Bulawayo, where, together, with South African Aerial Transport Limited, they established the first passenger flying service in Southern Rhodesia. From these beginnings, aviation soon gained a firm toehold in the colony.

In 1927, a Rhodesian Aviation Syndicate was formed, and by 1930 a Civil Aviation Department under the Department of Defence had been introduced, sanctioned by an Aviation Act. By 1931 Salisbury was a well established staging point for the Imperial Airways London to Cape Town route. At the same time internal air routes had been established between the major towns and cities within Rhodesia and Nyasaland. Such is the generous climate of this part of Africa that ideal flying conditions prevail for most of the year. As civil aviation prospered so also did flying schools. Thus, by the outbreak of European war in September 1939, aviation was well established in Rhodesia, inclusive of an aircraft manufacturing industry, albeit under licence.

Military aviation first appeared in the colony in 1926 when RAF aircraft were pioneering the air route from Cairo to Cape Town. However, in the same year arrangements were finalised for Southern Rhodesians to train and gain experience in the RAF before returning home for local military duty. The Air Section of the Territorial Force came into being in November 1935 as the forerunner of an established air force. By 1938, the Air Section had outgrown itself and those pupils who had gained their wings were commissioned directly into the RAF Volunteer Reserve. On 12 May that year, the distinctive Rhodesian flying wings first appeared. Instead of bearing the lettering 'RAF', at the centre of the wings the Rhodesian Coat of Arms was incorporated. The next logical step was to constitute the Southern Rhodesian Air Force (SRAF) which was established on 19 September 1939.

It should be remembered that at this time Italian Somaliland bordered with Kenya. Southern Rhodesia had, by 3 September 1939, established two detached flights in Kenya, having the distinction of being the first colony in the Empire to establish 'war stations' outside its own borders. The visionary figure behind the build-up of the SRAF was Lieutenant Colonel C. W. Meredith, who had a sharp grasp of what was required. The SRAF base at Cranborne was quickly built up with an Air Headquarters established in Salisbury. Meredith later visited England in December 1939 offering the services of his colony and its air force to support the mother country. In particular, he offered the colony's resources as air training facilities utilising the civil airport at Belvedere and the military airfield at Cranborne. The British government jumped at the chance, tasking Meredith to prepare further airfield sites. Meredith, now promoted to the rank of Group Captain, returned home and set about the task in hand. By March 1940 the first RAF draft had arrived to set the foundations of what was to be

RRAF Pilots Wings

the Southern Rhodesia Air Training Group (SRATG). Such was the enterprise and urgency that the record time of eleven weeks was recorded for one of the sites which was completed from raw veld to air station.

As the war progressed, the attrition of Allied aircrews was horrendous. What started in Rhodesia as a small-scale training effort mushroomed, through necessity. In all, some 32 stations were operating by the end of the war, concerned with giving Allied aircrews basic and advanced flying training including specialist navigator, air gunner, air bomber and wireless operator instruction. At the same time language schools were opened to instruct Greek, Polish and French aircrews in English. Moreover, during the Allied campaign in North Africa, Southern Rhodesia became a key staging post in the ferrying of Allied aircraft from the Cape to the war theatre.

In the years from 1941 to 1945 it is estimated that over 90,000 Allied aircrews were trained under the Empire Air Training Scheme in Southern Rhodesia. In addition three Rhodesian squadrons flew as part of the RAF, Nos 237, 266 and 44 Squadrons. No 237 Squadron operated in the Western desert flying Hurricane and then Spitfire aircraft, No 266 Squadron flew Fairey Battles, latterly converting to Typhoons operating from the UK, while No 44 Squadron flew Lancaster bombers from the UK. Because of the casualty rate none of these squadrons were ever totally Rhodesian in establishment. Nevertheless, all were given the distinction of bearing the title 'Rhodesia' and all had a strong Rhodesian flavour. In addition, it is worth remembering that Marshal of the Royal Air Force Sir Arthur Harris had, as a young man, served in the British South Africa Police and the 1st Rhodesia Regiment before joining the RFC in England. Two other notables were Squadron Leaders Learoyd and Nettleton, both of whom gained the VC and served with No 44 (Rhodesia) Squadron.

At the end of the war the RATG was wound up leaving a small but well-equipped air force to look after the colony's defence. In 1946 and in gratitude for the colony's contribution to the Allied war effort, the King granted permission for the SRAF to adopt the 'Royal' prefix and so the Royal Rhodesian Air Force formally came into existence. The RRAF lasted until the announcement of UDI. Later constitutional changes have, of course, produced the independent state of Zimbabwe. Whatever the politics, rights and wrongs of the last twenty years, there is no doubting the contribution made by Rhodesia to the RAF as part of the Empire Air Training Scheme, nor that of the countless Rhodesian personnel who served in the three (RAF) Rhodesian squadrons and the RAF at large. It is also worth remembering the contribution made by the native black Rhodesians who formed the Rhodesian Air Askari Corps and who so generously supported the war effort.

The Royal Indian Air Force (RIAF)
On 12 March 1945 King George VI gave his approval for the Royal prefix to be added to the Indian Air Force (IAF) title. This designation lasted until 26 January 1950, when the Force title reverted to "Indian Air Force" on India becoming a Republic. As in the other Dominion and Commonwealth countries, the basis of the IAF was the Royal Air Force. Similarities between the two services remain to the present day both in organisation and in operation, as well as in dress style. Of all the Royal Air Forces, perhaps the Royal Indian Air Force is the least remembered. Although it was not formally created until the dying days of the Second World War, its contribution in that war and the Far East campaign in particular, was no less magnificent than any other Commonwealth or Dominion country. Indeed, the granting of the "Royal" prefix was made in recognition of the loyalty, devotion and courage of members of the IAF in support of Great Britain against the Japanese offensive in Burma, the Dutch East Indies and general Far Eastern theatre of war. The IAF soon gained an enviable reputation for professionalism, discipline and airmanship with an apparent natural aptitude for low-flying skills, hedge-hopping over the jungle canopy to

inflict surprise on the enemy. A skill to be later copied by other Allied aviators.

The history of the IAF is distinguished; it dates before the Second World War to the halcyon days of the British Raj. Aviation development in a country the size of India seemed a natural path to follow, if, for no other reason, than to improve the lines of communication. Following the First World War, the potential of military aviation was soon recognised. The Government of India first set up a Committee to look at air power in early 1925. The findings of the Committee were published in April 1927 which recommended the formation of an Air Arm as part of the Indian Army. This recommendation was accepted by the British government and by 1930, the first new pilots started training at the RAF College, Cranwell. However, it would be wrong to suggest that flying expertise had not previously existed amongst the Indians. During the First World War, several Indians had been commissioned into the RFC where they had flown earning great distinction. At the end of the War and on return home, these pioneers provided the driving force to established civilian flying clubs near the major towns of Dehli, Bombay and Madras. The perception to realise the potential of aviation in India was not slow to materialise, and the adeptness of Indian craftsman to manufacture aircraft components, provided the basis of an aviation industry. Aviation expertise was available in India from the very beginning. Bureaucracy, however, insisted that everything be regularised.

Air Headquarters, Baghdad, 1927.

From these strained and diverse beginnings blossomed the IAF. The first batch of military Indian pilots received the King's Commission on 8 October 1932 concurrent with the date on which the Indian Air Force Act became effective. From these humble beginnings and under the husbandry of the Royal Air Force, the IAF soon grew in stature. 'A' Flight IAF was formed at RAF Drigh Road, Karachi, on 1 April 1933 and commenced a programme of training to reach operational effectiveness. For many years the IAF were to be equipped with obsolete aircraft, such as the Westland Wapiti which remained in use until the early days of the Second World War. It was in these aircraft that the IAF first saw active operations in the rebellion which broke out in Waziristan in the autumn of 1936. On 1 October 1937 'A' Flight IAF moved to this troubled North West Frontier area carrying out bombing and reconnaissance missions in support of the 50,000 ground troops also deployed. The IAF soon proved itself with 'A' Flight latterly expanding to become No 1 Squadron of the IAF, under the command of an IAF officer.

With the outbreak of war in Europe in September 1939 many RAF squadrons were withdrawn to Great Britain leaving only 2 RAF squadrons resident in India. As a result, the IAF was to begin a period of expansion in order that it could provide the national air cover and thus, wholly releasing the RAF units for the European War. To meet the new task, the Government of India announced the Indian Air Force Volunteer Reserve scheme which sought to mobilise the air-minded from the many civilian flying clubs that had sprung up. There was no shortage of enthusiasm and, by the end of 1939, five coastal Defence Flights had been recruited, trained and equipped. During this same period, further bases were opened for the specialist training of Navigators, Air Gunners and Wireless Operators. However, no new aircraft were available from the UK. The IAF had to make do and mend with what was already in theatre. It is a marvel of Indian ingenuity, enterprise and initiative that those obsolete aircraft, the Harts, Audaxes, Rapidis and Wapatis were ever kept flying at all! India was nowhere in the defence plan for Britain and the home government could spare nothing, but verbal encouragement, for the IAF. The external defence investment that had existed was now being centralised in the Far East for the defence of Singapore and Malaya.

Eagle Arm Badge, India

The situation was to change when, on 7 December 1941, the Japanese carried out the joint attack against Pearl Harbor and targets in Malaya. The ruthless efficiency of this surprise attack was followed, at lightning speed, by mass ground assaults which in a matter of months was to threaten the very coastline of India itself. So began the First Burma Campaign as a defensive measure to secure the Indian border. During this campaign and flying in their obsolete aircraft the IAF first gained its reputation for accurate low flying. Some IAF units were now equipped with the Lysander aircraft. At first the IAF flew army co-operation, reconnaissance and surveillance missions, employing their obsolete aircraft on bombing missions, often achieving great success through 'hedge-hopping' surprise. Such was the success achieved by the IAF that in late 1942 the decision was made to expand the Force to ten squadrons, with some squadrons to be equipped with more up-to-date Spitfire and Hurricane aircraft.

The year 1943 saw the ending of the First Burma Campaign with a stalemate; but at least the borders of India were secure. In the period 1942-43 Allied troops had been pouring into India, whilst at the same time, local recruitment had greatly enhanced the power and punch of the Indian Army. Recruitment for the IAF had exceeded demands and the new Air Force was ready for the next stage in the offensive war to clear the Japanese from Burma.

In August 1943 the Allies agreed to form South East Asia Command under the leadership of Lord Louis Mountbatten. In December of the same year the Second Burma Campaign began

with the IAF to play a key role first on the Arakan front and later on the Imphal front in support of the beleaguered town of Kohima. There was to be no doubting the professionalism of the IAF which now flew DC3s in the transport role moving whole armies at a time, as well as operating fighter, ground attack and reconnaissance aircraft in support of the ground armies. Few knew and understood the rolling jungle terrain as well as the IAF aircrews.

When Rangoon fell to Allied troops on 3 May 1945, the Second Burma Campaign was all but over. Although some IAF squadrons remained for the final mopping up of the enemy operations, the majority of IAF squadrons returned to India. However, thousands of IAF officers and men never actually saw the IAF in action, but instead worked for the RAF throughout the length and breadth of India, Burma and Ceylon. For these personnel, the war was to continue to the bitter end. The contribution made by both the IAF on its own and the members of the IAF who worked for the RAF is inestimable. One figure given is that over 1 million Indians were employed by the RAF in support of RAF and IAF operations.

In 1946 the now RIAF began to demobilise in line with the political plans which were announced to give India full independence. On 15 August 1947 India was granted full Dominion status within the Commonwealth with Air Marshal Sir Thomas Elmhirst being appointed as the first Chief of The Indian Air Staff. In the early post Second World War years the RIAF was reorganised on a national basis with Regional Air Headquarters. In a country the size of India re-organisation was not easy and it is greatly to the Indians credit that out of the confusion of independence and partition, strong foundations were to be laid for the Republic of India's New Air Force in 1950.

In the years to the present day the IAF has matured into a proud and dedicated Air Force with a professionalism second to none. At the same time, civil aviation has expanded into a major growth industry.

Chapter 10
Colours and Standards

The origin of Colours and Standards in the RAF dates back to 1943 when, on the 25th Anniversary of the Service, King George VI announced his intention of awarding a ceremonial flag to be known as The Standard to operational squadrons, and King's Colours, equivalent to the Regimental Colours of the Army to honoured formations. But the custom and tradition of military colours dates back as far as biblical times, if not before. History records that the Israelites carried into battle the sacred standard of the Maccabees on which was written in Hebrew the text 'Who is like unto thee O Lord, among the Gods'. The standard of the Maccabees was used as a rallying symbol and this meaning is perpetuated in the Colours and Standards of the present day. Other historians suggest that the origins of our present military colours date back to the Middle Ages, when it was customary for each lord or baron to have his own flag or banner displaying the family crest or coat of arms. Whatever the origin, flags and banners were carried at the head of an army and used as a rallying and identifying feature, particularly on the battle field. Seen from a vantage point, the progress of a battle could be observed by following the movement of banners. Furthermore, since all banners were held in an elevated position, the rank and file had a good idea of how the battle was faring, particularly if the banner was seen being carried hastily to the rear! The seal upon a battle won was to secure the opponent's banner.

The introduction of the term 'Colour' appears much later in history and is attributed to the captains of infantry during the reign of Elizabeth I. The suggestion is that many of the Elizabethan yeoman officers did not have a crest or coat of arms to display, and adopted flags of distinctive colours, from which the term colour is derived. Regimental Colours on the other hand first appeared during the English Civil War of 1642-50, but they were still very much the personal banners of the commanders who had raised the armies. It was not until the beginning of the 17th century that a specific Colour was allotted to a military formation and this practice continued for a further hundred years. Then in 1751 the King, through Parliament, decreed that each regiment should have two Colours, a King's and a Regimental Colour; the King's Colour to be based on the Union flag, the Regimental Colour to have its own distinctive badge. This custom remains in the Army to the present day where the Army usage of the term Colour also includes Cavalry Standards and Guidons.

Military Colours came to represent the spirit of the regiment and the tradition arose of recording battle honours on them. The first battle honour to be granted in the British Army was to the 15th Light Dragoons, to commemorate a successful action fought at Emsdorff on 16 July 1769, during the Seven Years War. (The tradition of displaying battle honours is not perpetuated on RAF Colours but rather on RAF Standards.) Not unnaturally, each regiment took great pride in — indeed venerated — its Colour and the custody and care was entrusted to a young officer whose task it was to defend it to the end. To assist him in his task, the Ensign, as he was called, had a small Colour guard of a Sergeant, known as the Colour Sergeant and supporting soldiers. The titles 'Ensign' and 'Colour Sergeant' remain in use in the Army today.

The last time a Colour was carried into action was on 26 January 1881 in South Africa. The regiment concerned was the 58th Foot (later the 2nd Battalion of the Northamptonshire Regiment), at the battle of Laing's Neck. Shortly before in 1880, Parliament had considered the merits of carrying Colours in battle and in 1881 sought the views of commanding officers. The outcome was that Colours should be retained for peacetime use, but not carried in battle since they were obvious targets. In January 1882 an order was published to that effect. However, not all Army regiments had carried Colours into battle; regiments such as the Light Infantry, whose task it was to skirmish ahead of main columns employing tactics of stealth and concealment, would have found a Colour a disadvantage. Similarly, the Royal Artillery (RA) does not have a regimental Colour. The RA has taken part in nearly every land campaign in support of the infantry. Its list of battle honours is, therefore, considerable, and impossible to include on a single Colour. Instead, a system of honour titles was instituted in 1925 where batteries were allowed to adopt the names of battles or of famous battery commanders. Thus, for example, the 12th Field Battery is known as the 'Minden' Battery, after the Battle of Minden on 1 August 1759. It was also considered that the sound of artillery firing in battle provided just as good a rallying and location marker as did the Colour. A Colour was therefore superfluous, but the RA does have a distinctive ceremonial flag bearing the Regiment's badge. The tradition attached to a Colour today gives it an almost reverential significance, which Peter Herring aptly describes in his book *Customs and Traditions of the RAF*: 'they fly not only for the living, but for all who have died in the regiment for the King; not only as an augury of battles won, but a token of every field of the past'.

Consecration of Colours

In the British Museum there is a 14th-century manuscript prescribing a form of religious service for the blessing of flags. Later, in 1634, Barry records that the first task of a Captain is 'to cause his Colour to be blest'. It was not, however, until 1830 that any standardised form of religious service was considered in the British Army, and even then it was not brought into general use. The earliest references to a standardised ceremony appear in the 1867 edition of Queen's Regulations for the Army. Today, a special form of service has been devised by the Chaplain in Chief which is used at the consecration of all RAF Colours. It is customary for the monarch or her representative to present a Colour which has the full title 'The Queen's Colour'. When a Colour is to be retired or renewed, the 'Old Colour' is ceremonially laid up in a church or cathedral.

The RAF Colours

As noted earlier, it was King George VI who first announced an intention to present the RAF with Colours. However, it was not until after the relaxation of austerity measures following the Second World War that anything positive could be done. All RAF Colours are designed by the Inspector of RAF Badges in consultation with the Air Force Board. Each Colour is 3ft 9in square and made of silk; the background colour is RAF blue bearing a hand-embroidered badge or crest. It is supported on an 8ft 6in pike, which is capped by a gilded crown. The Colour bearer wears a special cross body brace made of blue-grey barathea edged with gold and bearing the Royal Cypher at the front. RAF Colours are paraded for guards of honour for royalty and heads of state, and on occasions directed by the Air Force Board.

The King's (Now Queen's) Colour for the RAF College Cranwell

The first Colour was presented by King George VI at Cranwell on 6 July 1948. Her Majesty Queen Elizabeth II presented a new Colour to the College on 25 July 1960, which was replaced by a new Colour, again presented by Her Majesty, on 30 May 1975. The present Colour is displayed in the main dining room of College Hall Officers' Mess and both old Colours have been laid up at the RAF Cranwell Church of St Michael and All Angels. In the centre of the blue silk square, the Colour carries the College Crest, and around the square is a blue and silver silk thread embroidered fringe. Normally only badges are borne on Colours, but since a grant of arms was made to the College in 1929 (see Chapter 6) this was permitted.

The King's (now Queen's) Colour for the RAF in the UK

The King's Colour for the RAF in the United Kingdom was first presented by Princess Elizabeth on 16 May 1951. King George VI took a personal interest in this Colour and rejected the first design on the grounds that it did not represent his own personal associations with the RAF; the late King had served in the RAF for a brief period in 1918. He asked that the Royal Cypher be added to the Union flag and roundel of the design. Sadly the King became seriously ill and was unable to present the Colour himself. At first the Colour was kept at the Royal Air Force Regiment Depot at Catterick but was later moved to the RAF Depot at Uxbridge, where it remains under the care of the Queen's Colour Squadron for the Royal Air Force. The Colour was renewed by Her Majesty Queen Elizabeth II on the 50th Anniversary of the RAF.

The Queen's Colour for No. 1 School of Technical Training RAF Halton

The Queen's Colour for No. 1 School of Technical Training, RAF Halton was presented by Queen Elizabeth II in the presence of Lord Trenchard (founder of the school) on 25 July 1952. It was designed at the same time as the College Colour and depicts the school badge of a beech tree of learning and the motto *Crescentes discimus* meaning 'We grow as we learn'. The Colour is paraded on Founder's Day and at graduation parades.

The Queen's Colour for the Royal Air Force Regiment

The Queen's Colour for the Royal Air Force Regiment was the fourth Colour to be presented and was granted to mark the 10th Anniversary of the Corps' formation. It was presented by Her Majesty Queen Elizabeth II on 17 March 1953. A second Colour was presented by Her Majesty in 1967. The Colour displays the Union flag, Royal Cypher with the Corps' own badge of Astral Crown and crossed rifles. The Colour is held at the RAF Regiment Depot at RAF Catterick.

The Queen's Colour for the Near East Air Force

The Royal Air Force has maintained a presence wherever there has been a requirement for a military force. The RAF's presence in the Mediterranean, Near East, South Arabia and Cyprus was marked on 14 October 1960 when the late Duke of Gloucester presented the Queen's Colour for the Near East Air Force at RAF Akrotiri in Cyprus. When the Near East Air Force was disbanded this Colour was formally laid up at the RAF Church of St Clement Danes in the Strand on 31 May 1976. The Colour displays the Union flag, with the Royal Cypher and the Astral Crown placed before a setting sun.

The Queen's Colour for the Far East Air Force

To mark the RAF presence in the Far East, including Malaysia, Singapore and Hong Kong, the Queen's Colour for the Far East Air Force was presented by Her Majesty on 13 July 1961, at RAF Changi. This Colour was formally laid up at the RAF Church of St Clement Danes on 13 June 1972, when the military garrisons and airfields in the Far East were closed. The Colour depicts the Union flag, Royal Cypher and an oriental junk.

The Queen's Colour for the Central Flying School

On 26 June 1969, at RAF Little Rissington, Her Majesty Queen Elizabeth II presented the Queen's Colour for the Central Flying School. The Colour displays the Central Flying School coat of arms and Royal Cypher on a blue silk background. The Colour is now kept at the School's new location at RAF Scampton. (See also Chapter 8 for a more detailed description of the coat of arms).

The Queen's Colour for Royal Air Force Germany

To mark the presence of the RAF in Germany, HRH the Princess Anne presented the Queen's Colour for Royal Air Force Germany on 16 September 1970 at RAF Bruggen. The Colour is lodged at Headquarters RAF Germany, RAF Rheindahlen. (See also Chapter 8.)

Squadron Standards

Royal Air Force Standards rank second in precedence to RAF Colours. For a squadron to qualify for the award of Standard, King George VI directed alternative requirements: a squadron must either have completed twenty-five years service in the RAF, Royal Auxiliary Air Force, Royal Flying Corps or Royal Naval Air Service, or it must have earned the King's appreciation for 'outstanding operations'. These requirements were formally announced in Air Ministry Order A. 866 of 1943. Thirty RAF squadrons were to qualify immediately, with 617 Squadron, the Dam Busters, being the first Squadron to earn the King's appreciation for outstanding operations; 120 Squadron was the only other squadron to qualify under this heading. Austerity measures again determined that the manufacture and final presentation of squadron Standards would not take place until the early 1950s. Unlike a Colour, which is normally presented by the Sovereign (or her representative), a squadron Standard may be presented by the Air Officer Commanding-in-Chief of the Command to which the squadron belongs. In some cases, however, where a member of the Royal Family might be the Honorary Air Commodore, they may wish to undertake this task. The form of service for the blessing of a Standard is the same as that for a Colour, but it may be undertaken by the officiating chaplain instead of the RAF Chaplain in Chief. The other difference is that the service is termed a dedication, rather than a consecration.

When a Colour and Standard are paraded together, the Standard is paraded on the right-hand side of the Colour. The most senior flag *of a type* (Colour or Standard) is to the right. On occasions when Colours and Standards are paraded together it is usual to have the Colours in front. (If only one Colour and one Standard then side by side with the Colour as right marker to the pair.) RAF squadron Standards are again hand-made in silk, to a uniform size of 4ft by 2ft 8ins. The squadron's own badge is embroidered in the centre of the silk, with background scrolls either side of the badge detailing battle honours. The silk-embroidered border is composed of the national emblem of the home countries: the thistle, rose, shamrock and leek. The staff which supports the standard is 8ft 1in long, capped by a gilded eagle with wings outstretched. The Standard bearer wears a similiar supporting brace to that described for a Colour bearer, but instead of the Royal Cypher, the squadron badge is depicted at the front. Some early Standards did not include the leek in the silk-embroidered fringe of flowers edging the Standard, and this embarrassing omission was noticed by Mr. H. R. Gower, MP for Barry, who brought this point to the attention of Parliament in May 1953. The Air Ministry were duly embarrassed and on 11 March 1954 the first Standard to include the leek in the fringe design was presented by HRH Princess Margaret to No. 605 (County of Warwick) Squadron of the Royal Auxiliary Air Force. The first squadron to be presented with a Standard by Her Majesty Queen Elizabeth II was appropriately No. 1 Squadron, on 25 April 1953 at RAF Tangmere. The first auxiliary squadron to receive a standard was No. 600 (City of London) Squadron, presented by HRH Queen Elizabeth The Queen Mother in May 1953. When a squadron is disbanded, its Standard may be laid up. Several disbanded squadron Standards are now kept on permanent display in the rotunda of College Hall Officers' Mess at the RAF College Cranwell.

Battle Honours

Apart from the Falkland Island campaign and Northern Ireland, there are ninety-five listed battles and campaigns in which RAF squadrons have fought. Squadrons which have taken part in more than eight battles may select those they wish to appear on their Standard. The tradition of recording battle honours is solely perpetuated on squadron Standards. A list of RAF battle honours is given in Appendix I.

Chapter 11
Medals, Decorations and Awards

The present-day usage of the word medal is as a collective title and in Service parlance may also cover military decorations and awards. The word medal comes from the French medaille, which simply means coin. Some early medals had a coin value and were given in payment for tasks undertaken — there were also medal coins struck to commemorate victories, coronations and other historic events. Much later, medals were awarded by monarchs and governments in recognition of acts of gallantry, war service and outstanding public duty. The origin of the commemorative medal is obscure. However, it is known that the Italians produced commemorative medals during the 15th century and that the Germans adopted the idea in the 16th century. The earliest English medal is thought to have been struck in 1588 to commemorate the defeat of the Spanish Armada. By vote of the House of Commons a medal was struck in 1650 and awarded to all parliamentary forces who took part in the battle of Dunbar, with further medals in 1653 for officers and seamen involved in various naval campaigns. In 1794, a medal celebrated Lord Howe's naval victory against the French.

The first recorded issue of the General Service Medal (GSM) was in 1816, to all ranks who took part in the Battle of Waterloo. From the Napoleonic wars onwards, Parliament took a much greater interest in military awards, so much so that by the late 19th century a form of structured organisation and administrative procedure was in evidence for granting the various medal distinctions. Campaign medals were regularly issued with gallantry and bravery awards, of which the Victoria Cross, instituted on 29 January 1856, is probably the most famous. Each medal has its own distinctive ribbon, or riband, which is used to support the medal and is the point of attachment to the uniform. The wearing of medals today is reserved for full ceremonial occasions, though miniature medals are always worn on Mess dress. Medal ribbons, on the other hand, are

The first GSM to all Ranks Waterloo 1815   *Victoria Cross*

displayed on the RAF No. 1 and No. 2 uniform jackets and equivalent tropical dress for normal day-to-day wear. Medal ribbons are positioned above the left breast pocket, but below any flying badge.

Medals

The word medal is taken to mean campaign medal, such as the General Service Medal or more recently the Falkland Island Medal, Coronation or Jubilee medal, or Long Service and Good Conduct Medal (LS & GCM). The last of these is issued only to airmen ranks after fifteen years faultless service, although officers commissioned from the ranks may also wear this medal. The double award of a medal, and this would only apply to the LS & GCM to show twenty-four years' service, is distinguished by a small silver rose in the centre of the medal ribbon. This same small silver rose is also used in other circumstances — for example, when worn with the Falkland Island Medal it means that the individual served under active service conditions and in the Falklands theatre. The same medal worn without the rose signifies that the individual served outside the active service area, but supported the campaign. The GSM may be awarded for different campaigns. To identify the

ROYAL AIR FORCE SQUADRON BADGES

FLYING SQUADRONS

OCULI EXERCITUS

PER DIEM PER NOCTEM

USPIAM ET PASSIM

POSSUNT QUIA POSSE VIDENTUR

FACTA NON VERBA

PREUX ET AUDACIEUX

SEEK AND DESTROY

SCORPIONES PUNGUNT

FORTITER IN RE

GLORIA FINIS

SWIFT

HIC ET UBIQUE

AUT PUGNA AUT MORERE

DESPITE THE ELEMENTS

ENDURANCE

PER NOCTEM VOLAMUS

REM ACU TANGERE

OCCORES ACRIORESQUE AQUILIS

LEADS THE FIELD

IN OMNIBUS PRINCEPS

HEREWARD

TERTIUS PRIMUS ERIT

IN FUTURUM VIDERE

FRANGAS NON FLECTAS

AIM SURE

OPERTA APERTA

EXCUBITERE CONTENDE

ANIMO ET FIDE

IMPIGER ET ACER

VENTRE A TERRE

IN CAELUM INDICUM PRIMUS

ADESTE COMITES

LOYALTY

NIL NOS TREMEFACIT

QUID SI COELUM RUAT

CORPUS NON ANIMUM MUTO

PER ARDUA AD AETHERA TENDO

USQUAM

RAF REGIMENT SQUADRONS

*Queen's Colour for the RAF
College, Cranwell*

Queen's Colour for the RAF in the UK

*Queen's Colour for No. 1 School
of Technical Training, RAF Halton.*

Queen's Colour for the RAF Regiment

*Queen's Colour for the Near East
Air Force*

*Queen's Colour for the
Central Flying School*

*Queen's Colour for the Far East
Air Force*

Queen's Colour for RAF Germany

Standard for 201 Squadron

Standards held in safe custody hanging in College Hall Officers Mess notice the Silk Embroidered Border and the Gilt Eagle which surmounts the Pike.

The rotunda of College Hall Officers' Mess

The First General Service Medal to all Ranks

Selection of Military Medals

National Awards

'The Most Excellent Order of The British Empire'

'The Most Noble Order of The Garter'

'The Most Noble and Ancient Order of The Thistle'

'The Most Honourable Order of the Bath'

'The Most Distinguished Order of St Michael and St George'

'The Order of Merit'

'The Royal Victorian Order'

theatres of operation, clasps are worn attached to the medal ribbon which state the campaign for which the medal was awarded. The current 1962 General Service Medal, for example, has clasps for military campaigns in Radfan, South Arabia, Dhofar and finally Northern Ireland. For the owner of one or all of these clasps, only one medal is presented and only one ribbon is worn on the uniform jacket. Other current medals include the Rhodesia Medal, and the distinctive blue and white United Nations medal which is worn by all British servicemen who have served as part of a UN peacekeeping force. Criteria for the award of medals are published in Queen's Regulations or Defence Council Instructions. Medal precedence will be dealt with later in this chapter but it is worth noting that campaign medals come before conduct and foreign medals.

Mention in despatches
One medal award first introduced in 1902 and revised in 1939 has no coin medal of its own but is rather a distinctive emblem. It is the small bronze oak leaf worn on the tunic as if it were a medal ribbon, with the stalk furthest from the shoulder. The distinction is titled 'Mention in Despatches'. The award is made for brave or gallant conduct and if earned during a period when a campaign was under way, may be worn attached to the campaign medal ribbon. Otherwise, it is worn attached to a small piece of grey backing material on Mess dress and uniform alike. The oak leaf emblem is also worn to signify those who earned the distinction of the 'Queen's Commendation for Valuable Service in the Air'.

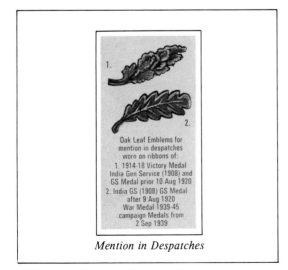

Oak Leaf Emblems for
mention in despatches
worn on ribbons of:
1. 1914-18 Victory Medal
India Gen Service (1908) and
GS Medal prior 10 Aug 1920
2. India GS (1908) GS Medal
after 9 Aug 1920
War Medal 1939-45
campaign Medals from
2 Sep 1939

Mention in Despatches

Decorations
The decoration medal is a little easier to define. Decorations are medals awarded for specific acts of gallantry or bravery (but not always in the face of the enemy). Classic examples are the Victoria Cross, Distinguished Flying Cross, Distinguished Service Order, Air Force Cross and Medal, George Cross and Medal. Some distinction is made between presenting decorations to officers and to airmen. As a rough guide, the Cross or Order title is presented to Warrant Officers and commissioned officers, while the medal title is awarded to non-commissioned ranks. The exceptions are the Victoria Cross and George Cross, which may be presented regardless of rank. There is also some difference between the Medal and Cross ribbon design, though the colours may be the same. The double award of a decoration is signified by a plain silver clasp worn across the medal ribbon when the medal is attached. For flying decorations this will include an eagle with outstretched wings embossed on the clasp. When only the ribbon is worn a small silver rose is sewn on to the ribbon to acknowledge the double award. The double decoration award is termed 'and bar'. There is no limit to the number of 'bars' that may be displayed. Some further information on specific military decorations appears at the end of this chapter. All citations to decorations are promulgated in the *London Gazette*.

Awards
Awards, such as 'The Royal Victorian Order', 'The Order of the Companions of Honour', 'The Most Excellent Order of the British Empire', may be made in time of peace and war. These national awards are given in recognition of outstanding devotion to duty, or achievement, or as a reward for personal services performed on behalf of the Sovereign. The recipients of awards are usually notified through either the Queen's New Year's Honours List, or the Birthday Honours List. These lists are published in division, to account for both a military and civil list. In exceptional circumstances, such as the Falklands campaign, awards may be notified through the *London Gazette*. From a Service point of view, the most widely known award is 'The Most Excellent Order of the British Empire'.

This Order was founded on 4 June 1917 by King George V. Originally, the award was to be

Naval General Service *1793-1940* *Camperdown 1797*	*Frigate Action* *1799*	*First India Medal* *1799-1826*	*Copenhagen* *1801*	*Egypt (Navy)* *1801*

Early Military Medals

granted to those who had rendered conspicuous service at Home or in India, the Dominions or Colonies, other than to Navy or Army personnel. It could, however, be conferred on military personnel for services of a non-combatant nature. In 1918 the Order was formally divided into civil and military divisions. The Order is now used to reward service in every civil and military activity. The two highest classes of the Order entail admission into knighthood and, as with all knights, the right to bear the title 'Sir' or 'Dame'. Foreigners, on the other hand, are only admitted as honorary members. The reigning monarch is the Sovereign of the Order, and the Duke of Edinburgh is the Grand Master of the Order. There are five classes to the Order: the Knight Grand Cross or Dame Grand Cross (GBE) wear the badge of the Order on a sash or on a collar, with the Star of the Order. The second class is the Knight Commander or Dame Commander (KBE or DBE). The incumbents of this award wear the Badge of the Order on a neckband for gentlemen, or on a bow for ladies, together with the Star of the Order. The Commander of the Most Excellent Order of the British Empire is the third class of the Order (CBE). Recipients here wear the badge of the Order on a neckband, for gentlemen, or on a bow for ladies. The fourth class of the Order is the OBE, or Officer. Gentlemen wear the badge of the Order on a chest 'riband'; ladies wear the Order on a bow. The final Class of the Order is that of Member (MBE) and here the badge of the Order is again worn on a chest riband for gentlemen or a bow for ladies. Associated with this Order is the

British Empire Medal (BEM), which again has a civil and a military division. This medal was instituted on 21 April 1941 for people who have given deserving service which justifies a token of Royal appreciation. The award is worn as a coin medal and recipients are entitled to add the letters BEM after their name. The medal has one class and is worn on a chest riband. If the BEM is awarded more than once, it is provided with an oak leaf made of silver sewn on to the ribbon. In December 1975 a new status to this award was added which differentiated between the acts of gallantry for which the award was made, and meritorious service. Gallantry awards are distinguished by the wearing of an emblem composed of two silver oak leaves on the appropriate riband. (Notes on other national awards are given at the end of this chapter.)

Precedence in wearing and displaying medals
Medal ribbons should be displayed according to a strict order of precedence. The rule is that the VC, GC come first, followed by national awards such as the MVO or MBE; then by decorations (such as the MC or DFC) and Campaign medals; General Service Medals, with Good Conduct Medals last. Any foreign medal is worn after the last home medal.

Medal mounting
Medals may be displayed in one of two ways: court or plain mounted. When medals are court mounted, the medal ribbon extends to below the clasp to provide a backing to the 'coin'; this backing is stiffened by card of the same size as the ribbon. In plain mounting, medal ribbon loops through the clasp of the medal; all medals arrive plain mounted.

SOME FAMOUS NATIONAL AWARDS

The Most Noble Order of the Garter

This order was founded in 1348 by King Edward III. It originally consisted of the King and twenty-five knights or knights companion as they were known. The Order is considered to be the highest British civil and military honour. The conferment of the Order entails adoption into the knighthood and the letters KG (Knight of the Garter) may be added after the name of the recipients. Only Christians may receive the Order.

The Most Ancient and Most Noble Order of the Thistle

The Order of the Thistle did not become an established Order of Chivalry until 29 May 1687, when it was revived by King James II of England. However, a similar Order had been lurking, probably as a Scottish Order, during the 15th and 16th century. On restoration by King James II, the Order consisted of the King plus twelve knights, an allusion to the Saviour and his twelve Apostles. On King James' death the Order fell out of use until it was revived by Queen Anne in 1703, who modelled it on the lines of the Order of the Garter. In 1821 King George IV increased the number of knights to sixteen, which by 1827 became the established figure. Today, members of the Royal Family are known as the Royal Knights. King Olaf V of Norway is an extra Knight, and the only foreigner to be admitted to the Order. Conferment of the Order entails an individual admission to the knighthood and the letters KT (Knight of the Thistle) after the knight's name.

The Most Honourable Order of the Bath

The Order of the Bath was created by King George I in 1725 and fully recognised in 1815. The Order may be conferred upon the military for outstanding war service, or to civilians from the Home Civil Service. The highest class in the Order is recognised as the highest British military honour (as opposed to decoration) to be obtained. Admission to the Order entails a knighthood; foreigners may be admitted to the Order as honorary members. The Monarch is the Sovereign of the Order, and the Duke of Gloucester is the Grand Master of the Order. Finally, the Order has civil and military divisions, each of three classes: Knight Grand Cross (GCB), Knight Commander (KCB) and Companion (CB). These letters may be included after the recipient's name.

The Most Distinguished Order of St Michael and St George

This Order was founded by King George III on 12 August 1818, as a reward to the inhabitants of the Ionian Islands and Malta. The peoples of these islands came under British sovereignty in 1814, but more particularly had given staunch service to the Crown during various Mediterranean campaigns. Today the Order may be conferred on diplomats and others involved in foreign service on behalf of the Crown, as well as those who have done valuable service in Commonwealth countries. The Order may also be granted to foreigners, although this is rare. There are three classes to the Order: Knight Grand Cross or Dame Grand Cross (GCMG), Knight Commander or Dame Commander (KCMG or DCMG) and finally Companion (CMG). The two highest classes of the Order include admission to knighthood, and the appropriate letters may be included after the recipient's name. Foreigners may be admitted as honorary members. The Monarch is the Sovereign of the Order.

The Order of Merit

The Order of Merit was founded on 23 June 1902 by King Edward VII. It was instigated as the Monarch's personal reward for 'specially eminent Service in the Armed Forces' and 'for unusually deserving achievement in the promotion of the Arts, Literature or Science'. The Order ranks after the Grand Order of the Bath. The number of Ordinary members is restricted to twenty-four, excluding foreigners who may be admitted as honorary members. The holders of the Order may add the letters 'OM' after their name. There is a civil and military division to the Order, each of one class.

The Order of the Companion of Honour

This Order was founded by King George V on 4 June 1917. It ranks after the Grand Cross of the Order of the British Empire, and is open to both men and women in recognition of services of national importance. The number of ordinary members is restricted to sixty-five, but Prime Ministers of Commonwealth countries may make nominations for this award and foreigners are admitted as honorary members. Holders of the Order may add the letter 'CH' after their name; there is only one class to the Order.

The Royal Victorian Order

The Royal Victorian Order was founded by Queen Victoria on 21 April 1896 as a reward for personal services performed for the Sovereign. Presentation of this award remains the prerogative of the Monarch, not the Government. This order may be conferred on Britons or foreigners and is associated with Royal visits abroad, and visits by foreign heads of state to this country. There are five classes to the Order: Knight Grand Cross or Dame Grand Cross (GCVO), Knight Commander or Dame Commander (KCVO or DCVO), Commander (CVO), Licentiate 4th Class (LVO), Member 5th Class (MVO). The two highest classes of the Order entail admission into Knighthood. Foreigners may only be admitted as Honorary Members. The Monarch is the Sovereign of the Order and 20 June (Queen Victoria's accession) is the Day of the Order. Her Majesty Queen Elizabeth The Queen Mother is presently the Grand Master of the Order; ladies were admitted to the Order in 1936.

SOME FAMOUS MILITARY DECORATIONS

The Victoria Cross

The Victoria Cross (VC) was instituted by Queen Victoria at the behest of Prince Albert on 29 January 1856. The decoration is open to all ranks of the Services who qualify by outstanding valour or by devotion to their country in the face of the enemy. The decoration may also be awarded to civilians and members of the Merchant Navy. It ranks above all other decorations and Orders and carries with it a tax free life annuity of £100. The Cross is the Cross 'paty', and the medal is fashioned from the metal of bronze cannons captured during the Crimean War. The Cross bears the inscription 'For Valour'. The youngest person to win the VC was Hospital Apprentice Arthur Fitzgibbon, aged fourteen, for his bravery with the Indian Medical Services at the Taku forts in northern China on 21 August 1860. A bar to the VC has been awarded three times and a total of 1350 VCs have been awarded since 1856, including two during the Falklands campaign of 1982. Nineteen VCs were awarded to the RFC during the 1914-18 war, and thirty-two to the RAF during the Second World War. The VC may be awarded posthumously. The ribbon is crimson, bearing a miniature of the Cross in bronze.

The George Cross and Medal

The George Cross (GC-GM) was instituted by King George VI on 26 September 1940. This decoration may be given as a reward for valour or outstanding gallantry displayed under dangerous conditions. The GC-GM was designed primarily for civilians, but members of the Armed Forces may also qualify. The decoration ranks after the Victoria Cross but before all other British Orders and decorations. It carries a lifetime tax free annuity of £100. The Cross is a St George Cross made of silver, bearing the Royal Cypher 'GVI' and the inscription 'For Gallantry'. The George Medal was instituted at the same time as the Cross but for circumstances where the action did not merit the GC. The medal bears the effigy of Her Majesty with the legend 'Elizabeth II Die Gratia Regina FD'; the reverse bears St George on horseback killing the dragon. Both cross and medal may be awarded posthumously. No bar has ever been awarded to the GC, but has been awarded twenty-five times to the Medal. The most famous dedication was probably to the people of Malta for their outstanding courage during the 'blitz' on the Island during 1941-2. The GC ribbon is garter blue, while the GM ribbon consists of six red and four medium blue stripes.

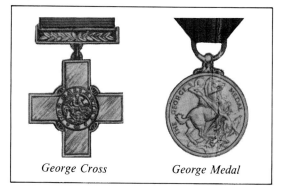

George Cross   George Medal

The Distinguished Service Order

The Distinguished Service Order (DSO) was instituted by Queen Victoria on 6 September 1886. It is awarded for distinguished service in war for officers of all services and officers of the Merchant Navy who, while serving with the Royal Navy, qualify for the award. Nomination for the Order may be made only if the person concerned has been mentioned in despatches. The badge is a gold cross paty, enamelled white and edged gold. The reverse of the Cross carries the Royal Cypher of the Monarch. The DSO takes precedence after Commander of the Order of the British Empire. A third bar to the Order has been awarded sixteen times. The ribbon is red with blue border stripes.

Distinguished Servce
Order

Distinguished Service
Cross

The Distinguished Service Cross

The Distinguished Service Cross was instituted by King Edward VII in 1901 as the Conspicuous Service Cross. In October 1914 it was slightly altered to its present title by King George V. It may be awarded to Naval and Royal Marine officers of the rank of Commander or below, or RAF officers of equivalent rank serving with the Fleet Air Arm. It is awarded for distinguished services that do not merit the award of the DSO. It may also be awarded to members of the WRNS for gallant and distinguished conduct ashore during enemy action, or officers of the Merchant Navy serving with the RN. A recipient of the award must have been mentioned in despatches. The design consists of a plain silver cross paty, bearing in its centre the Royal Cypher of the Monarch. A third bar to the DSC has been awarded only once. The ribbon has white and blue stripes of equal width.

The Military Cross and Medal

The Military Cross (MC) was instituted on 31 December 1914 and the Military Medal (MM) on 25 March 1916, both as an Army decoration. They are awarded for gallant and distinguished service in action. According to instructions published on 5 February 1931, the Military Cross may be awarded to officers of the rank of Major and below, including Warrant Officers. The other rank equivalent of the Military Cross is the Military Medal — which is a coin medal. The Military Cross is worn after British orders,

but before campaign medals. The Cross design is of an ornamented silver cross with narrow straight arms which widen slightly at their extremities. Each arm is surmounted by an Imperial Crown. The centre of the Cross contains the Royal Cypher of the Monarch. A third bar has been awarded four times to the MC and once to the MM. The MC ribbon consists of white, purple and white vertical stripes of equal width; the MM ribbon has three white and two crimson stripes in the centre and broad border stripes in navy blue.

Military Cross

Military Medal

The Distinguished Flying Cross and Medal

The Distinguished Flying Cross (DFC) was the first of the flying decorations, and replaced the Military Cross which had been awarded to some early military aviators. The DFC was instituted by King George V on 3 June 1918. It is awarded for displaying valour, gallantry and devotion to duty on one or more occasions while flying on active operations against the enemy. This decoration may be awarded to officers or Warrant Officers and equivalent ranking aviators of the other two Services. The other rank equivalent to the Distinguished Flying Cross is the Distinguished Flying Medal (DFM), which is a coin medal. The design of the DFC is of the 'Cross Flory', where the upper arm terminates in a rose, and the horizontal and lower arms with bombs. The upper and lower arms are surmounted by a propeller and the horizontal arms with outstretched wings. On the centre of the Cross are the letters RAF. During the two world wars a total of 20,347 awards were made. A second bar to the DFC has been made fifty-two times, but only once to the DFM. The ribbon for the DFC is violet and white in alternate stripes inclined at 45° to the horizontal. The DFM has the same colours, but narrower stripes.

Distinguished Flying Cross and Bar *Distinguished Flying Medal*

The Air Force Cross and Medal

Broadly, the AFC and AFM are peacetime counterparts of the DFC and DFM, though that does not prohibit their award during wartime. Both the AFC and the AFM were instituted by King George V on the same day as the DFC and DFM, 3 June 1918. These decorations are awarded for acts of valour, courage or devotion to duty while flying, though not in active operations against the enemy. It may also be granted to individuals not belonging to the RAF who render distinguished service to aviation.

Air Force Cross and Bar *Air Force Medal*

The Cross decoration is made of silver and consists of a thunderbolt in the form of a cross where the arms are conjoined by wings. In the centre of the cross is a roundel containing a representation of Hermes mounted on a hawk in flight 'bestowing a wreath'. On the reverse is the Royal Cypher above the date 1918. The AFC may be awarded to all officers, including Warrant Officers. The Air Force Medal is an oval-shaped coin medal awarded under the same criteria as the AFC but to non-commissioned officers. A second bar has been awarded twelve times to the AFC and eight times to the AFM. The ribbon for the AFC has white and red diagonal stripes at 45° to the horizontal; the AFM has the same colours but narrower stripes.

The Distinguished Conduct Medal

The Distinguished Conduct Medal (DCM) was instituted by Queen Victoria on 4 December 1854. It may be awarded to non-commissioned officers and men for gallant and distinguished conduct in the field. It is a silver coin medal and bears the inscription 'For Distinguished Conduct in the Field' on one side, with the Monarch's effigy on the other. The ribbon has blue and crimson vertical stripes of equal width.

Distinguished Conduct Medal and Bar *Conspicuous Gallantry Medal and Bar*

The Conspicuous Gallantry Medal

The Conspicuous Gallantry Medal (CGM) was instituted by Queen Victoria on 7 July 1874. This medal is the Naval counterpart of the Army's DCM and may be awarded to Petty Officers and ratings of the Royal Navy and non-commissioned officers of the Royal Marines for distinguished acts of conspicuous gallantry, in action against the enemy. It may also be awarded to members of the Merchant Navy and to members of the WRNS for gallantry on shore during enemy action. The medal is made of silver; on one side is an effigy of the Monarch and on the other the inscription 'For Conspicuous Gallantry'. The RAF version of the CGM, known as the CGM (Flying), is awarded for conspicuous gallantry while flying in active operations against the enemy and is superior to the DFM. The medal ribbon is light blue with dark blue edges; the Naval version is white with dark blue edges.

The Distinguished Service Medal

The Distinguished Service Medal (DSM) was instituted by King George V on 14 October 1914. It may be awarded for courageous service in war to Petty Officers and ratings of the Royal Navy, and to non-commissioned officers of the Royal Marines. However, in certain circumstances, by example of bravery and resource when under fire, the award may also be made to Merchant Navy seamen and members of the WRNS. The medal bears on one side an effigy of the Monarch and on the reverse the incription 'For Distinguished Service'. The ribbon is blue-white-blue stripes of equal width with a narrow blue stripe running down the centre.

Distinguished Service Medal and Bar

AIR VICTORIA CROSS RECIPIENTS

(including the RNAS, Fleet Air Arm, Air Transport Auxiliary)

1914-18
William Barnard Rhodes Moorhouse
Reginald Alexander Warneford
Lanot George Hawker
John Aidan Liddell
Gilbert Stuart Martin Insall
Richard Bell-Davies
Lional Wilmot Brabazon Rees
William Leek Robinson
Thomas Mottershead
Frank Hubert McNamara
William Avery Bishop
Albert Ball
Alan Arnett McLeod

Alan Jerrard
James Thomas Byford McCudden
Ferdinand Maurice Felixwest
William George Barker
Andrew Frederick Weatherby Beauchamp Prater
Edward Mannock

1939-45
Donald Edward Garland
Thomas Gray
Roderick Alastair Brook Learoyd
Eric James Brindley Nicolson
John Hannah
Kenneth Campbell
Hughie Idwal Edwards
James Allen Ward
Arthur Stewart King Scarf
Eugene Kingsmall Esmonde
John Deering Nettleton
Leslie Thomas Manser
Rawdon Hume Middleton
Hugh Gordon Malcolm
William Ellis Newton
Leonard Henry Trent
Guy Penrose Gibson
Lloyd Alan Trigg
Arthur Louis Aaron
William Reid
Cyril Joe Barton
Norman Cyril Jackson
Andrew Charles Mgnarski
David Ernest Hornell
John Alexander Cruickshank
Ian Willoughby Bazalgette
Geoffrey Leonard Cheshire
David Samuel Anthony Lord
Robert Anthony Maurice Palmer
George Thompson
Edwin Swales
Robert Hampton Gray

N.B. In order to keep memory alive, it is the custom to name barrack blocks after VC recipients. The VC10 aircraft of 10 Squadron based at RAF Brize Norton also proudly bear the names of some RAF VC holders.

Chapter 12
The Custom of Saluting

The origin of saluting as a military act is a little obscure. Major T. J. Edwards in his book *Military Customs* suggests that 'saluting and the paying of compliments may be said to proceed from the exercise of good manners'. Taking the world saluting literally, it is merely the offering of a salutation or greeting, which in a military context must be reciprocated. Gladiators in the Roman arena saluted the Emperor before their battles; it is not known if this was optional for lions.

One of the more romantic theories relating to the origin of this custom and dating from medieval times suggests that victors at tournaments shaded their eyes with their hands when receiving their prize from the Queen, rather than be blinded by the Queen's dazzling beauty — an unlikely origin but certainly very chivalrous. More believable is the suggestion

The Hand Salute

that the military salute, like the handshake, has its origin in the offering of the open hand as a token of respect and friendship. The open hand, devoid of weapon, was an obvious demonstration of friendliness, or at least friendly intention. It is interesting to note that the Red Indians of North America evolved their own particular gesture of friendliness by presenting the raised and open hand — whether it was always accompanied by the statement 'How!' is perhaps a Hollywood custom! In Europe during the Middle Ages when knights met each other, a peaceful greeting was to uncover the head or lift the visor. The *Chronicles* of Froissart, dated 1345, state: 'When Sir Argot saw them, he took off his cap and saluted them'. From historical records two practices appear to emerge; first, the offering of the open hand, and second, the raising of the hand to uncover or bare the head. If these two acts are combined into one gesture, the origin of today's military hand salute becomes a little more clear. The 17th-century custom of hat raising is an extension of the custom of uncovering the head. An account of this action can be found in military records of the 17th century which detailed that 'formal saluting was to be by removal of headdress'. In Europe a similar custom prevailed; John Locke recorded that during a review of the Gardes du Corps in Paris in 1678: 'The King passed at the head of the line as they stood drawn up, the officers at the head of their companies and regiments in armour, with pikes in their hands, saluting him with their pikes, then with their hats. He very courteously put off his hat to them again: so he did when, taking his stand, they marched before him.' For some time thereafter hat raising became an accepted form of the military salute. During the early part of the 18th century the Coldstream Guards decided to amend the hat-raising salute. A Regimental Order dated 1745 directed: 'The men are ordered not to pull off their hats when they pass an officer, or speak to him, but only to clap up their hands to their hats and bow as they pass by.' This amended form of

The Sword Salute

salute appears to have caught on and was adopted by many other foot regiments despite the fact that it was not officially approved. The cavalry regiments and the Horse Guards, on the other hand, were not so keen: which may or may not have accounted for the Army's Standing Order No. 135 dated 1755, which directed that 'NCOs and soldiers are to pull off their hats to all officers'. The wear and tear through the constant doffing of hats was a matter of great concern to the Royal Scots, who in 1762 ordered that '. . . the men for the future are only to raise the back of their hands to them [hats] with a brisk motion when they pass an officer.' This practice was later adopted as a standing order published in the *Rudiments of War,* dated 1777. By the early 19th century the salute further evolved with the open hand, palm to the front, which has since remained the established form of hand salute.

The RAF Salute is the same as that of the Army. When RAF personnel hand salute today they display to each other the open defenceless hand, positioned so that the finger tips almost, but not quite, touch the hat band. The Naval hand salute is different. The palm of the hand is not exposed, but is facing down towards the shoulder. The origin of the Naval salute dates back to the days of sail when copious quantities

of pitch and tar were used to seal the timber joints from sea water. To protect their hands Naval officers always wore white linen gloves. The gloves soon became dirty, of course, and it was considered most undignified to present the open palm of a dirty glove in the salute, so the hand was moved through 90 degrees to become the present Naval salute. A further Naval custom on both sea and shore establishments is to 'salute the quarterdeck'. To understand this practice requires an outline knowledge of the construction of early sailing ships. The quarterdeck was originally defined as the upper deck between the mainmast and the poopdeck but it was also the location of officers' quarters and the place on ship where the gangway to the quay was positioned. As a result, all who boarded ship had to pass by the officers' quarters, which led to the custom of saluting. (A glossary of terms which helps to explain other Royal Navy customs appears at the end of this book.)

Saluting in the British forces normally takes place out of doors and when hats are worn. However, one regiment of the British Army is permitted to hand salute with hats off — the Blues and Royals. This custom originated at the Battle of Waterloo on 18 June 1815, when an officer of that regiment was ordered to ride to the Duke of Wellington and report that the Household Cavalry had been successful in their charge. *En route* to the Duke's headquarters the officer unknowingly lost his helmet but he duly arrived by the Duke's side, saluted, and made his report. Instead of admonishing the officer for his bareheadedness, the Duke congratulated him on the success that had been achieved, and since that day the custom of hand saluting without headdress has been continued as part of the Blues and Royals' tradition. A further oddity with regard to the hand salute is that until 1918 it was possible to give and receive salutes using either the left or right hand. Which hand to use depended on which side of an officer the individual passed by — the rule was that the arm furthest away was to be used for saluting. Saluting with the left hand today is only done if the right hand is medically incapacitated.

The hand salute is only one of many ways of saluting; others have the same intention of signifying peaceable intent. In the 'present arms' using the rifle, the rifle is placed in a position where it can do no harm and is literally being presented away from the body as though offering it up. In the sword salute the tip of the sword is pointed toward the ground, thus rendering the body defenceless. The firing of salutes from cannons gave evidence that the cannons were empty and defenceless, as it took some time to reload a cannon after it had fired. In the modern formation flypast salute, aircraft fly low, slow, and in close formation, rendering themselves a large and vulnerable target. Saluting with regimental colours and standards dates back to the 17th century. An extract from a military work in 1639 states: 'If a king or great prince passeth by, the Ensign [colour bearer] is to veil his colours close to the ground with his knee bending in token allegiance and submission'. In 1799 this practice was officially recognised in Army Regulations and continues to the present day; saluting with colours is exclusively reserved for Royalty and heads of state. However, it is custom that when a colour or standard is paraded, all members of the Armed Forces should salute, or if in civilian clothes and wearing a hat, bare the head. Finally, a modern custom which has evolved in the RAF is to salute when entering the office of another officer, regardless of whether the officer is senior or junior. The origin of this custom is obscure but it is in the best traditions of chivalry.

The custom of saluting commissioned officers of all three Services pertains entirely to the commission given by Her Majesty The Queen to that officer to serve in her Armed Forces. Accordingly, when a subordinate airman salutes an officer that airman is indirectly acknowledging Her Majesty as Head of State. A salute returned by an officer is on behalf of the Queen. Saluting also serves as a means of greeting and is usually accompanied by 'Good morning', or whatever is appropriate. In the RAF there are three basic rules of saluting. All airmen, up to and including the rank of Warrant Officer, salute all commissioned officers, including commissioned officers of other British, foreign and Commonwealth services. The second rule is that all junior officers, the rank span from Pilot Officer to Flight Lieutenant, salute all senior officers and air officers. (Senior officers cover the rank span between Squadron Leader and Group Captain, and air officers include the ranks from Air Commodore to Marshal of the RAF.) The last rule is that all senior officers salute officers senior in rank to themselves. To help explain the RAF's rank structure a table of the relative ranks

Saluting with a Colour

of the three British Armed Services and the United States forces is given on page 105, and non-commissioned ranks between the three home Services on page 107. The military code states that all officers entitled should be saluted by their subordinates. Some problems do arise when, for example, an officer is riding a bicycle or driving a car. The question is, does he get a salute or not? The answer is yes, but it may not always be possible for the salute to be returned for common sense or safety reasons. When an officer is wearing civilian clothes it is tradition for him to raise his hat as an acknowledging gesture to a salute given to him or, if not wearing a hat, to acknowledge the individual. It has long been a custom of the Services to salute ladies at any time, as it is to salute when being passed by a funeral cortège or at ensign hoisting or lowering.

The salute represents one of the oldest traditions in the military and should never be confused with a servile act. A French writer put it thus: 'The salute and other military compliments have their own *raison d'être*. They encourage a proper pride in the uniform, they effectively combine discipline with the respect due to superiors, while at the same time elevating the soldier in his own eyes by reminding him of all that is implied by the profession of arms and its traditions of chivalry and courtesy.'

RELATIVE RANKS AND BADGES OF OFFICERS OF THE SERVICES

RAF	RN	ARMY	USAF
MARSHAL OF THE ROYAL AIR FORCE (MRAF)	ADMIRAL OF THE FLEET (AF)	FIELD-MARSHAL (FM)	GENERAL OF THE AIR FORCE
AIR CHIEF MARSHAL (Air Chf Mshl)	ADMIRAL (Adm)	GENERAL (Gen)	GENERAL (Gen)
AIR MARSHAL (Air Mshl)	VICE-ADMIRAL (V Adm)	LIEUTENANT-GENERAL (Lt Gen)	LIEUTENANT-GENERAL (Lt Gen)
AIR VICE-MARSHAL (AVM)	REAR ADMIRAL (R Adm)	MAJOR-GENERAL (Maj Gen)	MAJOR-GENERAL (Maj Gen)
AIR COMMODORE (Air Cdre)	COMMODORE (Cdre) *Commandant	BRIGADIER (Brig)	BRIGADIER GENERAL (Brig Gen)

*Shoulder boards are worn for Ceremonial duties only.

RAF	RN	ARMY	USAF
GROUP CAPTAIN (Gp Capt)	**CAPTAIN** (Capt) *Superintendent	**COLONEL** (Col)	**COLONEL** (Col)
WING COMMANDER (Wg Cdr)	**COMMANDER** (Cdr) *Chief Officer	**LIEUTENANT-COLONEL** (Lt Col)	**LIEUTENANT-COLONEL** (Lt Col)
SQUADRON LEADER (Sqn Ldr)	**LIEUTENANT - COMMANDER** (Lt Cdr) *1st Officer	**MAJOR** (Maj)	**MAJOR** (Maj)
FLIGHT-LIEUTENANT (Flt Lt)	**LIEUTENANT** (Lt)	**CAPTAIN** (Capt)	**CAPTAIN** (Capt)
FLYING OFFICER (Fg Off)	**SUB- LIEUTENANT** (S Lt) *3rd Officer	**LIEUTENANT** (Lt)	**FIRST LIEUTENANT** (1st Lt)
PILOT OFFICER (Plt Off)	**MIDSHIPMAN** (Mid) **Junior to Army and RAF ranks**	**2nd LIEUTENANT** (2 Lt)	**SECOND LIEUTENANT** (2nd Lt)

*Refers to WRNS ranks.

RELATIVE NON-COMMISSIONED RANKS

N.B. The ranks in bold type are those that may be directly equated

RAF	RN	ARMY
Warrant Officer or **Master Aircrew:** Master Pilot Master Navigator Master Signaller Master Engineer Master Air Electronics Op Master Air Loadmaster	**Fleet Chief Petty Officer**	**Warrant Officer Class I** Warrant Officer (but junior to Air Force Class II Warrant Officer and Master Aircrew) There are no Sgts in the Household Cavalry Corporal Major – Cavalry
Flight Sergeant Chief Technician	**Chief Petty Officer**	**Staff Corporal** – Cavalry **Staff Sergeant** **Colour Sergeant**, RM
Sergeant	**Petty Officer**	**Corporal-of-Horse** – Cavalry **Sergeant** **Band Sergeant**, RM

Corporal	**Leading Rating** (but junior to military rank of Corporal and Bombardier)	**Corporal**
		Bombardier – Royal Artillery
		Lance Corporal) (but junior to
		Lance Bombardier) Corporal and
		                        Bombardier and
		                        to all Naval and
		                        Air Force Ranks)

Junior Technician	Able Rating	Marine
Senior Aircraftman/Woman Leading Aircraftman/Woman **Aircraftman/Woman**	Ordinary Rating **Rating**	**Private** Trooper – Cavalry/SAS Gunner – Royal Artillery Sapper – Royal Engineer Signalman – Royal Signals Driver – Royal Corps of Transport Guardsman – Guards Regiments Fusilier – Royal Fusiliers Kingsman – Kings Own Rifleman – Light Infantry Ranger – Royal Irish Rangers Craftsman – Royal Electrical Mechanical Engineers

Chapter 13
Inside an Officers' Mess

The Officers' Mess is the home of all living-in (single or unaccompanied) officers of a station. It is also the social and recreational centre for all officers and should not be confused with the Sergeants' Mess, which is the senior non-commissioned officers equivalent to the Officers' Mess and open to all ranks from Sergeant to Warrant Officer; or the Airman's Mess which is not a 'home' at all, but a central eating facility provided for airmen and Corporals who live in the nearby barrack accommodation. The last title may be taken as a collective term describing both airman's barracks and eating facilities.

The name Officers' Mess conjures up a picture of resplendent gentlemen living in dubious circumstances. The word 'mess' dates back many hundreds of years, and was originally used to mean a portion of food, as in a 'mess of pottage'. During the 15th and 16th centuries the provision of food for a marching army was largely up to the stealth and cunning of the individual soldier, although officers made their own catering arrangements. Troops would be allowed to leave a marching column to forage for fresh meat, fish and other foods to make a decent meal perhaps once per day. The meal may have consisted of some meat or fish with grain or alternatively a porridge-like mixture based on a cereal. As time passed, some catering refinements were added and any commander worth his salt made efforts to ensure that adequate time was allowed to collect rations *en route* through hunting, bartering or plunder. The result for the rank and file simply became a more organised mess of food, most probably served up twice per day! From these humble beginnings and through later colloquial usage, the meaning of the word mess was expanded, first to include the eating of a meal, as in the verb 'to mess' and secondly to describe eating accommodation, as in the description 'messing facilities', or 'mess room'. A Naval extension appears in the descriptive title 'Mess deck', meaning the place on ship where meals were prepared, as well as eaten.

The collective term Officers' Mess today describes the messing facilities, living accommodation and a host of other resources. This was not always the case. Before the Army reforms of the mid-nineteenth century officers were charged with finding their own accommodation at their own expense, so boarding and lodging houses proliferated around Army barracks. Soon the custom arose of regimental officers dining together perhaps once or twice a week at a selected eating house. Later, the selected taverns were expanded to include accommodation. The next step was to incorporate boarding accommodation into barracks themselves. Although this is a simplified explanation of what happened, the wisdom of providing a central facility was soon recognised, if for no other reason than convenience. The Royal Artillery Mess at Woolwich, Lieutenant-Colonel R. V. Dickinson records in his book *Officers' Mess,* probably has the distinction of being the first purpose-built Mess, in the present sense of the word. When the architect prepared the original plan in 1783, an 'Officers Mess' was included. However, as early as 1772, some principles for establishing a Mess in the field were published in the *Military Guide for Young Officers.* 'Each field officer and Captain is to contribute 6 guineas and each subaltern and staff officer one day's pay each to the purchasing of a dining tent, a cart and two horses, table linen and kitchen furniture'. The idea of officers contributing from their own purse for the upkeep and maintenance of their own Mess is as true today as it was in 1772. But it would be a grave injustice to compare the Officers' Mess of the late 18th and 19th century with the modern Officers' Mess. To understand the changes that have taken place requires study of the lifestyle of the times. Records show that in 1811 a sum of £25 was made available from the Crown for each infantry company 'to enable the officers of a Regiment to enjoy the comforts and advantages of a Mess, without incurring expenses which their pay could not meet'. It was a drop in the ocean and had little practical

The original Royal Artillery Barracks and Officers' Mess, Woolwich. *(Courtesy of Brigadier D. F. Ryan, OBE, Royal Artillery Institution)*

benefit. The Mess bills received by officers of that era were often in excess of the salary they received! This fact of military life remained true well into the next century, despite Cardwell's Army Reforms of the late 1850s which abolished the purchasing of military commissions and introduced a form of pay structure based on rank and merit. For many years a private income was a prerequisite for acceptance into many regiments.

By the late 19th century the Mess had become firmly established as the home for bachelor officers. These were also the days when marriage required the colonel's approval and marriage allowance was only paid on reaching the age of thirty. Moreover, the Mess would be full of subalterns of many years' seniority waiting for a Captain's vacancy. The junior living-in officers thus formed their own closed society. The married officers, on the other hand, used the Mess facilities for rest and relaxation during the day and attended the prescribed Regimental dining-in or guest nights during the week. Life in the Mess was largely a reflection of the formal social life evident in Victorian society. There were many traps and pitfalls; the conventions that were laid down had to be strictly observed and Mess etiquette was based upon what were said to be 'the customs and traditions of the regiment'. One of the first customs to evolve was the dinner night. These occasions were presided over by the commanding officer on four or five occasions each week. Dinner nights were a parade, in full dress, where absence was considered 'bad form' and would ultimately invite a reprimand. An extension of the dinner night was the guest night, where married officers dined in and guests were invited into the Mess to dine with the regimental officers. The impression created by plays and films about Army life of that period tends to be misleading, as it portrays officers in Mess dress charging around on horses in an advanced state of alcoholism — a misguided and totally inaccurate picture. If there were instances of heavy drinking, they would be dealt with severely by the Colonel. Furthermore, for many years Mess bills were scrutinised by the Colonel or adjutant to ensure that a junior officer's lifestyle did not exceed his income or lead to overindulgence.

As the Officers' Mess evolved, so too did a structured administration which included the publication of 'Mess Rules' governing what was and what was not acceptable. One of the earliest sets of Mess rules appeared in 1811, prepared for the RA mess at Woolwich. Before this, the only guidance available appeared in the book *Advice to Officers of the British Army,* published in 1782, which commented: 'if you belong to mess eat with it as seldom as possible, to let folks see that you want neither money nor credit. And when you do, in order to show that you are used to good living, find fault with every dish that is set on the table, damn the wine and throw the plates

RAF Bentley Priory, Officers' Mess

at the mess man's head.' Perhaps it is just as well that Mess rules were introduced!

At first membership of an Officers' Mess was entirely voluntary, but by Regency times it had become compulsory. Coincident with compulsory membership came the payment of the 'Regent's' Allowance in 1818 to help with the overall expenses of running a Mess. This allowance did not amount to much and for the most part went towards improving the general fabric of a Mess rather than benefiting individuals. The responsibility for a Mess has always rested with the unit's commanding officer, who in turn delegates the task of order, conduct, discipline and organisation to one of his senior officers as President of the Mess Committee, or PMC. But is is not only his views that matter. Since the first Officers' Messes were the home of those officers who lived in, it was considered only fair that they too should be allowed a say in how the Mess was administered. Accordingly, the members of the Mess committee were drawn from junior officers ranks, who either volunteered or were appointed by their seniors. Further, to ensure the democracy and integrity of the Mess, meetings were held on frequent occasions where both officers and committee members alike could air their views in a forum, with a final democratic vote by the Mess membership on the proposals. Little has changed over the years and a similar tradition has developed in the Royal Navy, though the Naval equivalent of an Officers' Mess is termed the 'Wardroom'. This misleading term is simply a corruption of the former description

of a cabin where the ship's officers kept their booty — the Wardroberoom. It was normally adjacent to the officers' living quarters and when at the beginning of a cruise the wardrobe was empty it was used as an additional officers' anteroom.

The staff who ran the early Messes were drawn from the ranks of a regiment or ship. In the Army, the senior non-commissioned officers in charge of the Mess were known as the Mess Sergeant, and the Mess Corporal. The remaining staff were composed of volunteer soldiers, or paid civilians, serving as cooks, steward's mess hands with finally the ubiquitous batmen. The origin of the term 'batman' dates back to the earliest days of soldiering, when every knight had his squire. The word is derived from the French *bat*, meaning a pack saddle and was literally the man who looked after his master's baggage. He later became personal servant and valet to the officer (see also Glossary of Terms). In terms of early Mess organisation, he did not come under the control of the Mess Sergeant but the head batman whose responsibility it was to train him in his duties. He was essentially a soldier and was paid extra by his officer for the batting services he provided. A cautionary tale about a batman is taken from a memorial tablet in a church in Simla, India which states: 'Sacred to the memory of Brigadier Lancelot David Warnock of the Royal Hussars who was accidently killed by his batman on 15 October 1872'. Underneath, the inscription continued: 'Well done thou good and faithful servant'.

It is easy to understand how, when the Royal Flying Corps was formed in 1912, its traditions

RAF Netheravon, Officers' Mess

were simply borrowed from the Army. Despite a strong Naval influence from 1914 to 1918, the new RAF adopted a mainly Army orientated philosophy of life. The first RAF Messes copied similar Army Messes, including their customs and traditions, with perhaps just a dash of Navy here and there. Life in an RAF Officers' Mess between the two world wars perpetuated general military traditions and the form of the time. Officers dressed for dinner on two or three occasions each week, and there was the normal round of dining-in nights and guest nights. From time to time wives would be invited to dine in the Mess on what were to become ladies' guest nights. Otherwise the Mess was the bastion of the bachelor, as it had been in previous years. When plans were made in the early 1930s for an unprecedented expansion of RAF stations, including the construction of many new Mess buildings, the Air Ministry Works Directorate made every effort to achieve comfort and dignity with vastly improved Mess facilities. A total of eighty-four Officers' Messes were constructed during the RAF expansion programme 1935-9. The size of a Mess was governed by the accommodation provided, and from the one basic design there were three sub-designs — No. 1 for accommodating 36-45 officers, No. 2 for 85-100 officers, No. 3 in excess of one hundred officers. The graceful Georgian elegance of the chosen façade makes RAF Officers' Messes constructed during this period of architectural interest. A scale drawing of the design chosen and now a very familiar building on RAF stations, is given on page 112, with a ground floor plan on page 113.

The expansion programme Messes provided officers with a high standard of comfort, including well proportioned bedrooms, large airy anterooms, a billiard room, reading room and mess room. Some mess rooms also included a minstrels' gallery. The comfort was, however, to be short lived. The Second World War found Mess accommodation insufficient for the RAF's needs. Secco huts, Portal huts, Nissen huts and any other accepted design of hut sprang up around the Messes to provide additional accommodation. Never again would Messes be built on such a scale. War construction had to be cheap, functional and effective. During the war years some 500 temporary Messes were constructed by the Air Ministry Works Department, of which many have now disappeared. However, where existing

RAF Old Sarum, Officers' Mess

accommodation could be utilised, such as in manor houses and the like, the opportunity was not missed. Old-established houses such as Nocton Hall and Belton House in Lincolnshire, Medmenham in Berkshire, Castle Archdale in Northern Ireland and a host of other historic houses became famous officers' Messes. Perhaps one of the most interesting to visit these days is the Petwood Moat House Hotel in Lincolnshire, once the Officers' Mess of 617 Squadron when they were stationed at Woodhall Spa airfield.

Today's, RAF Officers' Mess serves three basic functions: as ever it is the home of all living-in officers, it is the club for all serving officers, and finally it is the social centre for all officers of a station. Every commissioned officer on a station is a member of the Mess, and he is also an honorary member of every other Mess within his own and the sister Services.

Mess organisation

Each Mess is run by a small local committee chaired, as in the past, by a senior officer appointed by the station commander to be PMC. This duty is known as one of the secondary duties; a PMC will be assessed by the station commander on his performance. This task carries no extra salary, and the incumbent may expect to do this thankless and demanding job for between six and eighteen months in addition to his own primary task as squadron commander or whatever. The minimum number for a Mess committee, including the PMC, is five. The officers who make up a committee are elected at

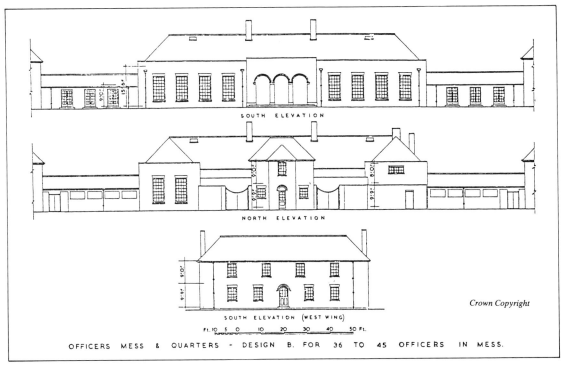

SOUTH ELEVATION

NORTH ELEVATION

SOUTH ELEVATION (WEST WING)

Ft. 10 5 0   10   20   30   40   50 Ft.

OFFICERS MESS & QUARTERS - DESIGN B. FOR 36 TO 45 OFFICERS IN MESS.

Crown Copyright

Basic design for an RAF Officers' Mess

general Mess meetings. They are 'volunteer' junior officers (volunteered by those anxious not to get the job!). Again, the Mess committee member responsibility is a secondary assessed duty without additional pay or privileges. The key committee appointments are Mess Secretary, Messing Member, Wines or Bar Member, House (furnishings and fabric) Member and Entertainments Member. Additionally there may be a Library Member, Gardens Member, Silver Member, and any other type of member deemed necessary. The Mess committee is responsible to the station commander and officers of a station for the conduct and observance of discipline by Mess members as well as the formulation of local Mess policy and the social calendar for the Mess. The Mess committee also represents an interface between the Mess members and the Mess staff.

The Officers' Mess staff
The day-to-day running of an Officers' Mess, including Mess staff management, is the responsibility of the Mess manager. The Mess staff may be all civilian or all Service, or a mixture of the two. The Mess staff are

established, like any other branch of the service, on the strength of the officers serving on the unit and their subordinate commander is normally the station catering officer. The Service staff of a Mess are drawn from the catering branch, including cooks and stewards; they are, therefore, professionals in their own right and are treated as such. Batmen (or women) are now civilian employees and receive a small wage for the duties they perform. As in the past, it is the responsibility of the living-in officers who benefit from the batting services to pay their batmen on a monthly basis. A batman is allocated to between five and eight officers, and at 1987 prices would expect to receive about £8 to £9 per month from each of his officers. The Service staff, on the other hand, should not be tipped as a small gratuity is paid to them from Mess funds at the end of the year. The Officers' Mess manager is the lynchpin of the Mess. If Service, he will be Flight Sergeant rank or above; if civilian, of the equivalent status to Warrant Officer. He is a most useful person for new living-in officers to get to know, though any complaints about Mess staff are dealt with through the Mess committee never directly with the Mess Manager. The mid 1980s have seen a swing towards the civilianisation of many catering sections. Thus, it is now more likely that a Mess will be run by a civilian contractor rather than Service staff. It is also fair to say that many stations no longer provide a batting service or, indeed early morning tea! There is little doubt that there has been an erosion in the quality of Mess life over the past 5 years due to new need for 'expedience and economy'. Simply, it is up to individual Mess committees to ensure that the quality of Mess life is not eroded and standards are maintained.

Mess meetings

The democratic forum of the Mess is the Mess meeting, at which minutes are formally recorded. There are three types of Mess meeting: general, extraordinary, and Mess committee. General Mess meetings must be held at least annually, but more usually six-monthly and

always to coincide with the end of an audit period, when the balance sheets will be available to the Mess for scrutiny. An announcement that a Mess meeting will take place will be posted on the Mess notice board, together with an agenda. These meetings are a parade, and unless on urgent operational duty all Mess members are expected to attend. Items that might be discussed include the minutes of the last meeting, the passing of the balance sheet, entertainment details, the purchase of fabric and furnishings for the Mess, the revision of any Mess rules, appointees to the Mess committee and the election of honorary Mess members. The nomination of appointees to the Mess committee is processed in true democratic fashion, based on an original volunteer. The normal procedure is that an individual will be proposed at a meeting and seconded by someone else, with the Mess membership voting to accept or otherwise. The

Ground plan for an RAF Officers' Mess   NB The East Wing is a mirror of the West Wing

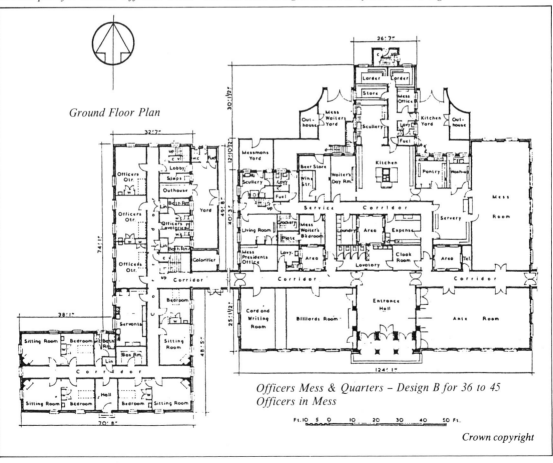

Ground Floor Plan

Officers Mess & Quarters – Design B for 36 to 45 Officers in Mess

Crown copyright

second category of meeting is the extraordinary Mess meeting. These meetings may be called to discuss pressing matters that cannot wait until the next scheduled general Mess meeting. Alternatively, the PMC or station commander may wish to call an extraordinary Mess meeting. Finally, one-fifth of the Mess membership may call an extraordinary Mess meeting, though this is rarely done. The Mess committee meeting is chaired by the PMC and held on an as-and-when basis. Where large functions are envisaged, such as a summer ball, Battle of Britain cocktail party or the Christmas draw, the Mess committee may authorise a sub-committee specifically to organise that function. All proposals put forward at a Mess meeting, or suggested by the Mess committee, are voted upon by the Mess membership.

There are three categories of Mess membership: full, affiliated and honorary. Full membership includes all RAF officers serving, or on temporary duty at a station. It also covers all Naval and military officers serving, or on temporary duty at the station and, moreover, all officers of Commonwealth Forces attached as individuals to the RAF and subject to the Air Force Act. Affiliated membership gathers in civilians of officer status working on a station, such as the executive grades of civil servant. It also includes all officers of the RAF Volunteer Reserve (RAFVR), the Auxiliary Air Force (R Aux AF), and officers of Commonwealth countries not subject to the Air Force Act, but serving on temporary duty at a station. The

RAF Shawbury, Officers' Mess

question of honorary membership is discussed at general Mess meetings. The Mess committee may with the commanding officer's approval and the consent of a general Mess meeting invite individuals to become honorary Mess members. Such invitations are limited, but might be offered to retired Naval or military officers living in the local area, civilian dignitaries, local VIPs and the like. Only full Mess members have voting rights at Mess meetings.

Mess facilities
All RAF Messes are comfortable, well furnished and self-contained. Apart from an officer's individual bedroom or perhaps suite, all remaining Mess facilities are shared with other station officers. Broadly, the facilities are described as public and non-public accommodation. Non-public means not open to non-Mess members except with the prior consent of the PMC. The non-public accommodation includes the bedrooms, dining room, anterooms, sitting rooms, TV and sports rooms, library and the bar other than at specified times. One room, the ladies room, a small comfortable anteroom, is provided for officers to entertain family and friends when Mess rules state that guests may be allowed into the Mess. In addition, tennis, squash and croquet facilities are normally available in the Mess garden area. For bachelor officers, laundry and ironing facilities are also provided.

Mess rules
The need for Mess rules dates back to the Woolwich Mess of 1811, and perhaps before. Every Mess will have its own set of rules, and although these are fundamentally the same throughout the three Services, they sometimes vary in accordance with local conditions and customs. Many of the RAF Mess rules were originally prepared for Army Messes and Wardrooms, so established custom and tradition is enshrined in many of them. Initially the rules may well have been designed to restrain the energies of the young officer, but more realistically they were designed to set standards as part of the grooming process for young officers in preparation for wider responsibilities. The task of Mess rules today is to define clearly the code of conduct expected in the Mess with guidance on what is and what is not acceptable. A copy of Mess rules is provided in each officer's bedroom: ignorance is never accepted as an excuse.

Dress in the Mess

Dress in the Mess has always been a matter of concern, particularly when RAF dress standards are compared with the trends and fashions of civilian life. Maintaining standards in dress, deportment and social behaviour is considered by the Service to be important. When Mess rules are written and later revised, what goes on in the equivalent strata of life outside is duly considered, but it would be fair to say that the RAF demands and expects high personal standards — higher than would normally be expected in some areas of civilian life. Mess rules will stipulate acceptable day and evening dress wear for its members.

Mess bills

Each month every station officer will receive a Mess bill; by tradition it must be paid by the 10th of the next month. The Mess bill will cover extra messing charges based on a daily rate (if the officer lives in), Mess subscriptions, fund payments such as for silver, library or garden funds, a bar bill and any other Mess expenses as a result of dinner nights, parties or other functions. Mess subscriptions are paid on a pro rata basis according to rank. The charges made by the Mess will depend on how long the officer was resident in the Mess during the month for which the bill is made out. To help the Mess clerks work out the bills, all officers are required to warn-in by completing details in a ledger held in the Mess foyer. This is done when an officer arrives on station for the first time, and thereafter he or she is required to warn-in and warn-out as and when resident. Other books are provided in the Mess foyer for officers to record any messing suggestions, general suggestions, with finally a book where officers may advertise any sales or wants. By tradition, the two suggestions books (for the Mess fabric and messing) are never used for complaints; these are always handled by the Mess committee.

Dining-in nights – the Loyal Toast

One of the oldest Mess customs is that of dining-in, ostensibly to drink the loyal toast. Dining-in nights are occasions when the station's officers dine together to celebrate the brotherhood and companionship of commissioned service in the Royal Air Force. The young officers of today are tasked to uphold this custom in the best traditions of the Service. There are three types of dinner evening: the dining-in night, when

RAF Swinderby, Officers' Mess

officers of a station dine together; the guest night when official guests are invited into the Mess to dine with the station officers; and ladies guest nights, when wives and girlfriends may also be invited to dine in. As a rule of thumb, dinner evenings occur about every month to six weeks, and are a parade for all the station's officers where absence is only permitted with the station commander's approval — and lateness is deemed inexcusable. The dress for dinner nights is Mess dress for officers (No. 5A or 5B) with the equivalent evening dress for ladies.

If a guest is to be invited to a Mess, a formal printed invitation will be sent; station officers will be notified through an announcement posted on the Mess notice board. The proceedings begin thirty minutes before the appointed hour for dinner, when all Mess members assemble in an anteroom for pre-dinner drinks. Diners should ensure that they are no more than five minutes late and certainly never early. On entering the anteroom, it is custom that before receiving or taking a drink all officers should 'call' on the PMC. This is done by simply standing before the PMC and saying 'Good evening, sir'. It is at this time that any guests should also be introduced. Once acknowledged, the officer may take a drink and circulate. At ladies' guest nights the station commander and his wife and the PMC and his wife may be present in the Mess foyer to greet Mess members and their guests as they arrive. Smoking may be permitted at the direction of the PMC.

Only sherry, spirits and non-alcoholic drinks are available during the half hour preceding dinner. Stewards are normally in attendance to exchange empty for charged glasses and in some Messes a bar may be provided. The general idea is for the officers and any guests to circulate as much as possible in the best tradition of friendliness and hospitality. During the pre-dinner drinks period diners should also check their position on the seating plan and make arrangements to escort into the dining room any lady who may be seated on the gentleman's right. Finally, it may be advisable to 'ease springs', as a need to leave the dining room during the meal to water the daisies is considered bad form.

At dinner nights the PMC appoints a vice-president, who is the most junior officer present and is known as Mr Vice. His first duty, when the Mess manager has announced 'Dinner is Served', is to lead the assemblage into dinner in reverse order of rank — junior officers first. If a band is in attendance the Mess manager's announcement may be preceded by a trumpet fanfare and followed by the playing of 'Roast Beef of Old England' as the diners go into dinner. Once in the dining room, members will stand behind their chairs, keeping talking to a whispered tone. The last to arrive will be the station commander, guest and PMC. The PMC will then bang his gavel and ask the padre to say grace. Following grace the diners may be seated. The dining room tables are normally set out in the form of a 'T' or 'E' with the PMC, guests and station commander seated on the top table. It is custom for the rest of the station's officers to be seated in accordance with their rank and position in the Air Force list of Officers, with the junior officers furthest from the top table. Mr Vice's position is at the very bottom end of the table. Normally the first course will be on the table, so that grace having been said, the meal may begin. However, the custom is that diners should not start a meal course before the top table, and this applies to every course. The stewards will only clear away empty plates when the last diner has finished eating. It is untrue that when the top table has finished, everybody else should also have finished. As already mentioned, it is considered most undignified to leave the dining room once dinner is in progress, but there may be exceptional circumstances

The RAF College Dining Hall

when an officer may wish to excuse himself for duty reasons. The procedure is that he must make his way up the aisle between the tables, stand before the PMC and ask formally to be excused! Smoking is not permitted between courses, and it is a time-honoured custom in all Service Messes to avoid any conversation to do with women, politics, religion or 'shop'.

At the conclusion of the meal and before any speeches, it is customary in all three Services to drink the 'loyal toast' to the health of the Sovereign. At the end of the meal, the Mess staff will clear all plates and glasses other than a port glass. A decanter each of port and madeira is then positioned in front of the PMC and Mr Vice. Mr Vice now concentrates on the PMC. When the PMC removes the decanter stoppers, Mr Vice does likewise. The PMC then passes the decanters to his left. He does not charge his glass, nor will he offer to charge another diner's glass. Each diner then charges his own glass to taste. A steward will be in attendance with a jug of water while the port is being passed for those who prefer a non-alcoholic drink. Eventually the PMC's set of decanters will reach Mr Vice, and Mr Vice's the PMC. (The decanters should never be passed back to the right.) The PMC then charges his own glass and replaces decanter stoppers, and Mr Vice likewise. On an evening where there is a large number dining, extra decanters will be placed at regular points around the tables. It is important that these extra decanters are handled in the same way. The tradition that the decanter should not touch the table until it reaches its final destination is obscure. Simply, passing the decanter by hand will prevent damage to the polished surface of the dining table. Mess rules will dictate which of the practices is to be enforced. As a note of interest in the Royal Navy, a round bottomed port decanter supported by a silver boat coaster is traditional. Thus, instead of being passed by hand, the coaster would be pushed from person to person along the table for each diner to lift out the decanter. The coaster was often made of silver in the form of a boat. From this Royal Navy tradition comes the saying, 'to push the boat out', meaning originally to pass the port.

When all diners have charged their glass the stage is set for the loyal toast. The PMC bangs his gavel and proclaims: 'Mr Vice — The Queen'. Mr Vice then rises and replies: 'Ladies and Gentlemen — The Queen'. The assembly rises, and if a band is in attendance the National

RAF Syreston, Officers' Mess

Anthem will be played. On completion of the anthem, glasses may be lifted, the toast to 'The Queen' is repeated by the assemblage and the port finally sipped. Seats are then resumed. If there are visiting dignitaries from foreign or commonwealth countries, toasts may be proposed to their head of state. The guest's individual host or the PMC will rise and propose the toast, 'Mr Vice — The President of the United States of America'. Mr Vice rises and replies: 'Ladies and Gentlemen, The President of the United States of America'. Again, if a band is present it will play the appropriate anthem; otherwise, all will then rise and lift their glasses and repeat the toast, 'The President of the United States'. When guests represent more than one foreign country, the individual host or PMC may propose a collective toast to the heads of state, naming them in order of rank and seniority of their respective representatives present, but not through Mr Vice. When the guest toasts have been proposed and drunk, the senior of the foreign visitors present will respond on behalf of all visitors by proposing the health of the Queen, but not through Mr Vice. When a band is present at a dinner night, light music will be played from the minstrels' gallery throughout the meal. Before the speeches start, and after the loyal toast, it is customary for the President to ask the band master and the chef to join him for a glass of port. This is intended as a token of thanks on behalf of the diners.

The origin of toasting goes back a long way and the custom is probably derived from the ancient religious rite of drinking to the gods and

RAF Upavon, Officers' Mess

the dead. The Greeks and Romans poured libations to their Gods at ceremonial banquets. In Stuart times it was the custom to put toast in the wine cup before drinking in the belief that it gave the liquor a better flavour; an extension perhaps of the Elizabethan idea of taking salt before a meal to cleanse the palate. It is also worth mentioning the origin of the 'backhander' as this pertains to passing the port at dining-in nights. If a diner inadvertently fails to fill his glass (waiting for a non-existent alternative decanter) the correct form is to send the glass to the left to overtake the decanter and then, after it has been filled, it comes back — hence backhander.

On completion of the loyal toast, coffee is served and the PMC recommences the circulation of the port and madeira decanters. Mess members will generally have no need to touch the Mess silver; indeed in some messes a diner may be fined for so doing. However, if there is a burning need to read a particular inscription or to admire more closely a piece of fine tableware, it is generally permitted to touch the silver after the Loyal Toast. Whilst coffee is being served, the PMC may bang his gavel, rise and announce, 'Gentlemen, you may smoke'. The silver cigarette and cigar boxes are then circulated from the PMC's position. Speeches follow. The station commander is normally first to speak and having been introduced by the PMC he will welcome guests, introduce new officers dining-in for the first time and say a few words about those officers who are being dined out or are leaving the service. At the end of his speech he will propose a toast to the guests or to those leaving (but not through Mr Vice). The senior guest present may then be introduced by the PMC to reply on behalf of the visitors and to thank the Mess and Mess staff for their hospitality. He may conclude his speech with a toast of his own dedication to the RAF or to the Mess in question. Other speeches may follow at the discretion of the PMC. To indicate the end of dinner, the President will bang his gavel and stand, the top table will rise and, led by the station commander, leave the dining room. During the exit, the remaining diners stand until all the top table have left. Once the PMC has left, Mr Vice moves to take over the PMC's chair at the top table, inviting other junior officers to join him. Other diners may then leave the dining room as they feel and later rejoin the anteroom for post-dinner refreshment. On ladies' guest nights a band may be in attendance for dancing. Post-dinner festivities on all evenings other than ladies' guest nights may include Mess games. Many of the Mess games have their origin in the Army and Navy and range from snooker to schooner racing to mess rugby. The lead is taken by the PMC. It is traditional for officers not to leave the Mess until the station commander and his guests have left.

Membership of an RAF Officers' Mess is more than a lifestyle — it is a cherished and civilised way of combining friendship and fellowship with a deep sense of purpose, towards achieving professional excellence as well as high standards of integrity and personal behaviour.

Chapter 14
Social Etiquette for the RAF

This Chapter is provided as an insight into the accepted social conventions in the RAF. Whilst it may be of passing interest to some, for those readers considering a commissioned career in the RAF, this Chapter is provided as constructive background reading.

To find an objective reference dealing with social conventions is like hunting for the Holy Grail. Many know of its existence, few know where to find it — but having believed it has been found, somebody further suggests that it is not the real thing! The social conventions of the RAF are largely inherited traditions that have evolved. Debrett's *Etiquette and Modern Manners,* together with *Debrett's Correct Form* are useful references and are recommended reading, but military social conventions are not always the same as their civilian counterpart. It may be necessary to cross refer to find a 'correct answer' on a point of etiquette or form. Moreover, what might be accepted behaviour for one social group may be anathema to another. Manners and etiquette, on the other hand, have remained the same.

Military invitations may come in any one of three categories — formal, informal or casual. These titles are given for convenience to tie in with the three corresponding styles of dress rather than representing definitions of personal behaviour.

Formal functions such as a guest night, wedding or dinner party, are always preceded by a written or printed invitation card. They are written in the third person and contain the following details: the date and time of the function, the type of function, where it is to take place, the dress required and the details for a reply. The tone and format is given at Figs 14.1-3. The wedding invitation is an exception; the guest's name may appear handwritten on the top left of the invitation, rather than appearing in the centre of the text. A change in formal invitations has been the introduction of the 'At Home' type card (Fig 14.5a & b) which is largely replacing the pre-printed card given at Fig 14.4. They are equally acceptable.

When an invitation is to a married couple, the practice is to address the envelope to the wife alone, but to include the names of both husband and wife on the top left hand of the card. For example, an envelope may be addressed to Mrs Robin Loxley, but the invitation card is annotated to Mr and Mrs Robin Loxley. If the invitation is to good friends, prefixes on the card may be dropped altogether using only first names.

Fig 14.1: Officers' Mess Guest Night formal invitation.

> The Commanding Officer
>
> and officers of
>
> Royal Air Force Benwell
>
> request the pleasure of the Company of
>
> Flight Lieutenant A. Bodger AFC
>
> at a Dining In Night
>
> on 15 August 1995 at 7.30 pm for 8 pm
>
> RSVP
> Mess Secretary
>
> No. 5b Mess Dress

Fig 14.2: Formal wedding invitation
(invitee's name is handwritten at top of card)

> Mr and Mrs Victor Snoad-Bloxley
> request the pleasure of your company
> at the marriage of their daughter
>
> Susan Fanny
> to
> Mr Simon Simple
>
> at St George's, Newcastle
> on Saturday the tenth of January
> at eleven o'clock
> and afterwards at
> 12 Acacia Gardens
>
> RSVP
> 2 Wallflower Road
> Beckingham, Kent

NB *On civilian invitation cards RSVP details may appear on the left hand side of the card, and the dress for 'At home' functions may not be stated.*

There is some variation here between the military and civilian form. Civilian invitation cards may not include prefixes (such as The Hon.) nor letters after the name signifying rank or awards, though this information will be included on the envelope. The military form is that when the invitation is to a couple, rank is included on the card but not decorations, awards or degrees, as in the example given at Fig 14.6.

Fig 14.3a: Civilian invitation to dinner

> Mrs Lotta Front
>
> At Home
>
> Wednesday October 15th
>
> RSVP
> 10 Rillington Place
> Surbiton   Dinner
> Surrey   8 for 8.30 pm

Fig 14.3b: Military invitation to dinner

> *Squadron Leader and Mrs Ivor Thrust*
>
> Request the pleasure of the Company of
>
> *Pilot Officer and Mrs Rupert Twinkle*
>
> for dinner
>
> *at 8 pm on Saturday 5th May 1994*
>
>   RSVP
>   12 Beagle Way
>   RAF Wellcran
> Black Tie   BFPO7

Fig 14.4: Pre-printed invitation card, useful for buffet, dinner or cocktal parties

> ....
>
> Request the pleasure of
>
> ....
>
> Company for
>
> ....
>
>   RSVP

Fig 14.5a: At Home invitation

> (Enter Guest's Name)
>
> (Hostess's Name) ....
>
>   At Home
>
> (date and time) ....
>
> (Enter Function   *RSVP
> and dress details)   (enter reply details)

Fig 14.5b: Personal printed At Home

> (Enter Guest's Name)
>
>   Mrs Delia Molestrangler
>
>
>   At Home
>
> (date) ....
>
> (Enter function time   *RSVP
> and dress and details)   Railway Cuttings
>   Gasworks End
>   Ramsbottom,
>   Lancashire

However, in the singular form, the reverse is true as in the example at Fig 14.7. The rule of thumb for suffixes, with the exception of VC and GC, is: awards followed by decorations followed by degrees. If the 'At Home' card were to be used in preference to those in the examples at Figs 14.6 and 14.7, the same titling rules apply.

Fig 14.6: Military invitation to a couple

> Wing Commander and Mrs B. J. Prune
>
> request the pleasure of the company of
>
> Squadron Leader and Mrs Jack Rock
>
> for dinner on Tuesday 4th July at 8 pm
>
>   RSVP
> Black Tie   Bentley House

Envelope address

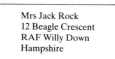

Mrs Jack Rock
12 Beagle Crescent
RAF Willy Down
Hampshire

Fig 14.7: Military invitation – singular

Wing Commander and Mrs B. J. Prune

request the pleasure of the company of

Squadron Leader J. Rock MBE, MC, BA, RAF

for dinner on Tuesday 4th July at 8 pm

RSVP

Black Tie   Bentley House

Envelope address

Squadron Leader J. Rock MBE, MC, BA, RAF
Officers' Mess
Royal Air Force
Brampstone
Kent

Fig 14.8: Acceptance letter

8 Cordington Crescent
Michinhampton
Gloucestershire
GL14 8BR

Mr and Mrs Robert Burke thank
Mr and Mrs Hyde Roxley for their kind
invitation to dinner on Friday 6 June
and have pleasure in accepting.

Fig 14.9: Regretting

.... 6 June, but regret that they are
unable to accept because of a prior engagement.

In the Services, where couples are both serving members of HM Forces, problems do arise when addressing invitations, particularly where the couple are of differing rank — for example, Flight Lieutenant Rosemary Black, and her husband Wing Commander Nigel Black. This invitation is recommended to be addressed to Wing Commander and Mrs Nigel Black, though the wife's rank may be included if wished. If the ranks were reversed, the recommendation is to address invitations as Flight Lieutenant and Mrs Nigel Black. In both cases the envelope should be addressed using the wife's name and rank.

The reply to the formal invitation
Formal replies are always written by hand in the third person and never typed. The civilian form is much the same as the military, with the exceptions that civilian replies may be written on headed notepaper, but not dated (Fig 14.8). For both civilian and military formal replies, only the centre third of unlined notepaper is used to write the text. The text will always take the same form: Mr and Mrs Guest (using the husband's Christian name), thank Mr and Mrs Host (no initials or Christian names) for their kind invitation to .... at .... on .... and, either, have great pleasure in accepting, or, if unable to attend, regret that they are unable to accept because of (due to) a previous engagement (Fig 14.9). On the military reply, the outline address of the officer replying together with the date is included (see examples at Fig 14.10a-b). Replies should be sent in plenty of time for the host to make suitable arrangements.

Fig 14.10a: Military reply accepting

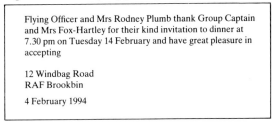

Flying Officer and Mrs Rodney Plumb thank Group Captain and Mrs Fox-Hartley for their kind invitation to dinner at 7.30 pm on Tuesday 14 February and have great pleasure in accepting

12 Windbag Road
RAF Brookbin

4 February 1994

Fig 14.10b: Military reply regretting

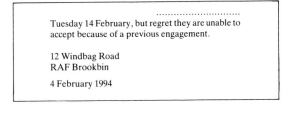

....
Tuesday 14 February, but regret they are unable to accept because of a previous engagement.

12 Windbag Road
RAF Brookbin

4 February 1994

Fig 14.10c: Envelope address

Mrs Rhenard Fox-Hartley
Astral Towers
Royal Air Force
Brookbin
Kent P25 OJ7

If the invitation card states the dress as being White Tie, Black Tie, No. 5a or b Mess Dress, or No. 1 Home Service Dress, the occasion may be said to be formal, regardless of the use of an 'At Home' invitation card.

Informal invitations and replies

Informal entertainment and social functions take in a tremendous variety of occasions for which the 'At Home' type of invitation card is ideally suited. The term informal is used to describe the dress for the evening and to suggest a more relaxed atmosphere than would be present on a formal occasion. Examples of suitable invitation cards are given at Figs 14.4 and 14.5, where it would be necessary only to change the formal dress stated to simply Lounge Suit or Sports jacket, which is the accepted form of informal dress. The hostess decides whether to request replies from guests: normally these days the letters RSVP are deleted from the card and the words 'regrets only' inserted in their place, with the address written underneath, as in the example at Fig 14.11. Moreover, the hostess may wish to add her telephone number if she is happy to accept regrets by telephone. If a written reply is called for, it should be written on normal home stationery using the first person, as in the example given, at Fig 14.12a for acceptance and Fig 14.12b for regrets. The decision on whether to use Christian names on the invitation card is personal. However, Christian names do add to the air of informality. A useful alternative to the 'RSVP' or 'regrets only' acknowledgement to an informal invitation is to use the 'Pour Memoire' or 'To Remind' annotation, having first struck through the 'RSVP'. In such cases the hostess will have first contacted all her guests by telephone and will then send out her 'At Home' invitation cards purely as a reminder to those who accepted.

Fig 14.11: Informal invitation

> (Pilot Officer and Mrs Black or Rupert and Candice)
>
> Mrs Bartholomew Drivil
>
> At Home
>
> Tuesday 26th March
>
> Buffet Supper   Regrets Only
> 7.30 for 8 pm   The Manse
> Lounge suit   Todworth
>   Lancashire
>   (Tel. No. Optional)

Envelope address

> Mrs Rupert Black
> 14 Beagle Grove
> Hatton
> Lancashire

Fig 14.12a: Informal reply accepting

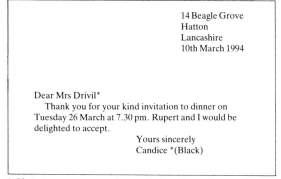

> 14 Beagle Grove
> Hatton
> Lancashire
> 10th March 1994
>
> Dear Mrs Drivil*
>   Thank you for your kind invitation to dinner on Tuesday 26 March at 7.30 pm. Rupert and I would be delighted to accept.
>   Yours sincerely
>   Candice *(Black)

*Christian name may be used if preferred

Fig 14.12b: Informal reply regretting:

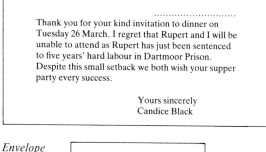

> ....
> Thank you for your kind invitation to dinner on Tuesday 26 March. I regret that Rupert and I will be unable to attend as Rupert has just been sentenced to five years' hard labour in Dartmoor Prison. Despite this small setback we both wish your supper party every success.
>
>   Yours sincerely
>   Candice Black

Envelope address

> Mrs Bartholomew Drivil
> The Manse
> Todworth
> Lancashire

Thank you letters

It is established custom to write a thank you letter to a hostess after attending a formal or informal function. For Service functions where the event takes place in the Officers' Mess, the letter should be addressed to the President of the Mess Committee and despatched within forty-eight hours of the function. The letter should always be written, not typed, with warmth and sincerity using the first person.

Casual invitations

The last category of entertainment covers casual functions. These are parties or celebrations of a very informal nature such as birthday parties, fancy dress parties or even just get togethers, where the dress is stipulated as costume or where collar and tie might be out of place in the relaxed atmosphere. A casual function may or may not be preceded by a written invitation. If it is, the 'At Home' type card may be used, as in the example given at Fig 14.13a, or a handwritten card similar to the example given at Fig 14.13b. However, more often than not a telephone call may take the place of a written invitation card. Dress for a casual function is entirely up to the hostess. The Service interpretation of 'casual dress' is of the slacks and open neck shirt mode, or female equivalent, rather than a 'kiss me quick' tee shirt worn with bleach dyed jeans and 'flip flops'. As with all functions where there might be some doubt about the type of dress to be worn, it is always acceptable to check with the host or hostess.

Fig 14.13a: Casual invitation cards

Mrs Simon Snoade	
At Home	
Friday 15 May	
Simon's Promotion Party	Regrets Only
Snacks	12 Toad Lane
8 pm	Cornford
Casual	Devon
	07-330 71212

Fig 14.13b: Handwritten invitation card to a casual party

Simon and Sadie Snoade	
invite you to celebrate Simon's promotion to substantive Pilot Officer at 8 pm on Friday 15 May at 8 pm	
Snacks	*Regrets Only*
Casual	07-330 7121

As with formal and informal functions, it is customary to offer thanks following the party. For casual functions a telephone call is quite acceptable, although the option to write is open if preferred.

Gifts to the hostess

In earlier times flowers were often sent to the hostess the day after the function. These days, it is quite acceptable to bring a gift to a party and present it to the hostess on arrival. A box of chocolates, a bottle of wine or a bunch of flowers are all considered acceptable, but not obligatory. A gift does not, however, replace a thank you letter.

Dress

Self-confidence is a key factor in success at social gatherings. Self-confidence is generated from the self-assurance and awareness that an individual looks and knows the part. Selecting the right dress is of paramount importance and the first step in gaining self-confidence. If the dress for a social occasion is not stipulated on the invitation card, it is always acceptable to seek advice from the host or hostess.

The dress for formal occasions will be stipulated as morning suit, white tie (top hat and tails), black tie (dinner jacket), No. 1 Home Service Dress or No. 5a or b Mess Dress. Morning suit and white tie are forms of formal dress made to a standardised pattern and obtainable on hire from the bespoke tailors for weddings, Royal or Court occasions. Black tie or dinner jacket, on the other hand, is a frequently requested dress for cocktail parties, dinner parties and the like. As with all forms of dress there are extremes in dinner jacket design from red velvet jackets to pink fluorescent bow-ties. Choice lies with the individual but the more conventional black barathea jacket worn with black bow tie and white dinner shirt will always be accepted. Where Service dress is stipulated, care should be taken to ensure that the dress is correct, including accoutrements, (hats, gloves, medals, etc). For the ladies the task to define suitable dress is more difficult. Debrett suggests that it is better for a lady to be underdressed than overdressed. Short dresses or tailored suits are recommended for formal daytime wear, but where evening dress is stipulated there is much more scope for imagination. Where black tie is requested, ladies may wear long or short evening dresses, or decorative evening trousers, according to personal preference and the prevailing fashion. However, extremes such as plunging necklines, fish-net tights and feather dusters are best avoided!! For cocktail parties a suitable short cocktail dress should be selected. Gloves for the ladies have become optional and are rarely seen. However, when they are worn with evening dress the recommendation is to keep then on when dancing, but to remove them while eating. Hats (or tiaras!) are, again, optional.

The dark lounge suit has always been most acceptable for the majority of informal functions and is an essential item for the male wardrobe. Sports suits, sports jackets, blazer and flannels, once daytime dress, are now accepted for wear throughout the day. The one clear exception is the cocktail party where, if dinner jacket is not stipulated, a dark lounge suit is the only alternative. Selecting informal clothing is a matter of personal taste and from a Service viewpoint the best advice is to avoid clashing colours, extremes of fashion and outlandish patterns. For ladies the spectrum of dress available is much wider, from the tailored suit or dress to the skirt and shirt or indeed jacket and trousers. Debrett recommends that ladies' informal dress should be simple and smart in accordance with the fashion.

Arrival times

It is generally accepted in most quarters that it is as rude to arrive at a function too early as it is to appear late. The recommended time to arrive is within ten minutes of a function starting, but never early. The exception to this advice is when a strict starting time has been declared, such as for a concert, in which case arrival must be in plenty of time to be seated, or prepared, for the performance to begin. Where dinner parties or gatherings are scheduled, for example, at 7.30pm for 8pm, guests should aim to arrive in the period 7.30pm to 7.40pm so that the remaining twenty minutes may be used for introductions and gentle ice-breaking conversation between guests. At a cocktail party where the timings are scheduled as, for example, 7.15pm to 8.45pm, the ten-minute arrival flexibility still stands but the last guest should have left by 8.45pm; it would be considered inconsiderate to remain longer. How long a dinner party should last is difficult: much will depend on the host and hostess. As a rough guide, between two and two and a half hours from the beginning of a meal normally signals the end of festivities, and time to leave.

Introductions

Making the correct introductions at a social gathering is important. There are four basic rules of introduction which are as follows: a gentleman is always introduced to a lady — 'Mrs Smith, may I introduce Flying Officer Colin Cad'; a single woman is always introduced to a married woman — 'Mrs Munroe, may I introduce Miss Daphne Wentwhistle'; a junior is always introduced to a senior — 'Group Captain Bog, may I introduce Pilot Officer Chain'; a younger person is always introduced to an older person — 'Air Marshal Prong, may I introduce Master Hugh Bean'. The alternative and more polished form of introduction is to disregard the 'may I introduce' bit, introducing the names

only: 'Flying Officer Cad — Mrs Smith', 'Miss Wentwhistle — Mrs Munroe', and so on. The use of Christian names in the introduction is optional and depends on how well the two parties are known. Having made the correct introduction, a simple salutation follows which is the same for both parties. The senior guest will reply to the introduction by saying, 'How do you do', 'How do you do Mr Brown', and offer the hand of friendship. There may be a temptation for the guest being introduced to take the question literally, energetically pump the other guest's hand and confess that he hasn't been feeling too well following an evening at the Dog and Whistle and eating a surfeit of carrots and mushrooms for tea! This sort of response is best avoided. The answer to 'How do you do' is always 'How do you do', or even better, 'How do you do, Sir' — or Mrs Smith. If the senior guest wishes Christian names to be used he or she may say during the opening salutation — 'How do you do Mr Cad — Alice Smith', for which the reply from Flying Officer Cad would be 'Colin Cad — how do you do, Alice'. This verbal exchange serves merely to break the ice and to open conversation. Following an introduction the host may then like to add a few words or information about the person being introduced to stimulate further conversation. The 'How do you dos' over, the host or hostess adds: 'Colin has just returned from a round the world trip flying a jumbo jet upside down and backwards, with nothing on the clock but the maker's name; he is also an accomplished tiddlywink player'. This provides background information that those being introduced may care to use to develop conversation. The host must then attend to the refreshment needs of the guests to ensure that their conversation is not impeded through lack of lubrication. At some functions it may be a case of directing a wine steward with his tray of goodies to the dried-up area, or alternatively, at a suitable opening in the conversation, it may be convenient to ask what the guests would like to drink — and fetch it. When there is no host to introduce guests, and this can sometimes happen, it may be necessary for one of the guests to instigate an unhosted introduction. 'Hello, I'm Rodney Bungtrotter, how do you do'. In which case the reply might be: 'Hello, I'm Doris Clack, how do you do'. Nature will then take its course. If momentarily, the host or hostess is unable to recall names during the introduction phase and to save embarrassment, it is acceptable to take action as for an unhosted introduction.

Circulating at a social function is important if for no other reason than it is an excellent way of broadening horizons and striking up new friendships. The action of circulating may be achieved by either the host taking an individual from one group to another or by the individual moving groups under his own steam. The two golden rules of circulating are: never leave a guest unattended, never forcibly barge in on another group. If by chance an unannounced person arrives, the unhosted introduction is recommended, followed by a group introduction.

Individual and group hosting

Young officers and executives alike are often called upon to host VIPs at formal and informal functions. The aim will be to introduce as many guests as possible to the VIP. This task needs to be done slowly and deliberately. At a large function it will be impossible to memorise a guest list of 345 names. Many large functions are organised on a group basis, where one person is responsible for hosting a small group of eight to ten guests. In the first instance the VIP's host should introduce the group host to the VIP — 'Air Marshal Prong — Mr Douglas Bogtrotter, who is the director of personnel for ICBM Ltd'. Following the 'How do you dos' and handshake Douglas Bogtrotter, as the group host, takes over from the VIP host to introduce his group. This is where the situation can become complicated. Two options are open. The group host may introduce the VIP, in a firm voice, to the members of his group in the form — 'Air Marshal Prong, may I introduce the members of my group'. Then, working around the group, but starting at the nearest guest to the VIP, introductions continue: 'Mr and Mrs Snodgrass — Mr Snodgrass is our personnel director; Pilot Officer Twicle — he is our military liaison officer' — and so on. At the end of the introducing phase, the onus is on the VIP to open conversation. Alternatively, the group host may introduce his group individually: 'Mr and Mrs Snodgrass — Air Marshal Prong' — 'How do you do' etc, 'Mr Snodgrass is our personnel director'. The group host is advised to acquaint his group beforehand on the method he will adopt. While the group introductions are going ahead, the VIP host remains in the background

ensuring that the VIP is provided with refreshment. Once all the introductions have been made, and depending upon the time available, it may then be necessary for the VIP host to escort the VIP to the next group. The VIP will then excuse himself, and with the VIP host move on to the next group. While in transit, the VIP host may care to brief the VIP on the next group host and say a little about that group — 'We are now going to Wing Commander Flap's group; Wing Commander Flap is the chief test pilot working with ICBM Ltd and his group includes all the military technicians'. As a rough guide, ten minutes per group of ten guests should be allowed for group introductions.

Conversation

The initial introduction stage is where first impressions are gained by both parties. The onus is on an individual to get to know his fellow man through friendly conversation. As mentioned earlier, a good introduction from the host or hostess can go a long way towards breaking the ice and providing the stimulus for further conversation. This in turn may lead to a topic of mutual interest. Risky topics include religion, flippancy, dirty jokes, politics and women. Some might not think that leaves much to talk about. On the other hand, the indirect question that does not offer the option of a 'yes', or 'no' answer can be useful in striking up a conversation. 'How far have you travelled here tonight?' — 'How long are you staying in the area?' — 'How did you start in business?' — 'What attracted you to the Services?' — 'I hear you went to Turkey for your holiday, what did you think of it?' The options are infinite; and with careful thought beforehand, in ninety-nine out of a hundred situations an engaging, interesting and informative conversation will soon develop.

It is the host and hostess's responsibility to see that refreshment is dispersed to guests. Legislation, however imposes hefty penalties for drinking and driving offences. Guests and hosts should always be aware of limits.

The ability to mix socially is a prerequisite for success in any profession. Not everybody is gregarious by nature, but those who try to broaden their horizons will be amply rewarded by the spirit of friendship, bonhomie and brotherhood that it brings. The key to success is simply courtesy and good manners.

Chapter 15
The RAF Regiment

A Royal Warrant declaring the RAF Regiment to be a Corps formed as an integral part of the RAF was signed by His Majesty King George VI on 6 January 1942. Shortly after this date, Air Ministry Order N221/1942 stated that all existing RAF ground defence squadrons and flights were to be reorganised, expanded, re-equipped and incorporated in the RAF Regiment with effect from 1 February 1942. The Corps was then placed under the command of Major General Liardet, who became the RAF's first Director General of Ground Defence, and Commandant of the RAF Regiment.

The story of the RAF Regiment begins much earlier than 1942. During the First World War the RFC was considered by many as simply another Corps of the Army. Airfields were sited well behind the lines in strongly defended areas where there was little need for a separate dedicated force for airfield defence. However, air power had also brought the threat of reciprocal air bombing. The RFC's solution was to invite the Royal Artillery to provide anti-aircraft weapons, with the RFC manning locally sighted machine-gun posts for close anti-aircraft defence. This system was seen to be efficient and effective.

In 1918 the new RAF had problems enough

RAF Regiment Badge

without considering aerodrome defence. It was assumed that the Army would again provide ground and anti-aircraft defence for the RAF, as it had done for the RFC from 1914 to 1918, and nothing further was considered. Meanwhile, as a way of extending the influence of the RAF and thus ensuring its existence, Trenchard had conceived the idea of providing a peacekeeping force for the Middle East based on a strong 'Air Umbrella' to police the vast desert expanses. This use of air power in underdeveloped and underpopulated areas was accepted as more economical than maintaining huge Army garrisons and by the end of 1922 the RAF had assumed responsibility for the defence of Iraq, Trans-Jordan and Kuwait. But air power alone was insufficient and required support on the ground from a fast mobile, hard-hitting force. The result was the formation of the RAF Armoured Car Companies, to be supported later by locally enlisted levy forces. The embryo of a specialist RAF Ground Defence Force had been born. No. 1 Armoured Car Company was the first of the new units to be formed at Heliopolis on 19 December 1921, for operations in Iraq. On 7 April 1922 No. 2 Armoured Car Company was formed, and stationed in Trans-Jordan. The supporting levy forces had been in existence since 1915 as the bodyguard for political officers in central and southern Mesopotamia. In October 1922, reconstituted as the Iraq levies, the force was placed under RAF control to work hand in hand with the RAF's flying and armoured car squadrons to police the Middle East. This levy force remained in existence, in later years falling under the command of RAF Regiment officers, until disbanded in 1955.

Trenchard's ideas for 'policing' the Middle East were an outstanding success and in early 1928 the policy of air control was extended to the protectorate of Aden. A levy force was raised under the command of Colonel Lake and titled the Aden Protectorate Levies (APL). From humble beginnings, this force was later equipped to include mounted, infantry, armoured car and

RAF Rolls-Royce armoured car circa. 1924

anti-aircraft companies, and saw distinguished service in the Middle East. Many APL officers were RAF, although replaced by RAF Regiment Officers after the Second World War. The British Army began to assume control of the APL from 1957 onwards but RAF Regiment officers were still being seconded to the force until the British withdrawal from Aden in 1967. Both the RAF levy forces (Iraq and APL) had a distinguished record in support of the Crown. This was particularly true during the Second World War where, although they did not fight outside the Middle East, their presence released British and Commonwealth forces for urgent duties in North Africa and elsewhere.

The Royal Air Force gained great admiration for its services in the Middle East during the interwar years, displaying both professionalism and punch. During the same period at home, on the other hand, the RAF was only concerned with aircraft. It was still taken for granted that war on land, and the protection of airfields from

air attack, was the traditional role of the Army. The Army, for reasons best known to the War Office, were reluctant to accept responsibility for this task, suggesting that RAF stations should 'undertake their own local defence'. In 1937 the Air Council directed that RAF stations would be responsible for their own local defence against ground forces and low-flying aircraft. Stations were scaled with eight Vickers machine-guns for air defence, but unfortunately there were no rifles available for personal issue to airmen, as someone (?) had previously made the decision to phase them out of the RAF! Instead, all that was available was a motley collection of automatic weapons. Despite some improvements in the supply of small arms by 1939, the RAF was still in no position to defend airfields from the threat posed by Germany and it had to go cap in hand to the Army for assistance to provide ground and low level air defence expertise.

The real problems of organising airfield defence became apparent in the operational

Rolls-Royce armoured car of No 2 Armoured Car Company RAF operating in Iraq (1927).   Crown Copyright

environment of France in late 1939 and proved a serious strain on the RAF's resources. This led to the attachment of Army officers to RAF stations to provide specialist ground defence commanders. From late 1939 onwards the situation gradually improved, until by the autumn of 1940, flights consisting of the new airman trade of ground gunner were being formed solely for airfield defence; in October 1940 there were some 35,000 ground gunners serving in the RAF. Light Anti-aircraft Defence, on the other hand, was largely in the hands of the Royal Artillery, with Bofors gun batteries supported by RAF ground gunners armed with an assortment of light machine-guns. There followed a further expansion in April 1941, when existing station defence personnel were formed into squadrons and plans were made to increase the number of ground gunners from 45,000 to

72,000. At the same time, the first cadre of RAF officers to command ground gunner squadrons began to pass through the Army Officer Training Units.

Then in May 1941 the Germans carried out a spectacular and daring assault on the island of Crete. The spearhead of this assult was provided by airborne forces dropped inland and tasked to neutralize airfields. Despite the earlier use of airborne forces by the Germans in Holland in 1940, their effectiveness had been underestimated. Crete soon awakened tired eyes, particularly with respect to the vulnerability of North African airfields. The Government ordered that a committee was to be convened under the chairmanship of Sir Findlater Stewart to examine ways of improving airfield defence. In November 1941 the committee recommended that the RAF should have its own defence force under Air Ministry control. The recommendation was accepted in December 1941 and the RAF Regiment was formally effective from 1 February 1942, absorbing the existing ground gunner defence flights and squadrons. Much to the relief of the Army, the new RAF Regiment assumed control and responsibility for the defence of all RAF installations in the UK by the end of 1942. At the same time plans were made to form more potent anti-aircraft units, and to mobilise the ground gunner forces overseas into RAF Regiment squadrons. By mid-1943 the corps had established a strong presence in all the war theatres — indeed, many of the units had been bloodied. In essence, RAF Regiment operations followed the pattern of providing close co-operation between air and ground forces, which had been pioneered in the Middle East during the mid-1920s. This was particularly apparent in North Africa, where the corps acted as the left (ground) hand to the Desert Air Force's right hand. At home an RAF Regiment depot was opened at Belton Park in Lincolnshire, with a further depot at Secunderabad in India, and the corps' anti-aircraft squadrons were re-equipped with the very effective Bofors L40/60 gun. Following the success of armoured cars in the Middle East and North Africa, these too were added to RAF Regiment squadrons at home, though the Middle East armoured car companies were to remain under RAF rather than RAF Regiment control until after the war.

The testing time for the new corps came with Operation Overlord, the invasion of France by the Allies on 6 June 1944. In early 1944 a manpower crisis had led to the transfer of some 40,000 trained airmen to make up Army forces. Although this depleted the corps' strength, recovery was swift. Light anti-aircraft (LAA) squadrons were earmarked for landing beaches and forward airfield air defence, and the field or infantry type of squadrons, together with the armoured car squadrons, were organised into rifle squadrons for ground offensive operations. Many of the rifle squadrons were paired under the command of an RAF Regiment Wing Headquarters (the equivalent of an Army battalion) and two RAF Regiment Wings sailed with the assault force on D-Day, landing on Juno beach in the early hours of D+1 Day. By 18 June 1944 there were ten Wings of RAF Regiment forces supporting the Allied offensive in Normandy. The flying bomb offensive then began against London and the south coast towns. Under the auspices of Operation Diver, home based RAF Regiment anti-aircraft units, together with Royal Artillery batteries, were moved to the south coast and claimed many V1s.

The RAF Regiment, acting independently or as part of the Allied armies, fought throughout the winter of 1944 and spring of 1945, achieving

L40/60 Bofors anti-aircraft position North Africa circa 1943   Crown Copyright

Rapier surface to air missiles introduced in the mid-1970s   Crown Copyright

distinction in many areas. No. 2875 Squadron based in Holland was the first anti-aircraft unit to shoot down a Messerschmitt 262 jet aircraft. In May 1945 Regiment squadrons accepted the surrender of fifteen airfields in Schleswig-Holstein. By VE Day there were seventy-four RAF Regiment squadrons in north-west Europe, twenty-four in the Mediterranean and thirty-three operating in the Far Eastern theatre. At its wartime peak, the RAF Regiment had

Scorpion light armoured vehicle introduced in the late 1970s   Crown Copyright

No. 2 Squadron RAF Regiment Crown Copyright

numbered over 85,000 officers and airmen, manning two hundred and forty operational squadrons. When peace came in 1945 the post-war policy for the RAF Regiment was that it should be given a reduced rôle. The prewar Middle East armoured car companies were absorbed into the corps in October 1946, and RAF Regiment officers and NCOs were to become responsible for the ground defence training of all RAF personnel. Moreover, RAF Regiment officers were to assume responsibility for the various levied forces in the Middle East. The corps' squadrons were trimmed down to twenty-nine in number and spread between the Middle East and Germany, At the same time the title Commandant of the RAF Regiment was retitled Commandant-General.

Since the war the RAF Regiment has served with distinction in all theatres of the world, including Malaya, where in 1947 the RAF Regiment (Malaya) was formed to meet the terrorist offensive. This was a locally enlisted force, with RAF Regiment officers and NCOs providing expertise and leadership. Five squadrons were formed between 1947 and 1948, with a sixth in 1956. The last squadron was finally disbanded in 1961. Thirteen Royal Auxiliary Air Force Regiment squadrons were raised in 1947 and affiliated to fighter squadrons of the Auxiliary Air Force as part of the national air defence plan. The early 1950s saw a brief expansion of the Regiment to include eighteen Wing Headquarters and forty-seven squadrons, plus the levy forces, with active involvement in several overseas peacekeeping campaigns. This expansion was short-lived and the corps was drastically pruned following the Defence White Paper published in 1957. The results of this policy left the corps with no Auxiliary squadrons and only four Wing Headquarters and twelve squadrons, distributed between the UK and the Middle and Far East. The RAF Regiment's strength has remained little altered since then. Despite its small numbers, squadrons of the RAF Regiment were actively involved in various operational campaigns throughout the 1960s and early 1970s, including the Indonesian confrontation in Malaya and Singapore, the Aden and Radfan campaigns in South Arabia, anti-terrorist activities in Cyprus and finally the peacekeeping task in Northern Ireland, as well as home defence activities as part of NATO. In 1971 RAF Regiment air defence squadrons returned to Germany to protect key RAF bases and have recently been re-equipped with the Rapier surface-to-air missile system. In the mid-

1970s the Belize Garrison in Central America was reinforced by a further Regiment air defence squadron, initially armed with the second-generation Bofors gun but later replaced by Rapier. The old rifle and field squadrons are now history, and the second arm of the corps has become mechanised with the Scorpion family of armoured fighting vehicles. The RAF Regiment also maintains one airborne parachute squadron (No. 2 Squadron), which is also equipped as a mechanized squadron. The 1987 task of the corps is to provide the ground and air defence of principal RAF airfields at home and overseas, including Harrier aircraft support operations.

The RAF Regiment Depot is now at RAF Catterick in Yorkshire, which has strong local ties with the town of Richmond.

On the 10th Anniversary of the corps' formation in 1952 the RAF Regiment was proud to be presented with its own King's Colour, which has since been twice renewed by Her Majesty. Furthermore, it is proud to have twelve squadron standards, as well as the care and protection of the Queen's Colour for the Royal Air Force which is maintained by the Queen's Colour Squadron, an RAF squadron manned by RAF Regimental personnel based at the former RAF Depot at Uxbridge in Middlesex. Finally, in 1979, Auxiliary Air Force Regiment squadrons were again raised to assist with the

defence of RAF stations at home (see also Chapter 17 — R Aux AF). Three squadrons were initially formed, followed by a further two squadrons in 1982. The RAF Regiment looks forward to a full and exciting future in support of air operations. A further two regular air defence squadrons armed with the Rapier missile system were raised in 1984 to defend the USAF Cruise bases and a new auxiliary regiment force is planned to provide the ground defence at Key Command Headquarters in 1987. The RAF Regiment badge is of crossed rifles enclosed by the Astral Crown. Some further RAF Regiment squadron badges are shown on page 133.

Badge of the RAF Regiment Depot Catterick

The Queen's Colour Squadron of the Royal Air Force on Royal Duties, Buckingham Palace.
(Courtesy of Sqn. Ldr. P. S.|C. Comina, RAF Regiment).

RAF Regiment Squadron and Wing badges including The R Aux AF Regt

Chapter 16
The Women in Blue

The Women's Royal Air Force

The Women's Royal Air Force was born of a need to release men for active service at the Front during the First World War. It was the product of the determination of a few single-minded women to support the national effort. The inspiration for the Corps came initially from the Marchioness of Londonderry, who in July 1915 suggested to the War Office that a 'Women's Legion' should be formed to undertake administrative tasks in support of the Army. The benefit of this scheme was that it would relieve able-bodied men from certain tasks such as cooking and cleaning, to provide additional combatant forces for front-line duties. The War Office gladly accepted the Marchioness's suggestion and for a trial period in late 1915 women were employed in convalescent camps, on catering and other domestic duties. The trial proved a huge success and by 1916 had been extended to military camps and headquarters. The scope of employment for women was gradually broadened to include clerical and storekeeping tasks. Such was the female impact on the Army that in February 1916 the War Office prescribed conditions of service for women drivers of the RFC and Army Service Corps.

The offensives of autumn 1916 and spring 1917 decimated the British Army. Although some reserves were available and Commonwealth forces were pouring into France in their thousands, finding sufficient numbers was still a constant problem to the War Office. Following the early success of the Women's Legion in releasing manpower the programme was again extended to include every possible suitable occupation outside the immediate front-line area. By March 1917 the Army Council issued instructions setting out the terms and conditions of service for women in France; the employment undertaken by women was further extended to include clerical and typing work, domestic duties, driving, storekeeping and various miscellaneous tasks within the postal and courier services. This third programme was equally successful and led on 7 July 1917 to the War Office announcing the formation of the Women's Auxiliary Army Corps (WAAC), the first ever women's military corps. Officers of the Corps were given the rank of controllers, which equated to staff officers, or administrators, which equated to lesser, but executive administrative officers. The rank and file were described as forewomen and assistant forewomen. The chief controller of the new Corps was a Mrs Chalmers-Watson, MD, for the WAAC at home, and Mrs H. C. I. Gwynne-Vaughan for the WAAC in France.

For the next seven months the WAAC consolidated its position as a Corps within the British Army. However, in February 1918 following interest and enthusiasm expressed by Queen Mary, the WAAC was retitled Queen Mary's Auxiliary Army Corps (QMAAC). By February 1918 the QMAAC was providing forces to assist the RN and RNAS as well as the various Army corps and regiments in the supreme task of supporting military and naval operations. At the same time, a sense of single-Service responsibility was beginning to emerge as a key factor within the structure of the national war organisation. Accordingly, on 4 February 1918 a separate women's force entitled the Women's Royal Naval Service (WRNS) was formed to meet the needs of the Royal Navy, inclusive of its air service. Coinciding with the formation of the RAF on 1 April 1918 came the formation of the third women's service, the Women's Royal Air Force (WRAF).

The first head of the WRAF was Lady Gertrude Crawford, who was given the rank of Chief Superintendent. A month later the rank was changed to that of Commandant and the Hon Violet Douglas-Pennant assumed the post, to be replaced in September 1918 by Mrs H. C. I. Gwynne-Vaughan, the former chief controller of the WAAC in France. The WRAF continued in existence beyond the First World War and formed part of the Army of Occupation in

WRAF personnel undertaking aircraft re-fuelling duties at RAF Swinderby.

Germany. But initial success was to be short-lived and in December 1920, in line with other economies, the WRAF was disbanded. This came as a bitter blow to those who had worked so hard in bringing to the attention of the nation the efforts of women to support the war effort. But the spirit and *esprit-de-corps* of the WRAF was kept alive after disbandment through the enthusiasm and determination of Mrs Gwynne-Vaughan and Miss Trefusis-Forbes. With the support of Lady Trenchard, they formed a Women's Emergency Service (WES) which was soon recognised by the Army and the Air Council. The WES was to train women to become officers should they be required in any future war. It was to be only eighteen years from disbandment before women were again called to the colours. Perhaps, too, the lessons of the past had been forgotten, for when a women's service was re-formed in July 1938 it was as the khaki-clad Auxiliary Training Service (ATS), rather

than the specialist WRAF. Appropriately enough, though, the by then Dame Helen Gwynne-Vaughan was appointed the first commander of the ATS with Miss Trefusis-Forbes as the chief instructor.

The ATS were formed into companies and allotted to Army and RAF formations. The training task was formidable and the specialist duties given to the ATS diverse; beyond basic training ATS companies had little in common. This single factor was to lead to the emergence of a separate women's force dedicated to serve alongside the RAF. The forerunner of the WRAF was No. 20 RAF (County of London) ATS Company — commanded by Miss Trefusis-Forbes. Thanks to her, and to Dame Gwynne-Vaughan's vociferous lobbying in late 1938 and early 1939, the War Office and Air Ministry jointly set about studying the case for a single women's service dedicated to the RAF and similar to the WRAF of 1918-20. The result was that on 28 June 1939 a Royal Warrant was issued authorising the formation of the Women's Auxiliary Air Force (WAAF) — and by 3 September of that year the WAAF comprised forty-eight companies

The aim of the new force was not only to release men for operational front-line duty but also to assume a wider and more active role within the Service itself. The khaki-clad pioneers of the ATS, RAF-dedicated companies duly exchanged their brown livery for one of Air Force blue and swung into action under the command of Miss Trefusis-Forbes who was given the rank of Air Commandant. The badges of rank of both officers and airwomen, as well as the style and colour of the uniform, conformed with that of officers and airmen in the RAF. This was a deliberate decision away from the 1918 concept to show a closer connection between the WAAF and its parent service. At the same time the trades open to the WAAF were vastly broadened to include armourer, balloon operator, balloon parachute hand, bomb plotter, electrician, flight mechanic, instrument mechanic, MT mechanic and many other skilled trades. The WAAF soon became an integral part of the RAF, and in early 1941 an Order in Council brought into existence the Defence (Women's Forces) Regulations, under which the WAAF, with the women's forces of the other two Services, became one of the Armed Forces of the Crown. The result of this legislation was that the WAAF could be posted for service with the RAF anywhere in the world. Prior to this date, on 12 March 1940, the Duchess of Gloucester was gazetted as an Air Commandant of the WAAF.

The contribution made by the WAAF in support of air operations was immeasurable. In the background and behind the scenes the WAAF worked tirelessly achieving distinction and the unending admiration of the parent service. Some readers may recall the excellent work done by Constance Babbington-Smith as part of the photographic interpretation team at Medmenham where she identified the V1 flying bomb. The measures taken by the Allies after this startling revelation probably saved thousands of lives. Although the WAAF were not actively involved with flying aircraft, a considerable amount of flying was done by women employed in the Air Transport Auxiliary, or ATA. The ATA was formed shortly after the outbreak of war with the object

1918 WRAF shoulder title

WRAF chief section leader's rank badge

Early WRAF badges and insignia of 1918

Air Commandant	Airwomen:
Group Officer	Warrant Officer
Wing Officer	Flight Sergeant
Squadron Officer	Sergeant
Flight Officer	Corporal
Section Officer	Leading Aircraftwoman
Assistant Section Officer	Aircraftwoman, 1st Cl.
	Aircraftwoman, 2nd Cl.

WAAF and airwomen's Rank 1940-48

of employing civilian pilots, including women, in so called second-line duties. These duties included ferrying aircraft and air communications tasks (transporting VIPs, etc). By the time the ATA was disbanded on 30 November 1945 it had been responsible for ferrying a total of 309,011 aircraft to destinations throughout the world.

At the end of the Second World War it was considered unwise to achieve any service economies through disbanding the WAAF. In the simplest terms, such was the contribution of the WAAF that the RAF could not do without them! However, a change in status came in 1948 when the Army and the Air Force (Women's Service) Act received Royal Assent. This Act enjoined the WAAF into the Royal Air Force and made its members subject to King's Regulations and the Air Force Act. At the same time the title of the WAAF reverted to the original First World War description of Women's Royal Air Force.

The WRAF is today a fundamental part of the Service, and its officers and airwomen serve in most of the non-flying branches. Equal opportunities exist for the WRAF to compete with their RAF counterparts for executive station and command headquarters appointments, including that of ground defence commander on front-line stations. In recent years the WRAF have been declared combatant and may take up arms. (Some early WRAF and ATA badges and rank equivalents are shown on page 136).

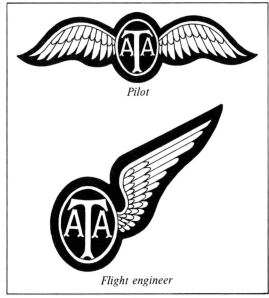

Pilot

Flight engineer

Insignia of the Air Transport Auxiliary

Air Transport Auxiliary cap badge

Princess Mary's Royal Air Force Nursing Service
The Royal Air Force Nursing Service was formed on 1 June 1918 as a wartime measure to support the RAF. Before this, Army nurses under the auspices of the Royal Army Medical Corps (RAMC) and assisted by staff of the Voluntary Aid Detachment had been responsible for staffing military hospitals, medical centres and convalescent homes. Flying stations were often situated in remote areas beyond easy reach of Navy and Army hospitals, and on the formation of the RAF in April 1918 it became clear that the new force should have its own nursing service, composed of trained nurses recruited for temporary wartime service. The return to peacetime conditions in 1919 saw the gradual withdrawal of nursing staff from the temporary field hospitals to the first permanent RAF hospitals at Cranwell and Halton. However, the continued existence of the nursing service was by no means sure, particularly in view of the disbandment of the WRAF in 1920. Fortunately the nurses survived, and in 1921 a Royal Warrant established the nursing service as a permanent branch of the RAF where sisters held officer status, though only professional titles were used. By 1923 new hospitals had been opened in the Middle East, and in June of that year the King consented to the Princess Royal's name being used to title the branch Princess Mary's Royal Air Force Nursing Service (PMRAFNS), a title that remains to the present day. The nursing service continued to grow from strength to strength, and during the expansion programme of 1935-9 several new hospitals were opened to replace the earlier hutted buildings. At the same time the Service began to develop its expertise in the field of aviation medicine.

During the war years, from 1939-45, the nursing service again expanded, providing hospital, casualty reception and convalescent care in every combat area in which the RAF was engaged. Of particular merit were the pioneering nursing skills developed by Sir Archibald Macindo's Unit in Surrey for the medical treatment of severe burn casualties from the Battle of Britain and later air offensives. But this was only one aspect of a global picture that also saw the development of aeromedical evacuation techniques in transporting serious casualties from the battle area, as well as the treatment and rehabilitation of other war wounded personnel.

After the war, the strength of the branch was reduced in line with other economies, but there was no question of disbandment — the PMRAFNS had become established as an essential element within the fighting Service. The temporary military hospitals were returned to their rightful owners and the Service's nursing facilities were centralised at various hospitals in the United Kingdom, with at least one hospital also being established in each of the Air Force Headquarter Zones overseas. The PMRAFNS again supported its parent Service in the Korean War of 1950-53 and later during the years of the Malayan emergency. More recently the branch has been actively involved in the evacuation of casualties from both Northern Ireland and the Falkland Islands campaign of 1982.

Although entry into the Service was originally at qualified nursing sister (SRN) level only, a non-commissioned element to the branch was formed in 1960. This element consists of student or pupil nurses who undertake a three-year training course as ward nurses, leading to the qualification of state enrolled nurse (SEN). On 1 April 1980 the commissioned male nurses (at SRN qualification) amalgamated with the sisters into a unified nursing service, and at the same time the commissioned ranks of the PMRAFNS became the same as those of the RAF and WRAF.

The PMRAFNS today is a branch of the RAF under the professional guidance of the Director General of Medical Services RAF and includes an auxiliary aeromedical evacuation squadron based at RAF Lyneham in Wiltshire (see also Chapter 17). It provides nurses to support doctors, dentists, medical technicians and medical secretarial staff in caring for the health of Service personnel and in some cases their dependants. Its hospitals and resources are also open to National Health Service patients. The motto of this small branch is *Nec Aspera Terrent* (Nothing Will Deter Us).

Chapter 17
The Royal Auxiliary Air Force, the Royal Air Force Volunteer Reserve and the Air Training Corps.

In October 1984 the RAuxAF celebrated sixty years of distinguished service. In August 1986 the RAFVR celebrated its 50th anniversary. Both the RAuxAF and the RAFVR represent the immediate reserve of trained personnel available to the mother Service in time of mobilisation. Their history and their pedigrees are, however, quite different.

The Royal Auxiliary Air Force
Today the Royal Auxiliary Air Force is a voluntary organisation comprising Maritime Headquarters units, Royal Auxiliary Air Force Regiment squadrons, a Royal Auxiliary Air Force Movements Squadron and a Royal Auxiliary Air Force Aeromedical Evacuation Squadron, in which members carry out part-time service while continuing to follow their civil occupations. Royal Auxiliary Air Force units are raised and maintained by Territorial Auxiliary and Volunteer Reserve Associations. Volunteers are enlisted for service in a unit or squadron administered by an association from which, except when the Royal Auxiliary Air Force is called out, they cannot be posted without their consent. During peacetime each unit is located in the area from which the RAuxAF personnel of the unit are recruited. Normally each unit is commanded by a Royal Auxiliary Air Force officer who has regular Royal Air Force officers on his staff. In addition in each unit there are a number of regular officers and airmen who assist in administration and the giving of instruction to Royal Auxiliary Air Force personnel.

Although a concept for an organised reserve for the Royal Air Force can be traced back to ideas first proposed by Sir Hugh Trenchard in 1919, the AuxAF was not formally established until 1924 when an Order in Council was published on 9 October of that year. The Auxiliary Air Force and Air Force Reserve Act of 1924 and was concerned solely with flying and pilot training. The first four Auxiliary squadrons were formed in 1925 and by the outbreak of war on 3 September 1939 some twenty Auxiliary flying squadrons and forty-four balloon squadrons were supporting the RAF. Squadrons were recruited by the County Territorial Army and Air Force Associations, while members were drawn from the district in which the Auxiliary squadron headquarters were situated. Training was carried out on weekday evenings and during weekends, with a fortnight summer camp of intensive training with the regular Air Force. Like the county regiments of the Army, the AuxAF squadrons had a local association and pride in their host county or city. All the Auxiliary squadrons were given a county or city title, such as 'No 500 County of Kent' or 'No 613 City of Manchester' Squadron. The first four squadrons were numbered 500 to 504 (excluding 503), and the remaining sixteen were numbered 600 to 616.

On the outbreak of the Second World War, Auxiliary Air Force recruiting was closed down so that there would be a single channel of entry into the RAF. Nevertheless, Auxiliary pilots were soon to gain fame, including the accolade for shooting down the first German bomber on British soil, on 16 October 1939. Later, it was an Auxiliary pilot who shot down Major Helmuth Weick, the German air ace credited with fifty-six victories, on 28 November 1940. The long list of awards and victories credited to AAF aircrew during the Second World War testifies to the fighting spirit and professionalism of the squadrons, but more particularly to the quality of their training in the pre-war days. A lesser-known but nonetheless key factor in the war effort, was the balloon squadrons. Auxiliary balloon squadrons, of which the first was formed in May 1938, had grown to forty-four in number by the outbreak of war and were absorbed into what was later to become Balloon Command. Their task was to provide balloon barrages around industrial and military targets. Balloons were a deterrent to low-flying aircraft and in the latter part of the war claimed several V-1 flying bombs.

In all the Auxiliaries flew 1500 barrage balloons. Throughout the Second World War the AAF squadrons flew alongside the regulars. They were equipped with up-to-date aircraft and introduced the first Allied Jet fighter — the Gloster Meteor — into the air battle in 1945. A notable 'first' for the AAF included a Meteor aircraft of 616 Squadron downing a V-1 flying bomb by tipping the bomb's wings. Some may be unaware too that the first U-boat sunk with the aid of air-to-surface radar was also at the hands of an Auxiliary squadron. In recognition of the distinguished service given by AAF personnel during the Second World War, the 'Royal' prefix was granted by King George VI on 16 December 1947 with the amended abbreviation RAuxAF.

At the end of the war Auxiliary balloon squadrons were disbanded, but the flying squadrons and Auxiliary headquarters units were retained, along with a new type of Auxiliary squadron born out of the RAF Regiment and titled the Royal Auxiliary Air Force Regiment (RAuxAF Regt). These Auxiliary Regiment squadrons, like their sister flying squadrons, were adopted by counties and cities and bore with pride the appropriate county or city title. The RAuxAF Regiment squadrons were to be recognised by their four-figure numbers, rather than the three figures of flying squadrons; all RAuxAF Regiment squadron numbers began with either 25 or 26. In total, thirteen of these squadrons were raised as anti-aircraft units to support the Auxiliary flying squadrons in the task of national air defence.

The cost to the Exchequer of maintaining all types of the Auxiliary squadrons rose sharply with the introduction of jet aircraft and more sophisticated ground equipment. Accordingly, all the flying and RAF Regiment Auxiliary squadrons were disbanded by the middle of 1957. Only a small nucleus of Auxiliary Air Force personnel was to be retained to man the RAF Maritime headquarters at Pitreavie Castle in Scotland, Plymouth in south-west England and Northwood near London. The demise of the Auxiliary flying squadrons, many of which proudly displayed their own squadron standards, was greeted with great sadness and even some disbelief that such action could be taken. The only voluntary fliers to be left with the RAF were a few previously qualified pilots, who flew part-time with the Voluntary Reserve

(VR). In 1979, to the delight of many, the phoenix of the RAuxAF Regiment rose from the ashes with the announcement that three Auxiliary Regiment squadrons were to be re-formed on a trial basis with the task of defending principal UK airfields.

These squadrons were No 2503 (County of Lincoln) Squadron, RAuxAF Regt, based at RAF Scampton; No 2623 (East Anglian) Squadron, RAuxAF Regt, based at RAF Honington; and No 2622 (Highland) Squadron, RAuxAF Regt, based at RAF Lossiemouth. Recruiting for the new AuxAF Regiment squadrons was so successful that a decision was made in 1984 to further expand the force by three additional squadrons which brought 'on line' No 2620 (County of Norfolk) Squadron based at RAF Marham, No 2624 (County of Oxford) Squadron based at RAF Brize Norton and No 2625 (County of Cornwall) Squadron based at RAF St Mawgan. During 1985 and as a result of salvaged Oerlikon 35 mm anti-aircraft guns — the spoils of the Falklands' Island Campaign — it was decided to form a new Anti-Aircraft RAuxAF Regiment unit to be numbered and titled 2729 (City of Lincoln) Squadron and to be based at RAF Waddington. In the same year No 2503 Squadron moved to RAF Waddington from its former home at RAF Scampton. Unlike the regular RAF Regiment, women play an important role in the RAuxAF Regiment squadrons. They are employed in a variety of both combat and non-combat tasks including first aid, signals, driving, fieldcraft and providing ammunition loaders for the Oerlikons. They are particularly adept in the running of the communication links where staffing of information (command post) displays are essential.

There has also been an expansion in other areas of the RAuxAF. At RAF Brize Norton No 4624 (County of Oxford) RAuxAF Squadron has been formed as an Air Movements Unit. This squadron is involved directly with the operation of the VC10 and Hercules aircraft and members of the squadron regularly fly to Ascension Island. The squadron plans to have a total of eight flights making it the largest of all the RAuxAF squadrons. A further new addition to the orbat is No 4626 (County of Wiltshire) Aero Medical Evacuation Squadron, RAuxAF. Formed at the RAF Hospital Wroughton on 9 September 1983, it provides vacancies for thirteen medical officers, 23 nursing officers and

168 airmen and airwomen. Both the Air Movements and Aero Medical units were used extensively during Exercise 'Lionheart' (the major British Army of the Rhine [BAOR] reinforcement exercise) in September 1985. In 1986 the RAuxAF has expanded even further to now include an additional RAuxAF Support Force.

This new element of the Royal Auxiliary Air Force has one flight being formed at RAF Lyneham with three similar units based at RAF St Athan, RAF High Wycombe and RAF Brampton. The aim of these units is to provide assistance to the parent station by supplementing Regular forces with auxiliaries to serve in the ground defence organization as guards, or to take over Station tasks and thus release Regulars for guarding duties. The Royal Auxiliary Air Force Support Flight at Lyneham will consist of 100 personnel, comprising a small Force HQ with an Officer Commanding and a SNCO who will work 150 days per year and a full-time civilian Clerical Officer. Other personnel will be required to complete eight days' (64 hours') training per year.

Membership of the Royal Auxiliary Air Force Support Force is open to men and women between the ages of seventeen and fifty (ex-Servicemen may be accepted to 55 years). Recruits will be given a free issue of uniform and will be paid according to the current rates of pay for the RAuxAF for each day's training completed. In addition there will be certain allowances to cover out-of-pocket expenses. Personnel who complete their annual training commitment will also be eligible for a tax-free bounty.

RAuxAF training standards are high and equal to the standard expected of the Regulars. On average an Auxiliary (other than the Support Force) will be expected to complete 150 hours of non-continuous training annually. This may be completed on evenings and weekends as well as the fifteen days' continuous training during the annual camp.

The Royal Air Force Volunteer Reserve

The Royal Air Force Volunteer Reserve chiefly consists of University Air Squadrons with a few air experience units and small photographic interpretation units. The University Air Squadrons are provided to give flying training to full-time undergraduates studying for a recognised degree pending a possible further career as a Regular RAF officer, though this is not obligatory. These squadrons are commanded by a Regular RAF officer who has a complement of Regular RAF officer flying instructors and ground support staff to assist him. Although not absolute in definition, the RAFVR was formed to provide a reserve of individuals rather than fully-fledged units vis-à-vis the Auxiliary squadrons. Very roughly, the RAFVR was seen to equate to the Army's Officer Training Corps (OTC) at universities whereas the RAuxAF appeared to parallel the Territorial Army.

Although the University Air Squadron concept had been realised in 1925, it was not absorbed into the RAFVR until much later, in May 1939. The initial aim of the RAFVR was to provide an immediate reserve of 2400 pilots capable of supporting and augmenting the Regular Air Force. The concept was timed to come to fruition over a period of four years. The RAFVR actually got underway in January 1937 utilising civil airfields, and even flying clubs to provide the instructional cadre. Most of the training was done at weekends. However, producing a reserve of trained pilots was not enough. It soon became apparent that the overall scheme would have to be broadened to include other aircrew categories (navigators and air gunners) as well as engineering tradesmen, general duties (ground) personnel, doctors, and so forth.

Rapid expansion with only part-time training also brought its problems. Part-time VR pilot training, for example, took nearly four times as

Bulldog aircraft – the primary training aircraft for the University Air Squadrons.

long to complete as did similar training for Regular students. Although there is no doubting that progress was made with the VR, by 1938 it was but a pool resource of semi-trained aircrews who on mobilisation would be allocated where needed, ie, 'plugging the holes'. The Auxiliary Air Force, on the other hand, had been organised into squadrons with a much greater identity and esprit de corps. Moreover, many of the Auxiliary pilots had paid for their training through private means. The RAFVR and RAuxAF had little in common in those days. In May 1939 the University Air Squadrons merged with the VR providing a better structure and more depth to the reserve. On 24 August 1939, normal RAF recruitment ended when the nation mobilised for war. Thereafter most of the aircrew who entered the RAF simply became VR. But the scheme did live up to its ideals and during the Battle of Britain period it provided a reservoir of 2493 pilots for the air force as a whole. During the war the total for all RAFVR, all branches, rose to 563,000. Although the RAFVR remained in existence during the early post-war years, it was destined to be drastically reduced, save for a few isolated units, under the Duncan Sandys Defence Cuts of 1957. The wheel has now turned full circle with a revival of the VR concept in the 1980s.

During 1986, the RAFVR's Golden Jubilee, the VR expanded from a strength of 55 officers and 19 airmen to a total of 110 officers and 44 airmen. The RAFVR has now a vital role within NATO in support of intelligence duties concerned with photographic reconnaissance. Later in 1986 and outside of the University Air Squadrons a flying element to the VR was reintroduced to evaluate the feasibility of having a full VC10 passenger aircraft crew and VR Air Electronic Officers (AEOs) available to support Nimrod aircraft undertaking maritime operations. Finally, with regard to the current expansion plans, it is intended to part staff University Air Squadrons with their own RAFVR flying instructors. The following is a list of the current University Air Squadrons:

Royal Air Force University Air Squadrons

Squadron title	Date founded	Base
Aberdeen, Dundee & St Andrews UAS	1941	RAF Leuchars
University of Birmingham AS	1941	RAF Cosford
Bristol UAS	1941	Filton
Cambridge UAS	1925	Duxford
East Lowlands UAS	1969	RAF Turnhouse
East Midlands UAS	1941	RAF Newton
University of Glasgow & Strathclyde AS	1946	Glasgow Airport
Liverpool UAS	1941	RAF Woodvale
University of London AS	1935	RAF Abingdon
Manchester & Salford UAS	1941	RAF Woodvale
Northumbrian UAS	1941	RAF Leeming
Oxford UAS	1925	RAF Abingdon
Queens UAS	1941	Sydenham
Southampton UAS	1941	Hurn Airport
University of Wales AS	1963	RAF St Athan
Yorkshire UAS	1969	RAF Finningley

Further information about the RAuxAF or RAFVR can be obtained from any RAF Careers Information Office.

The Air Training Corps

The youth-associated branch of the RAF is the Air Training Corps (ATC), which was created by Royal Warrant on 1 February 1941. In 1938 the Air League of the British Empire had founded the Air Defence Cadet Corps (ADCC) to foster interest in military aviation. The ADCC had a tremendous initial success and by 1940 mustered 200 squadrons including over 20,000 cadets. Not unnaturally, the Air Ministry took a great interest in the Corps and in 1941 assumed responsibility and control under a new title of Air Training Corps. The squadrons could then be staffed and commanded by Auxiliary or Volunteer Reserve officers.

In the early days the aim of the Corps was to act as a reservoir from which the Fleet Air Arm and RAF could draw their future air and ground crew and most of the training was given in preparation for later military service. By 1943 the Corps numbers had risen to well over 150,000.

After the war the Corps continued in existence, and, during the National Service years from 1949 to 1963 former ATC cadets were allowed to express a preference for the Service they wished to join. However, the end of National Service brought a decline in the Corps' popularity which resulted in many squadrons disbanding. The Air Training Corps of today is expanding beyond even our national boundaries. Although an ATC squadron has existed in Cyprus for many years, 1984 saw authority given for additional overseas squadrons, one in Gibraltar and three in Germany. Gibraltar was the first to form, officially opening on 1 March 85. All are attached to RAF Stations.

The ATC is a voluntary youth organisation which aims to promote and encourage a practical interest in aviation and the RAF. It does so by providing training which will be useful both in the Services and in civilian life. The Corps' aim is to foster the spirit of adventure and to develop qualities of leadership and good citizenship. In so doing, it provides a great deal for the young people of this country. But there is no pressure on ATC Cadets to join the RAF. The developed attitudes within the ATC will prove invaluable in any walk of life; whether physical fitness, or simply a pride in appearance. In recent years too, the ATC has been opened to entry by girls.

The ATC is the largest youth organisation participating in the Duke of Edinburgh's Award Scheme, but that is only one of the very many activities or studies on offer. (A list of activities is shown at the end of this chapter.) Some squadrons have a military band and some undertake special projects, extra-mural activities and citizenship training in addition to the normal progressive training syllabus. Perhaps the most popular activities are flying, gliding and small or full bore shooting which come under the general term of adventure training. Adventure training is at a very high level throughout the Corps. Squadron projects are varied and imaginative from rock climbing to sailing. The special courses organized for skiing, offshore sailing, parachuting and outward bound have been particularly successful. One key advantage in the Corps adventure training programme is the availability of the Adventure Training Centre at Windermere, in the Lake District, which was used by over 1200 cadets and 300 adults in 1986

The Corps is organised on a regional basis under the command of a Regional Commandant. There are seven regions. From

Chipmunks of 7 AEF at RAF Newton.

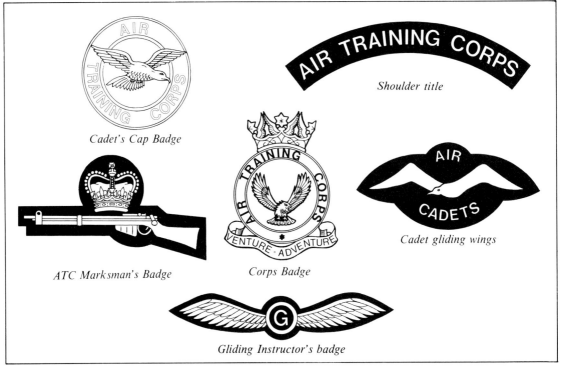

Cadet's Cap Badge

Shoulder title

ATC Marksman's Badge

Corps Badge

Cadet gliding wings

Gliding Instructor's badge

Insignia and Badges of the Air Training Corps

the regions, authority is devolved to Wing Headquarters, which are roughly organised on a county or area basis. However, the most important part of the chain is the ATC Squadron. A squadron will support thirty to fifty boys and girls and may be hosted within a school, or have its own accommodation. Most squadrons carry out training on two evenings per week and there is the opportunity to attend a week's camp on an RAF Station during the summer or Easter holiday. Some cadets are lucky enough to attend overseas camps in Germany, Cyprus or Gibraltar and others are selected for the International Air Cadet Exchange Scheme in Canada, the USA, Sweden, Belgium, the Netherlands, Hong Kong, West Germany, Israel, France, Norway or Turkey. In 1985 a total of 84 cadets benefited from this scheme, and they included a high percentage of girls.

The Ministry of Defence (Air) funds the basic equipment, clothing, flying and gliding activities. Cadets are expected to make a contribution towards unit welfare activities, sports and some adventure pursuits. The staffing of the squadrons and wings is on a volunteer basis, although there are some full-time paid appointments at Wing and Regional Headquarters. In most cases, however, staff will receive travel expenses, and uniformed officers and warrant officers may receive up to 28 days' pay per year. The uniformed officers who look after the ATC are commissioned into the RAF or WRAF Volunteer Reserve (Training Branch), abbreviated as RAF (or WRAF) VR(T). Warrant Officers who have previous senior NCO service or have given eight years' satisfactory service to the Corps may wear their insignia of a Royal Coat of Arms. Other Warrant Officers wear the large woven and embroidered Crown badge.

In addition to the squadron, Wing and Region organisation, the Corps maintains both powered flying and gliding centres. Powered flying is in the hands of the thirteen Air Experience Flights (AEFs), twelve of which are commanded by Regular RAF officers. However, the pilots are recruited from volunteer civilians who hold a full Service pilot's flying badge and have at least 300 Service hours as a first pilot; they are commissioned into the RAFVR(T). The gliding schools, on the other hand, are staffed entirely by RAFVR(T) officers and civilian instructors. There are 27 gliding schools throughout the country and some 2000 cadets achieve a solo standard each year. A recent innovation in the gliding schools has been the addition of powered gliders with an extensive replacement programme of the old wooden gliders.

Overall, and on behalf of the Ministry of Defence, the Air Cadet organisation is looked after by Headquarters Air Cadets at RAF Newton. This headquarters has its own full time Air Officer Commanding with an appropriate staff to manage and lead the Corps. The Corps badge, which is recognised as a splendid piece of heraldry, was designed by Sir James Heaton Armstrong. It consists of a red circlet bearing in gold the words 'Air Training Corps', and a gold falcon is displayed over the circlet, with the Astral Crown above it. The motto is 'Venture Adventure'. Some ATC insignia are shown on page 144.

The ATC is proud of its history and its unstinting support of the youth of this country. However, the Corps would be nothing without the personal sacrifice, devotion and energy of the civilian instructors, Warrant Officers and commissioned officers who have made the ATC what it is today.

Further details about the Air Training Corps can be obtained from any RAF Careers Information Officer or by writing direct to the local Region or Wing Headquarters whose address may be obtained from the local telephone directory.

Typical training and recreational activities undertaken by the Corps are listed below:

Aero-modelling
Aircraft operation
Airframes
Air navigation
Amateur radio
Athletics
Camping
Canoeing
Citizenship training
Community relations
Competitive shooting
Cross-country running
Debating
Drill
Duke of Edinburgh's Award Scheme
Engines
First aid
Flying experience
Gliding
Helping the community
Hovercraft building
Initiative training
Local historical surveys
Map-reading
Meteorology
Orienteering
Overseas visits
Parades
Photography
Principles of flight
Projects
Radar and radio
Rock climbing
Rugby
Sailing
Skiing
Soccer
Space travel study
Squadron bands
Swimming
Table tennis
Visits to RAF Stations, air museums and air displays

Chapter 18
The Royal Observer Corps (ROC)

In 1985 the ROC celebrated its 60th anniversary. Sadly, few are aware of this, or of the selfless contribution members of the ROC have given to the defence of the nation. The RAF has maintained a strong and proud association with the ROC which was originally founded as the early warning eyes and ears against air attack. However, the story of the ROC starts before 1925 and even before the formation of the RAF in 1918.

On 31 May 1915 East London erupted following the attack of a German airship which had dropped 3000 lbs of bombs. Seven people were killed, 35 injured and an estimated £18,000 worth of damage was caused. Although this was not the first air raid, since there had been seven previously on the north-east of England and down the east coast, the London air raid had struck at the heart of the nation. Something had to be done to improve London's air defences — the twelve anti-aircraft guns sited around the capital were clearly ineffective. Moreover, without some form of early warning system, how could the guns react in time? As a first step in providing an alerting force, special constables were tasked to keep their eyes open and report *ad lib,* using the telephone network, any airship sightings. The telephone network of the time was certainly not up to this and not surprisingly no airships were brought down in 1915!

By the next year, however, there had been some innovations. RFC fighter squadrons were allocated for the air defence of London and some searchlights were provided to assist the anti-aircraft guns during night firing. A further major step was to establish an observation organisation involving 200 carefully selected posts. At first, posts were manned by soldiers, later by policemen. The biggest flaw in the system, as before, was poor communication. There were no dedicated telephone lines or immediate means of contact with the defenders. Nevertheless, it was an improvement and by trial and error progress was being made.

On 13 June 1917 the nation witnessed the first massed enemy bomber raid, in daylight, on London, provided by twenty Gotha aircraft. Having just sorted out the airship problem, the government again was shaken to the core. Prime Minister, Lloyd George looked immediately for help to the then Lieutenant General John Smuts, remembering that it had been he who had earlier looked at the problems that had been brewing within the RFC and RNAS. Smuts, being the perceptive and innovative individual that he was and recognising the true qualities of leadership in his subordinates, appointed Major General E. B. Ashmore to solve the problem. General Ashmore was well chosen; he had been an early flying enthusiast before the war and had commanded an RFC Wing in France in 1915. At the date of appointment he was commanding a 'Gunner' Division in France — his nickname was 'Splash'.

Ashmore returned from France in 1917 and set about his new appointment with diligence and energy. By July of the same year and with War Office approval, the London Air Defence Area (LADA) was established. Ashmore had blended the RFC and RNAS resources to provide one layer of air defence backed up on the ground by deployed anti-aircraft batteries supported by searchlights. The scene was ready for the next Gotha attack. This took place on 12 August 1917 — and was totally repulsed.

The next stage in Ashmore's plan was to provide a greater depth to his air defence. This he did by incorporating balloons. At the same time, he woke up to the need to improve the 'warning and reporting' organisation. He now turned his attention to the Metropolitan Observation Service which had earlier been established to provide visual early warning of attacks against London. He extended the Services' network, introduced a standardised reporting format and did what he could to improve the lines of communication. The new format was an instant success and proved beyond doubt the effectiveness of a coordinated early warning and a complementary air defence system. The cast

Two war-time observers using 'Heath Robinson' height-finding apparatus for aircraft monitoring.

for an Observer Corps had been struck, although not by that title. At the same time, fundamental principles for air defence had been established.

With the announcement of the Armistice on 11 November 1918 Ashmore turned his attention to the future and on 22 November submitted his peacetime proposals for national air defence to the War Office. These were accepted and with little change became the blueprint for the future. However, by 1920 the ground control and reporting network had totally disappeared. This was a time of stringency and funds could not be found by the government of the day to support such an organisation. However, all was not lost, least of all the former expertise and knowledge and when the Romer committee sat in 1924 to review the air defence situation it was clear that a ground control, observation organisation would be needed. It may come as no surprise to learn that 'Splash' Ashmore was a key member on

Major General Romer's Committee! Later in the same year, tests and trials involving 32 Squadron aircraft were carried out over the Weald of Kent. The findings and recommendations from the trials were forwarded to the Committee of Imperial Defence who agreed the conclusions. The 'Observer Corps' was established on 25 October 1925. The Corps came under the auspices of the Home Office; it was to be organised by an Army Major General but to work for the RAF!

At first the Corps was centred on London, but in 1926 it expanded into the Home Counties where Group Headquarters and further observation posts were established. As awareness of the potential air threat grew, the RAF expanded accordingly; close behind came the Observer Corps. In the autumn of 1928 the Home Defence Sub-Committee recommended to the Committee of Imperial Defence that the Observer Corps, for now obvious reasons, be transferred to Air Ministry sponsorship. This was actioned on 1 January 1929. The Observer Corps consolidated its position in the following years. Exercises were held regularly with the RAF and the Corps' level of expertise steadily began to rise. New instruments to aid observation were developed and dedicated lines of telephone communication installed in the posts. In particular, the Corps has Heath Robinson to thank for the height-finding apparatus which although simple was effective.

In 1934 both the RAF and Observer Corps entered an unprecedented period of accelerated expansion. It was clear even then that war clouds were looming over Germany. Under the leadership of Air Commodore O. T. Boyd, rapid advances were made which finally established an integrated home air defence network in Great Britain incorporating the Observer Corps, Fighter Command of the RAF and the Chain Home (Link) Network (Radar) — all with dedicated lines of communication. By 1939, the Observer Corps was ready and prepared.

What had not been decided, however, and perhaps of less importance at the time, was a command structure, uniform and a pay scale. Not to overlook these points, Air Vice-Marshal Dowding set up a committee in mid 1939 to suggest recommendations. One idea was to give the Observer Corps officers the equivalent to RAF(VR) ranks. This was not accepted, although at first ex-serving officers of the Corps went on duty in the livery of their former Service.

The character of the Corps was, after all, essentially civilian. Nevertheless, in April 1941 King George VI kindly consented to the Royal prefix in recognition of the Corps' contribution to national air defence. At the same time, officers of the ROC adopted RAF uniform, but worn with ROC buttons, cap badge and shoulder flashes. Officers' rank was to be shown by rings of midnight blue braid. The rank and file on the other hand continued to wear civilian dress, but with Corps' distinguishing armlets and brassards.

The contribution by the ROC during the war years is inestimable. They are undoubtedly the unsung heroes of the time. The Observer's task was to keep track of enemy aircraft and report their movement to a military air defence (fighter) operations centre. They were able to do this through a national network of observation posts sited at vantage points with excellent panoramic views. Posts were sited 5 to 10 miles apart, each reporting to a Group HQ. Each Group had its own headquarters which fed information directly into an RAF Sector Air Operations Room where an ROC liaison officer was also available. The facts and figures reported would then be visually displayed on a plotting board so that RAF controllers would know where to send fighter aircraft to intercept. Despite the simplicity of the system by today's standards, it worked extremely well and was undoubtedly a key factor in the success of the Battle of Britain. Surprisingly, too, tracking by night or in cloudy weather was also very effective! This came into its own during the Allied bombing campaign in Europe, when damaged bombers, out of radio

Underground Monitoring Post.

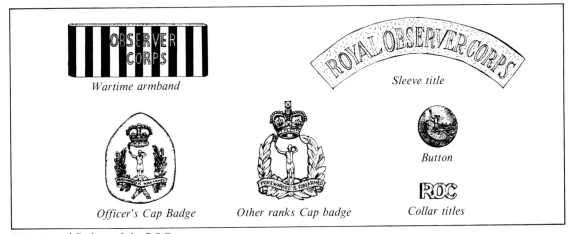

Wartime armband

Sleeve title

Officer's Cap Badge   *Other ranks Cap badge*   *Button*

Collar titles

Insignia and Badges of the ROC

contact and with injured crews on board were guided home to safe havens through procedures then operated by the ROC.

Throughout the Second World War the Corps gained an enviable reputation for professionalism and accuracy, and despite advances in radar provided the only reliable warning of low-flying enemy aircraft. This was to be particularly useful during the V-1 flying bomb offensive sustained in late 1944 and early 1945. Of particular merit, and largely unknown, is the fact that hundreds of ROC personnel sailed with the Allied Invasion Force and saw active duty during the sea crossings. Proposals were also in hand to provide advance warning of possible enemy air attack from forward observation posts beyond the invasion beaches but this was never practised. Outside of aircraft observation, the Corps also worked with the Royal Navy plotting shipping movement from coastal posts, whilst also looking out for an invasion fleet for the Army during the early part of the war.

When peace came in May 1945, the ROC was stood down from active duty. In June of the same year King George VI presented the ROC with its own ensign in recognition of its magnificent contribution to the nation's defence.

During the early post-war years many new schemes were looked at to improve the Observer's lot. By 1950 the ROC was placed under the control of Fighter Command and in the same year the King agreed to become the Corps' Air Commodore in Chief. But the atom bomb had changed the face of warfare. In 1955 an assessment was carried out, looking at the implications of nuclear warfare. The findings were that the ROC was best placed to provide the warning and reporting organisation against this horrendous threat. At first this aspect was absorbed as a secondary task, but by the summer of 1965 it was the primary task. Since then, the ROC has been wholly involved in nuclear reporting, as it is called, forming an integral part of the United Kingdom Warning and Monitoring Organization (UKWMO).

To accomplish this new task the ROC has twenty-five reinforced Group Control Centres looking after 870 reinforced monitoring posts. The Coprs task now is to supply essential data on nuclear strikes and the arrival and intensity of fallout. This information enables officers of the UKWMO to provide national advice on the path radioactive dust is likely to take. It is universally accepted that the ROC's advice could save countless lives in any future nuclear war.

As in the past, the ROC remains a voluntary organisation with a current strength of 11,000, staffed by seventy full-time officers who provide the training element. There is a graded rank structure from senior officers down to Observers. All members wear the RAF style uniform, but with ROC insignia. The Corps badge consists of an Elizabethan Coast Watcher holding a lighted torch in his right hand and shielding his eyes with his left, above a scroll bearing the apt motto 'Forewarned is Forearmed'. (Some ROC insignia is shown on page 149).

Further details about the ROC can be obtained from: Headquarters Royal Observer Corps, Bentley Priory, Stanmore, Middlesex.

Appendix 1

BATTLE HONOURS OF THE ROYAL AIR
FORCE
First World War 1914-1918
(Note: The dates shown below are limiting dates.
The dates inscribed on the Standard of any
particular squadron are within those limiting
dates, eg, a squadron which went to France in
1916 and stayed to the end of the war would bear
the honour 'Western Front 1916-1918'.)

Battles	Conditions of Eligibility
Home Waters 1914-1918	For operations over home water, whether by land-based or carrier-borne aircraft.
Home Defence 1916-1918	For interception operations against enemy aircraft and Zeppelins raiding Great Britain.
Western Front 1914-1918	For operations in support of the Allied armies in Belgium and France.
Independent Force and Germany 1914-1918	For squadrons based in France as part of the Independent Force; and for operations over Germany, whether by squadrons based in France (as part of the Independent Force or not) or by carrier-borne aircraft.
Italian Front and Adriatic 1917-1918	For operations over the Trentino and neighbouring areas, in support of the Allied Armies on the Italian front; and for operations over the Adriatic and attacks on targets on the Dalmatian coast.
Aegean 1915-1918	For operations in the Aegean area against the German/Turkish land, sea, and air forces, including the attempt to force the Dardanelles, the Gallipoli campaign, and the various operations over the Aegean Sea and against Turkish coastal targets.
Macedonia 1916-1918	For operations in support of the Allied forces at Salonika and in their eventual advance and defeats of the Bulgarian armies in Macedonia and adjoining territories.
Mesopotamia 1915-1918	For operations over Mesopotamia and Persia in the liberation of Mesopotamia from the Turks.
Palestine 1916-1918	For operations over Palestine, Trans-Jordan and Syria, in the liberation of those territories from the Turks.
Arabia 1916-1917	For operations over Arabia, in support of the Arab revolt against the Turks.
Egypt 1914-1917	For operations by squadrons based in Egypt during the Turkish advance on the Suez Canal across Sinia; and for operations in the Western Desert against the Senussi.
East Africa 1915-1917	For operations over German East Africa during its conquest, whether by aircraft based in the country or operating from exterior seaplane bases.

South-West Africa 1915	For operations by South African personnel during the conquest of German South-West Africa.
Further battles to be selected from Army battle honours as required.	These battle honours are to be awarded to squadrons for intimate participation in land battles and will be determined ad hoc by the Air Council.

BETWEEN THE FIRST AND SECOND WORLD WAR

(Note: These honours are not inscribed on squadron Standards and are determined by the Air Council after scrutiny of squadron records).

Battles
South Persia 1918-1919
Iraq 1919-1920
Kurdistan 1919
Kurdistan 1922-1924
North-West Persia 1920
Afghanistan 1919-1920
Mahsud 1919-1920
Waziristan 1919-1920
North-West Frontier 1930-1931
Burma 1930-1932
Northern Kurdistan 1932
Mohmand 1933
North-West Frontier 1935-1939
Palestine 1936-1939
North Russia 1918-1919
South Russia 1919-1920
Somaliland 1920
Sudan 1920
Iraq 1923-1925
Iraq 1928-1929
Transjordan 1924
Mohmand 1927
Aden 1928
Aden 1929
Kurdistan 1930-1931
Aden 1934

SECOND WORLD WAR 1939-1945

(Note: The dates shown below are limiting dates. The dates inscribed on the Standard of any particular squadron are within those limiting dates, eg, a squadron which went to the Middle East in 1941 and stayed to the end of the war in Africa would bear the honour 'Egypt and Libya 1941-1943'.)

Battles	*Conditions of Eligibility*
Battle of Britain 1940	For interception operations by fighter squadrons in the Battle of Britain (August to October inclusive 1940).
Home Defence 1940-1945	For interception operations after the Battle of Britain, in defence of Great Britain and Northern Ireland against enemy aircraft and flying bombs (November 1940 to 1945).
Invasion Ports 1940	For bombing operations against German-occupied Channel ports, to dislocate enemy preparations for the invasion of England.
France and Low Countries 1939-1940	For operations in France and the Low Countries between the outbreak of war and the fall of France (3 September 1939 and 25 June 1940). Applicable both to squadrons operating from home and overseas bases.
Dunkirk	For operations covering the evacuation of the British Expeditionary Force and the French from Dunkirk, 26 May to 4 June 1940.
Meuse Bridges	For squadrons which participated in bombing operations against the crossings of the Meuse during the German breakthrough between Sedan and Dinant (12 to 14 May 1940).
Atlantic 1939-1945	For operations by aircraft of Coastal Command and others employed in the coastal role over the Atlantic Ocean from the outbreak of war to VE Day.
Bismarck	For operations by aircraft of Coastal Command associated with the action against the *Bismarck* (24 to 29 May 1941).

Channel and North Sea 1939-1945

For ship attack, anti-submarine and mining operations over the English Channel and North Sea from the outbreak of war to VE Day.

Tirpitz

For operations resulting in the sinking of the *Tirpitz*.

Norway 1940

For operations over Norway during the German invasion (9 April to 9 June 1940): applicable both to squadrons based in Norway and to those operating from home bases.

Baltic 1939-1945

For operations over the Baltic and its approach by squadrons of Bomber and Coastal Commands from the outbreak of war to VE Day.

Fortress Europe 1940-1944

For operations by aircraft based in the British Isles against targets in Germany, Italy and enemy-occupied Europe, from the fall of France to the invasion of Normandy.

The Dams

For squadrons participating in the operations for breeching the Moehne, Eider, Sopre and Kembs Dams (May 1943 to October 1944).

Dieppe

For squadrons which participated in the combined operations against Dieppe on 19 August 1942.

France and Germany

For operations over France, Belgium, Holland and Germany during the liberation of north-west Europe and the advance into the enemy's homeland, from the initiation of air action preparatory to the invasion of France to VE Day (April 1944 to 8 May 1945).

Biscay Ports 1940-1945

For operations over the Bay of Biscay ports from the fall of France to VE Day.

Ruhr 1940-1945

For bombardment of the Ruhr by aircraft of Bomber Command.

Berlin 1940-1945

For bombardment of Berlin by aircraft of Bomber Command.

German Ports 1940-1945

For bombardment of the German ports by aircraft of Bomber Command and Coastal Command.

Normandy 1944

For operations supporting the Allied landings in Normandy, and the establishment of the lodgement area.

Arnhem

For squadrons participating in the operations of the Allied Airborne Army (17 to 26 September 1944).

Walcheren

For operations in support of the capture of the Island of Walcheren (3 October to 9 November 1944).

Rhine

For operations in support of the battle for the Rhine crossing (8 February to 24 March 1945).

Biscay 1940-1945

For operations over the Bay of Biscay by aircraft of Coastal Command and Bomber Command aircraft loaned to Coastal Command, between the fall of France and VE Day (25 June 1940 to 8 May 1945).

East Africa 1940-1941

For operations over Kenya, the Sudan, Abyssinia, Italian Somaliland, British Somaliland, Eritrea and the Red Sea during the campaign which resulted in the conquest of Italian East Africa (10 June 1940 to 27 November 1941).

Greece 1940-1941

For operations over Albania and Greece during the Italian and German invasion, whether carried out by squadrons based in Greece or operating from external bases (28 October 1940 to 30 April 1941).

South-East
Europe 1942-1945 For operations over Yugo-slavia, Hungary, Romania, Bulgaria and Greece.

Egypt and
Libya 1940-1943 For operations in the defence of Egypt and the conquest of Libya, from the outbreak of war against Italy to the retreat of the Axis Forces into Tunisia (10 June 1940 to 6 February 1943).

El Alamein For operations during the retreat to El Alamein and subsequent actions (June 1942 to November 1942).

El Hamma For operations at El Hamma in support of the Battle of Mareth Line, by squadrons operationally controlled by Air Head-quarters, Western Desert (including No 205 Group squadrons engaged in tactical bombing), during the period 20/21 March to 28 March 1943 inclusive.

Malta
1940-1942 For squadrons participating in defensive, offensive and reconnaissance operations from Malta during the period of enemy action against the island (10 June 1940 to 31 December 1942).

North Africa
1942-1943 For operations in connection with the campaign in French North Africa, from the initial landings in Algeria to the explusion of the Axis Powers from Tunisia (8 November 1942 to 13 May 1943).

Mediterranean
1940-1943 For operations over Italy, Sicily and the Medi-terranean and Aegean Seas by aircraft based in the Mediterranean area (includ-ing reconnaissance convoy protection, mining, and attacks on enemy ports and shipping) between the entry of Italy into the war and the initiation of air action pre-

Mediterranean
(continued) paratory to the Sicilian campaign (10 June 1940 to 30 June 1943).

Sicily 1943 For operations in further-ance of the conquest of Sicily (1 July to 17 August 1943) by aircraft based in Africa, Malta and Sicily or operations over Italy.

Italy 1943-1945
Salerno For operations in support of the Allied landings in Italy (9 September to 16 September 1943).

Gustav Line For operations participating in the operations against the Gustav Line (May 1944).

Gothic Line For air operations in support of the breaching of the Gothic Line (August to September 1944).

Pacific
1941-1945 For operations against the Japanese in the Pacific theatre, throughout the war with Japan (8 December 1941 to 15 August 1945).

Malaya
1941-1942 For operations against the Japanese in Malaya, Sumatra and Java, from 8 December 1941 until the final capitulation in Java on 12 March 1942.

Eastern Waters
1941-1945 For operations over waters east of the Mediterranean and Red Sea, including the Indian Ocean, the Bay of Bengal, the Java Sea and South China Sea, through-out the war with Japan (this honour is not only for coastal squadrons).

Burma
1941-1942 For operations in defence of Rangoon and in support of British Forces during the Japanese invasion of Burma (December 1941 to May 1942).

Arakan
1942-1944 For operations by fighter, bomber, and transport squadrons in support of the first and second Arakan campaigns (November 1942

Arakan *(continued)*	to February 1943, and November 1943 to March 1944.	Iraq 1941	For operations in the defeat of Rashid Ali's rebellion (2 May to 31 May 1941).
North Burma 1943-1944	For the air supply of General Wingate's first long-range penetration into North Burma (February-June 1943) and for the air supply and support of his second expedition (5 March to 26 June 1944).	Habbaniya	For units engaged in the defence of Habbaniya (30 April to 6 May 1941).
		Syria 1941	For operations over Syria during the campaign against the Vichy French (8 June to 12 July 1941).
Manipur 1944	For operations in support of the besieged forces at Imphal (March to July 1944).	Madagascar 1942	For operations by squadrons of the South African Air Force during and after the landings in Madagascar in 1942.

Burma 1944-1945 — For operations during the 14th Army's advance from Imphal to Rangoon, the coastal amphibious assaults, and the Battle of Pegu Yomas (August 1944 to August 1945).

Special Operations — For operations by squadrons regularly assigned to special duties, ie, the succour of resistance movements in enemy-occupied countries by dropping supplies and by introducing and evacuating personnel by air, from the formation of the first special duty flight (20 August 1940) after the fall of France to VE and VJ Days.

Arctic 1940-1945 — For operations over the Arctic by squadrons of Coastal Command in Iceland, Russia and the Shetlands.

Russia 1941-1945 — For operations from Russian bases in support of Russian offensive operations.

RAF SQUADRONS TO RECEIVE THE BATTLE HONOUR 'SOUTH ATLANTIC 1982'

Extract from MOD News release 61/83 dated 25 October 'Falklands Battle Honours Announced'.
The Squadrons of the Royal Air Force, which saw service between 2 April and 14 June 1982 south of 35° South and north of 60° South or took part in an operational sortie south of Ascension Island will be awarded the battle honour 'South Atlantic 1982'. The squadrons concerned are set out below.

No 1 (F) Squadron)	Harrier
No 18 Squadron	Chinook
No 42 Squadron	Nimrod
No 44 Squadron	Vulcan
No 47 Squadron	Hercules
No 50 Squadron	Vulcan
No 51 Squadron	Nimrod
No 55 Squadron	Victor
No 57 Squadron	Victor
No 63 Squadron RAF Regiment	Rapier
No 70 Squadron	Hercules
No 101 Squadron	Vulcan
No 120 Squadron	Nimrod
No 201 Squadron	Nimrod
No 206 Squadron	Nimrod

Glossary:
Naval, Military and Air Force Terms

The Services have a language all their own, where speech is essentially free speech evolved from centuries of tradition. Likely, but not exclusive, explanations of some sayings are given below. First the Navy:

Freeze the balls of a brass monkey — Despite first thoughts, this is all to do with gunnery. The round lead shot fired from early cannons was made to a critical size. Very hot or very cold weather would cause the shot to expand or contract. To slow down this process, shot would be prepared on brass trays which acted as an insulator. However, in very cold weather, the shot was prone to stick to the softer brass tray surface — hence the saying. The brass tray was known colloquially as a 'monkey', which to the sailor meant small. A Powder Monkey was the small keg of powder used as a propellant to the shot. The boys who brought the powder from the magazine to the cannon lines were also known as 'powder monkeys'.

Wait till you see the whites of their eyes — This was coined by ships' gunners in Nelson's time. Ship to ship bombardment took place in close proximity, and while ship's guns had no sights nor any mechanical means of judging distance, experience dictated that at 400 yards it was possible to hear the conversation on an opponent's ship, and at 200 yards the whites of the enemy's eyes could be seen. Using these rough and ready methods of measurement, Nelson's sailors were able to fire with reasonable accuracy. Nelson is believed to have used the expression frequently in battle. Nelson was also the first to realise the effect of bouncing cannon balls of the sea to achieve a greater effect. An effect later taken up by Barnes Wallis in his bouncing bomb.

Left hanging Judas — A rope is said to be left hanging Judas when it is dangling over the ship's side for no good reason. The phrase is used colloquially by sailors who having arranged a date with a girlfriend, wait and she does not turn up.

Soojey-moojey — This is a slang term used by sailors to describe a mixture of soda, soft soap, soda ash and other cleaning materials dissolved in a tub of hot water, and used for scrubbing decks.

To be three sheets to the wind — This is a sailing term when the ship, through the poor setting of sail, veers and luffs almost out of control. Hence the colloquial meaning for being drunk.

Tell it to the Marines — King Charles II was reputed to be talking to one of his captains when a sailor mentioned that he had seen fish that flew. King Charles was rather doubtful of the accuracy of the statement and, turning to a Marine officer, asked his opinion. The Marine officer informed the King that he had also seen fish that flew. 'Flying fish, flying fish!' the King announced. 'Well, should I in future have occasion to doubt any statement, I will first tell it to the Marines'.

It's an ill wind that blows no man good — This is derived from the fact that every wind is a fair wind for some ship under sail. The expression is found in Shakespeare's *Henry VI* Part II and also *Henry VI* Part III.

Like the Navy, the Army has its own peculiar way of saying things with a jargon and list of abbreviations almost unintelligible to the common man. The Army's approach to terminology is perhaps more clincial than the Navy's with the emphasis on accuracy, clarity and brevity. Many RAF terms are derived from, or at least owe their origin to military rather than naval descriptions. It is perhaps for their profound utterances Army commanders are remembered, such as those attributed to Arthur Wellesley, Duke of Wellington (1769 to 1852):

'Nothing except a battle lost can be half so melancholy as a battle won.' (Despatch from Waterloo, June 1815)

'What a glorious thing must be a victory, sir'. 'The greatest tragedy in the world, madam, except a defeat.' (1835)

'My rule always was to do the business of the day in the day'. (1835)

'I don't know what effect these men will have upon the enemy, but by God, they terrify me.' (1809)

'All the business of war, and indeed all the business of life, is to endeavour to find out what you don't know by what you do; that's what I called guessing what was on the other side of the hill.'

Although phrases such as 'whizz oh', 'prang', 'in the drink' and even 'Prunery' have evolved as essentially RAF expressions, they represent slang born of a particular era, which was not really perpetuated in the post-war RAF. Perhaps it was not encouraged as part of the new Service's refined jet-age image. However the following provides a short Glossary of RAF slang.

Balbo, A — A large formation of aircraft.
Bale out — To take to one's parachute.
Bind, A — People who obstruct one.
Black, A — Something badly done, a 'bad show'.
Blitz, A solid lump of — Large formation of enemy aircraft.
Blonde job, A — Young woman with fair hair.
Bomphleteers — Airmen engaged on the early pamphlet raids.
Brassed off — Diminutive of 'browned off'.
Brolly — Parachute.
Browned off, To be — 'Fed up'.
Bumps and Circuits — Circuits and landings.
Bus driver — A bomber pilot.
Buttoned up — A job properly completed, 'mastered'.
Completely Cheesed — No hope at all.
Cope — To accomplish, to deal with.
Crabbing along — Flying near the ground or water.
Deck, Crack down on — To 'pancake' an aircraft.
Dog Fight — Aerial scrap.
Drill, The right — Correct method of doing anything.
Drink, In the — To come down into the sea.
Dud — Applied to weather when unfit to fly.
Duff gen. — Dud information.
Dust bin — Rear gunner's lower position in aircraft.
Erk, An — A beginner in any job.
Fan — The propeller.
Fireworks, Mr — Armaments Officer.
Flak — Anti-aircraft fire.
Flap — A disturbance, general excitement.
Fox, To — To do something clever or rather cunning.
Gen. (pron. jen) — General information of any kind whatever.
George — The automatic pilot.
Get Cracking — Get going.

Gong, To collect a — To get a medal.
Greenhouse — Cockpit cover.
Hedge-hopping — Flying so low that the aircraft appears to hop over the hedges.
Hurryback — A Hurricane fighter.
Jink away — Sharp manoeuvre. Sudden evasive action of aircraft.
Kipper Kite — Coastal Command aircraft which convoy fishing fleets in the North and Irish Seas.
Kite — An aeroplane.
Laid on, To have — To produce anything, such as supplies.
Mae West — Life-saving stole, or waistcoat, inflated if wearer falls into sea.
Mickey Mouse — Bomb-dropping mechanism.
Muscle in — To take advantage of a good thing.
Office — Cockpit of aircraft.
Organize — To 'win' a wanted article.
Pack up — Cease to function.
Peel off, To — Break formation to engage enemy.
Play pussy — Hide in the clouds.
Pleep — A squeak, rather like a high note klaxon.
Plug away — Continue to fire. Keep after target.
Pukka gen. — Accurate information.
Pulpit — Cockpit of aircraft.
Quick squirt — Short sharp burst of machine-gun fire.
Quickie — Short for above.
Rang the bell — Got good results.
Rings — Rank designation on officer's cuffs.
Ropey — Uncomplimentary adjective. 'A ropey landing', 'A ropey type', 'A ropey evening', etc.
Scraper — The thin ring on Squadron Leader's rank braid.
Screamed downhill — Executed a power dive.
Scrub — To washout.
Second Dickey — Second pilot.
Shooting a line — Exaggerated talk, generally about one's own prowess.
Shot Down in Flames — Crossed in love. Severe reprimand.
Snake about — Operational aerobatics.
Spun in — A bad mistake. Analogy from an aircraft spinning out of control into the ground.
Stationmaster — Commanding Officer of Station.
Stooge — Deputy, ie, second pilot, or any assistant.
Stooging about — Delayed landing for various reasons. Flying slowly over an area. Patrolling.
Synthetic — Not the real thing. Also applied to ground training.
Tail End Charlie — Rear gunner in large bombing aircraft or rear aircraft of a formation.
Tear off a strip — To reprimand, take down a peg.
Touch bottom — Crash.
Toys — A great deal of training equipment is termed toys.
Train, Driving the — Leading more than one squadron into battle.
Type — Classification — usually referring to people. Good, Bad, Ropey, Poor type.

View — RAF personnel always take a 'view' of things. Good view, Poor view, Dim view. Long-distance view, Lean view, Outside view, 'Ropey' view.

Wizard — Really first class, superlative, attractive, ingenious.

Most RAF terms and expressions are derived from the two parent services. This glossary is designed to give an insight into the more widely used Service terms.

Adjutant — From the Latin *aduitans,* meaning assisting. A commanding officer's principal staff officer; the office confers no additional rank. The title was first used by Jesuits, founded by Ignatius Loyola in 1543, but it is not known how it crept into military usage.

Adjutant General — The member of the Army Board responsible for personnel.

Air Officer — Collective description given to the five most senior commissioned ranks in the RAF, (in ascending order) Air Commodore, Air Vice-Marshal, Air Marshal, Air Chief Marshal, Marshal of the Royal Air Force.

Admiral (Adm) — The word has been traced from the Arabic Amir-al-Bahr, which means Commander of the Seas. The word is believed to have been brought to this country by the Crusaders. The four ranks derived, in ascending order, are: Rear-Admiral, Vice-Admiral, Admiral, Admiral of the Fleet. In the same order the ranks in the RAF would be: Air Vice-Marshal, Air Marshal, Air Chief Marshal, Marshal of the Royal Air Force, and in the Army: Major General, Lieutenant-General, General, Field Marshal.

Aide-de-Camp (ADC) — The title for a commissioned officer in personal attendance on a general staff officer. There may be honorary ADCs appointed to HM The Queen, or these may be full-time appointments. It is a French term which originally denoted an officer attached to a commander as a carrier of his orders.

Aiguillette — The corded ornamentation worn over the shoulder, particularly by aides-de-camp, but also including other officers and soldiers assigned to duties with the Royal Household. The term dates back to when armour was worn. The 'Aglets', as they were called, were small lengths of plaited cord attached to a leather undergarment and used to attach armour. When armour was no longer worn, aiguillettes remained as a symbol of knightly chivalrousness, and an association with the monarch. The word is French in origin.

Articles of War — This refers to the Naval discipline act and defines the offences and their penalties under the act.

Artillery — A generic term which previously denoted a tube weapon that fired shells as opposed to bullets, and was too heavy to be operated by a single soldier. Today its use covers field guns, mortars and missiles.

Air Member for Personnel (AMP) — The Air Force Board representative for all manning and personnel matters.

Air Member for Supply and Organisation (AMSO) — The Air Force Board representative for all supply and organisation matters.

Assistant and Adjutant and Quartermaster General (AA and QMG) — The title given to the senior administrative staff officer in a division. Now replaced by the title Deputy Chief of Staff (DCOS).

Avast — From the Italian word *basta,* meaning enough; its usage today means stop.

Aye-Aye — From the old English 'aye', meaning eyes, a term used by sailors when a boat containing officers approached. Today it is used as an acknowledgement to an order.

Bag or Baggage — An army on the move was traditionally supported by the 'camp followers' who travelled with the equipment (baggage) at the rear of the column. Man's need being what it is, a proportion of the camp followers were women, hence the rather discourteous slang for a woman. More to the point, however, supplies were carried on pack saddles called 'bats', so hence the title 'batman' (qv).

Batman — From the French *bat* meaning pack saddle. A batman was placed in charge of baggage horses. Today the term is used for a Mess steward who looks after an officer's personal accommodation and clothing.

Battalion — A collective term similar in usage to the RAF Wing, which denotes the basic infantry unit commanded by a Lieutenant-Colonel and consisting of 500 to 700 all ranks. A battalion may contain three or four companies plus a company of support weapons. The word comes from the Latin *battuere* meaning to strike, and *battalia,* meaning an army in battle array. Strictly, therefore, the word battalion could be interpreted as 'battle unit'.

Battery — The title given to an artillery sub-unit of the equivalent size to a company; a battery is sub-divided into troops.

Battle Honour — A title, gained from a successful battle encounter, enscribed on Regimental colours or accoutrements. The earliest battle honour is Tangier and is borne by the Royal Scots, The Queens, Grenadier and Coldstream Guards, 1662-1689.

Bayonet — A short sword attached to a rifle for close quarter fighting. Known in infantry regiments as a sword. It was originally designed as an addition to the musket to enable it to be used as a pike.

Bearskin — The ceremonial headdress of the foot guards. The origin is to be found in a simple type of fisherman's cap around which a strip of fur was attached. The fur hat became traditional headdress for Grenadiers, horse and foot soldiers throughout Europe. It was adopted by foot guards in Britain prior to the Crimean War in 1854. Sometimes referred to, incorrectly, as a busby.

Berserk — Scandinavian mythology recalls a 'rambo' type war hero who always went into battle dressed in a bearskin. Whilst being 'macho' it was also quite warm! However, the Norse name for this individual was 'Ber Sark' meaning bear shirt. When the Vikings came on their cultural visits to the north-east of England, history recalls that the visits sadly degenerated into rape and pillage with quite a lot of shouting! Ber Sark was known to be on one or two of these unsolicited visits and gained quite a reputation amongst the local inhabitants for his colourful performances: hence — going Berserk.

Bikini — Bikini Atoll lies within the Marshall Islands and was chosen as the American testing zone for the atomic bomb. A nuclear explosion is characterised by a blinding flash of light (amongst other things). In the same year as the Bikini Atoll tests, a French fashion designer (Louis Reard) produced his first designs for a two-piece swim suit. He called his design a Bikini because of the stunning effect it had on a woman in enhancing her beauty, equating this beauty to the power and brilliance of the atomic explosion.

Billet — Literally the word means a piece of wood with which those requiring lodging used to bang or knock on a door. The word is taken from the French *billet,* — meaning a letter. The letter referred to the written demand from a king to provide accommodation for soldiers.

Biscuit — A term used to describe a military mattress in the shape of two squares of coir-filled canvas placed on top of a soldier's bed. The new type of mattress has replaced the biscuit.

Boatswain — This is the oldest rank in the RN and is derived from the Saxon *Swein,* meaning servant. Today it describes a special duties officer in charge of anchors, cables, hawsers, rigging and other sea gear; it is pronounced Bo'sun.

Bombardier — A rank in the Royal Artillery equivalent to a Corporal in the Army and slightly senior to a Leading Rating in the Navy.

Brevet — As a reward for distinguished service an officer may be awarded brevet rank above that for which he is paid. This confers seniority in the Army but not within his Regiment. Also a title sometimes given to RAF flying badges.

Brig — An abbreviation of Brigantine or Brigandine, a fast two-masted sailing vessel used by brigands or pirates in the Mediterranean Sea.

Brigade — A tactical formation comprising three or more battalions with supporting arms.

Brigade major — The senior staff officer in a brigade. Now replaced by the title Chief of Staff (COS).

Brigadier (Brig) — The most junior general staff officer, one rank above Colonel and one rank below Major-General. He may command a brigade or be a staff officer. Traditionally the commander of a brigade. The rank is the equivalent of Commodore in the RN and Air Commodore in the RAF.

Buccaneer — A French term which originally meant the beef sellers who dwelt in Haiti, derived from the word *boucan,* a dealer in dried beef. When their meat-selling trade died out, they took to lawlessness and the word became synonymous with pirates.

Bulwarks — Solid woodwork, waist high or higher, running round the weather deck of a ship.

Bulkhead — Originally, the removable partitions between cabins; today the word refers to the permanent vertical partitions within the ship's structure.

Bumboat — This term is believed to have come from the word boomboat, a boat that tied up at the ship's boom to trade with the crew.

Busby — The ceremonial headdress of the Hussar regiments and the Royal Horse Artillery *(see* Bearskin). It was first worn by Hungarian light horsemen and was later adopted by other nations. British Hussars adopted the busby in the mid-19th century after a short romance with the shako.

Captain — This title may in part owe its origin to the Saxon title or honour *caput,* meaning the head or chief. It was first established as a rank in 1380. Captain lies between the ranks of Commander and Commodore in the Royal Navy. There is no such rank in the mercantile marine — the commander of a merchant ship is titled Master and his ship's officers equate to mates. In the RAF Group Captain is the equivalent rank. In the Army the rank of Captain is senior to a full Lieutenant but junior to a Major; and equivalent in the RAF to a Flight Lieutenant. The modern derivation for the army comes from the French *capitaine,* which means the head of a company or small unit of soldiers.

Carabiner(s) — The title is derived from the long horse pistol with which regiments of horses were armed. The pistol was later replaced by the rifle and mounted cavalry with rifles were known as carabiners *(see* Dragoon, Hussar and Lancer).

Cashier — A title used when an officer is court martialled for financial offences.

Char — A slang term for tea used by soldiers, from the Urdu word.

Chart — From the Latin *charta* and Greek *charte* meaning a kind of papyrus. Early English nautical charts were known as 'sea cards' or 'scacards'.

Chevron — The distinguishing mark of rank worn on the sleeve by NCOs. The term is believed to be derived from the 'V' formation used by Roman soldiers in battle. The commanding soldier of the formation wore a V on his arm to distinguish him as the leader.

Chief Petty Officer (CPO) — Rank given to a rating one below Fleet Chief Petty Officer and next above Petty Officer. This rank equates to Staff Sergeant in the Army and Flight Sergeant in the RAF.

Close Quarters — In the days of Pirate ships it was customary for the attacking ship to draw alongside its prey. Then, the 'Burt Lancasters' of the time would swing across (at the same time clutching a cutlass in their teeth), knock hell out of the poor merchantman's crew, scuttle off with the booty and then put it in the wardrobe room *(see* Wardroom). This formula worked well for a time, but the merchant ship Captains (Masters) soon got wise and built 'Close fights', or wooden defence positions on the decks. Pirates who so boarded these 'close fight'-protected ships came in for a rude awakening. Instead of hand-to-hand fighting the boarders received a hail of shot from the 'close fight' and subsequently gave up pirateering as a bad job. In modern usage close came to mean 'close' as in near, as opposed to the original 'closed'.

Colonel — From the Italian *colonello,* a little column. The rank between Lieutenant-Colonel and Brigadier in the Army. In the RAF the rank equates to Group Captain, and in the RN to Captain.

Colour — The term used to denote the banners of infantry regiments. There are two kinds: a Queen's Colour and a Regimental Colour. The Royal Artillery and rifle regiments do not have colours. The Royal Artillery use the guns themselves as a rallying point, and as rifle regiments were often used as scouts they saw no need to advertise their presence.

Commander — A Naval title introduced by William III in 1827, one rank below Captain and one rank above Lieutenant Commander. In the RAF the rank equates to Wing Commander, and in the Army to Lieutenant-Colonel.

Compo — A shortened title for composite rations — a ration made up of a number of items all with a high nutritive value.

Commodore — This is a temporary rank to which a naval Captain may be appointed. On ending his tour as a Commodore he will either revert to the rank of Captain or be promoted to Rear-Admiral. In the RAF the rank equates to Air Commodore, and in the Army to Brigadier, but the Army and RAF equivalents are permanent ranks.

Corporal (Cpl) — From the French word *caporal* but originally from the Italian *Capo di* meaning head of a section. A junior non-commissioned rank in the Army senior to a Lance-Corporal but junior to a Sergeant. In the RAF the rank equates to Corporal. The Naval equivalent is Leading Rating, which is a slightly junior rank.

Court martial. — A legally constituted court for the purpose of trying persons subject to military law.

Coxswain — A title given to a sailor in charge of a boat, today a senior rating in small ships. The word comes from the Saxon word *cock,* meaning a small rowing boat, and *swain* meaning servant.

Crab — (as in RAF personnel) This affectionate, not derogatory, title was coined by the members of the RNAS. Naval aircraft suffered more than land aircraft due to the erosion effect of salt-sea spray. To reduce the erosion RNAS ratings applied a thick jelly-like graphite grease to the exposed metal parts of the Naval aircraft. The grease bore the local name of 'Crabfat' and was the same hue as the first blue RAF uniform that appeared. At first 'Crabfat' described the RAF, later shortened to just 'Crab'.

Cruiser — Today this title refers to a large surface gun- or missile-armed warship capable of spending long periods at sea without support. The word comes from *crusal,* meaning a fast, light vessel used by pirates in the Mediterranean Sea. They were not fighting ships but rather raiding ships carrying few guns.

Deadline — During the American Civil War of 1861-1865, Captain Henry Wirz looked after a PoW Camp at Andersonville which contained over 30,000 Union prisoners. To prevent their escape Wirz established a literal deadline — a line around the camp but inside the walls. If any prisoner crossed this, it would be assumed that he would be escaping and he would be shot. Wirz was subsequently hanged as a war criminal, but his legacy is a term that means a fixed and unchangeable date.

Destroyer — A medium-size high-speed warship normally tasked to support strike and amphibious forces. This type of ship is similar to a frigate but more powerful and strongly armed.

Dhobi — This is believed to be an old Indian term dating back to the days of the Raj, and is a much used word today referring to personal laundry.

Division — A common naval term referring to the tactical sub-division of a squadron or an administrative unit of a ship's company. A ship's company may, for example, 'muster by divisions'. Also an Army term describing two or more brigades.

Dragoon — The name dragoon comes from dragon, which was the nickname of a blunderbus-type musket with which some early cavalry units were armed. Troops were at first called dragooners. Dragoons were officially introduced into the British Army at the time of the Civil War. They were essentially cavalrymen who could also fight on foot, and were sometimes referred to as mounted infantry (*see* Hussar, Lancer).

Draught — The vertical depth from waterline to the lowest point of the keel or propellers.

Echelon — A term used to denote a sub-divison of an HQ or a separate level of command or formation.

Ensign — The title given to a national flag flown by warships. The word comes from the old Norman *enseigne* and the Anglo-Saxon *segne,* each meaning flag. The RN borrowed the word from the Army in the 16th century. The word was also used to describe the lowest commissioned rank in the infantry, equivalent to a Cornet in the cavalry.

Epaulette — Originally a strap on the shoulder to prevent a belt slipping off, it has become more decorative and serves to indicate the rank of the wearer.

Executive Officer — The second in command of a ship.

Exon — An appointment held by retired Army Captains, of whom there are four relating to a rank within the Yeoman of the Guard.

Face the music — Those caught fiddling the books in the Army would, after Court Martial, be cashiered. Part of the ceremony included a full parade with drummers. The officer being cashiered would face the drummers whilst his misdemeanours were read out to the assembly and his uniform stripped of its insignia — hence to face the music. History does not record if the tune was 'Hey Big Spender'!

Field Marshal (FM) — The highest rank in the Army. A Field Marshal never retires. In the RAF the equivalent rank is Marshal of the RAF, and in the RN Admiral of the Fleet.

Fifth Column — This term dates from the Spanish Civil War and was coined by General Emile Mola in 1936. He was asked if his four columns of troops advancing on Madrid were sufficient to take the city. He replied that he already had a 'Fifth Column' inside Madrid ready to strike. He was referring to his covert spies and saboteurs. Ernest Hemingway later popularised this expression in his play of the same name.

Flag Captain — An officer appointed to command a flag ship.

Flag Lieutenant — An officer of Lieutenant or Lieutenant Commander rank on the personal staff of a flag officer, equating to a personal staff officer (PSO) in the RAF.

Flak — The term Flak is simply an acronym from the German Fliegerabwehrkanone, meaning anti-aircraft gun.

Flash in the pan — The flintlock rifle depended on a flint to spark and ignite the primary charge in the 'pan' which was positioned below the hammer. This would then set off the charge in the barrel and off went the shot. However, this was not a guaranteed method; quite often there would be a flash in the pan as the primary charge ignited, but nothing else. Hence our meaning today as an initial burst of enthusiasm or effort, but nothing to follow it up.

Flight — A collective term used to describe a group of men equivalent in the Army to platoon. It may also describe a group of aircraft, where two to four flights may comprise a squadron.

Foot Guards — The Guards Regiments of the Grenadier, Coldstream, Scots, Irish and Welsh Guards.

Forecastle — On early sailing ships high wooden castles were often built at the fore and after end of ships. However, they were not totally successful and soon fell out of use. Today the term means the foremost weather deck, pronounced fo'csle.

Free Lance — This term is believed to have been put about by Sir Walter Scott circa 1820. The allusion is to mediaeval mercenary knights who, for a few extra bob, would support the best payer, thus they were free from allegiance (see also Lance Corporal). There is a suggestion also that the Lance Corporal's one Chevron badge is representative of a broken lance.

Frigate — This name was given to ships used in the Mediterranean Sea which had both oars and sail. Today the title refers to a medium-sized warship of good speed tasked as an escort ship, or available for independent deployment.

Full Tilt — The suggestion here is that only when a Mediaeval knight was close to his opponent did he lower or tilt his lance as it was difficult to hold it in the tilted position for long periods. Thus, and after the run-in to the prey, he would be travelling at great speed — the slang usage to mean at top speed.

Fusilier — The title originally referred to infantry armed with a light weapon or 'fusil', which could be worn over the back and shoulders supported by a sling. The first fusiliers, the Royal Fusiliers, were raised to guard an artillery train. A private soldier in the Royal Fusiliers is known as a Fusilier.

Gash — A slang term shared by the three Services, but with different meanings. The Navy and Royal Marine usage is to describe rubbish, in the RAF it means free or bonus.

General (Gen) — The rank immediately below that of Field Marshal. In the RAF the rank equates to Air Chief Marshal and in the RN to Admiral.

Geneva Convention — A code of behaviour in wartime governing the treatment of the sick, wounded, civilians and prisoners of war, first agreed by the European powers in 1865 and subsequently much amended.

Gentlemen-at-Arms — Members of Her Majesty's bodyguard of the Honourable Corps of Gentlemen-at-Arms, a small bodyguard of retired officers of field rank.

Glass House — Simply from the Victorian military prison at Aldershot which, in keeping with the time, had an extensive glass roof.

Gollock — A Malay term which describes a heavy-duty field knife or machete used for cutting undergrowth. The term is confined to the RN and RM.

Gone for a Burton — An RAF expression meaning to have been shot down or lost from use. The expression was derived from a Burton Ales advert which always showed a group of people, but with quite obviously one person missing — the caption was 'Gone for a Burton'. Weight was added to this expression since the sea was known in slang as 'the drink'.

Gorget — Originally a piece of armour worn around the neck. When the wearing of armour fell into disuse, the gorget continued to be worn as an officer's badge of rank up to its abolition in 1830. In the course of time, the patch of cloth, button and small cord which had supported the gorget became themselves a distinction to be worn on the collar in a variety of colours to indicate the wearer's status. They are sometimes referred to as 'tabs'. Today, scarlet gorgets are worn by full Colonels and higher ranks. RAF officer cadets at Cranwell are distinguished by white gorgets.

Gremlin — An RAF expression dating from the between the war years on the North-West frontier of India. The word is an amalgam of 'Grimm' (as in Grimm's Fairy Tales) and 'Fremlin', the brewer. The hot and dusty atmosphere of India caused many problems in aircraft leading to considerable unserviceability. The name conjured up by the aircrew to place blame was the Gremlins. Seemingly the only book in the Station library was Grimm's Fairy Tales and the only beer in the bar was Fremlins.

Grenadier — Literally the word means a man who throws a grenade. In former days each regiment had a grenadier company, but now the grenade is a general infantry weapon. Grenades were first used in 1594; the first regular troops to be armed with them were the French Army in 1667. The first grenadiers in the British Army appeared in 1677 as a company attached to each regiment of foot guards and troop of Household Cavalry. Grenadiers were considered as elite troops and in later times the word was associated with a mark of honour.

Grenade — From the French nickname of 'pomme granate' — seed apple — the seed representing the fragmentation when the bomb explodes.

Grog — A measure of rum watered to the ratio two of water to one of rum. The word dates back to Admiral Vernon's time; in 1740 he first ordered the issue of rum with water. His naval dress was made of a coarse material called grogram, a kind of taffeta, whence came the nickname 'Old Grog'.

Grot — Royal Navy and Royal Marine slang to describe living quarters, particularly sleeping accommodation.

Guardsman — A soldier of the foot guards, equivalent to a Private in other regiments and to an Aircraftman in the RAF.

Guidons — The swallow-tailed banners that were the colours of regiments of Hussars, Dragoons and Lancers; the Lancers and Hussars no longer have them. Guidons should be saluted like Colours and Standards in the RAF. Guidons should not be confused with the swallow-tailed Gonfannons, which are purely religious banners that hang vertically from transverse bars at the top of the staff.

Gun — An artillery weapon that is breech loaded, as opposed to a mortar which is muzzle loaded, or a rifle which is hand held.

Gunwale — From the Anglo-Saxon word *Wala* or *wale,* meaning a strip or ridge. On the upper decks of early sailing ships guns were fired over plankings that had been reinforced by 'wales', hence the term 'gunwale', pronounced 'gunn'l'.

Hammock — A hanging canvas bed formerly allotted to midshipmen and ratings. The word is ascribed to Christoper Columbus, who in 1498 noticed that natives of the Bahamas slept on woven cotton nets called 'hammacs'.

Havoc — This term is believed originally to have been a battle cry that meant to attack without mercy or quarters.

Hawse — The area between the bows of a vessel where the anchor is stowed, a hawser being the long length of rope or cable that secures the anchor to the ship.

Heads — Title given to the latrine on board a ship.

Hooker — An American expression coined from the antics of General Joseph Hooker. During the American Civil War thousands of troops were concentrated in defence of Washington under his command. Morale being important, an extensive red light district grew up to look after the Army's needs. The red light district soon became known as Hooker Division and the ladies of fortune 'Hookers'.

Horse Artillery (The Royal) — The title given to the *corps d'élite* of the Royal Regiment of Artillery. It maintains one horsed battery for ceremonial duties.

Horse Marine — A title originally given to the 17th Lancers when they were embarked aboard ship for a brief period. Today the term is used as slang for an unhandy man.

Household Cavalry — The regiments that form the Household Cavalry are the Life Guards and the Royal Horse and Dragoon Guards, all of which were raised by Charles II. The Life Guards were formed from the Cavaliers who fought for Charles I, and the Royal Horse Guards were recruited from members of Colonel Crook's Regiment, which had fought for the Parliamentarians.

Hussar —Believed to be of Polish or Hungarian origin, relating to light cavalry around 1458-90. King Carvinus Matthias of Hungary ordered that every twenty houses were to provide one horseman for his army, and the word derived from the Hungarian *huzz,* meaning twenty, and *ar,* meaning pay. The British Hussars first appeared between 1681 and 1684 called dragoons, but later became hussar regiments in line with the Continental description of light cavalry. The term was adopted in 1807 and the dress uniform is a modification of Hungarian national costume. Today the hussar regiments are armoured (*see* Lancer/Dragoon).

Jacob's Ladder — A flexible portable ladder consisting of rope strings and wooden rounds.

Jerry Can — The quartermaster petrol cans on issue in North Africa during the early days the Second World War lacked the durability of the Africa Korps equivalent, so much so that home-produced cans were dumped in favour of the German edition. The better-designed German petrol cans were simply known as 'Jerry Cans'.

Khaki — From the Urdu *khak* meaning dusty, drab or off colour. The khaki-coloured dress was first introduced in India in 1840. Its introduction was the result of observation and trial by Sir Harry Lumsden to produce a more comfortable and lighter dress to wear than the traditional red. It was also a first attempt at camouflage dress. It was fully adopted as hot climate wear in 1880-82, and became the home colour for battle dress in 1913-14.

Killick — A small general-purpose anchor; the badge design of a leading seaman included a small anchor, so the nickname arose, relating to the leading seaman badge.

Lance Corporal — The original title was *lance spesate,* an Italian word which means 'broken lance'. It is believed that a Lance Corporal was a man at arms or a trooper who, having broken his lance on the enemy and lost his horse, was used as an assistant or additional foot soldier until such time as he got his horse back or found a new mount. Today, Lance Corporal is a rank between Private and Corporal distinguished by one chevron worn on each arm.

Lancer — The title of lancer was introduced in the British Army in 1816, based upon a Polish idea. During the Napoleonic wars and after, lancer regiments proliferated throughout Europe. They were essentially light cavalry, of which the senior regiment was the Fifth Royal Irish Lancers dating from 1858. Lancers were among the hussars and dragoons of the light cavalry brigade who achieved fame during the Charge of the Light Brigade at Balaclava in 1854.

Landsman — A term, not necessarily derogatory, often used by seamen to describe a non-sailor.

Larboard — An old name describing the port side of a ship.

Leading Seaman — A naval non-commissioned rank, junior to Petty Officer, and senior to Able Seaman. In the RAF the rank equates to Corporal.

Lieutenant (Lt RN) — The word is derived from the French *lieu* meaning 'in place of'. By the mid-

19th century, Captains were given executive officers to replace them on watches, etc. Thus the Lieutenant on watch was 'in place of' the Captain. There are three ranks of Lieutenant: Sub-Lieutenant, Lieutenant, Lieutenant Commander. In the RAF, and in the same order, these ranks equate to Flying Officer, Flight Lieutenant, Squadron Leader; and in the Army to Lieutenant, Captain and Major.

Lieutenant (Lt Army) — A title of French origin meaning one who acts as a substitute for a Captain, Colonel or General. The rank today is senior to a Second Lieutenant and junior to a Captain, and equates to Sub-Lieutenant in the RN and to Flying Officer in the RAF. The junior Lieutenants are known as Second Lieutenants, for which there is no equivalent in the RN but equates to Pilot Officer in the RAF.

Lieutenant (First) — A Royal Navy term used to describe an executive officer, sometimes the second in command. He may also be called 'Number One' or the 'Jimmy'.

Lieutenant-Colonel (Lt Col) — A rank between Major and Colonel which equates to Wing Commander in the RAF and Commander in the RN.

Lieutenant-General (Lt Gen) — A rank between Major-General and General which equates to Air Marshal in the RAF and Vice-Admiral in the RN.

Lock, Stock and Barrel — Today describing the whole lot, the term formerly described the flintlock which consisted of three main components: the lock (firing mechanism), the stock and the barrel.

Magazine — The compartment of a ship specially designed to store ammunition and pyrotechnics.

Major (Maj) — Meaning a 'greater' or more important person than a company officer. It is the rank next above Captain and one below Lieutenant-Colonel in the Army, and equates to Lieutenant-Commander in the RN and Squadron Leader in the RAF.

Major-General (Maj Gen) — The rank above Brigadier but below Lieutenant-General. Formerly the title was Sergeant-Major General, but the 'Sergeant' was dropped in the late 19th century. The rank equates to Rear-Admiral in the Navy and to Air Vice-Marshal in the RAF.

Marines (Royal) — Originally the marines were the fighting men of a ship while the seamen were concerned with the sailing of the ship. The first corps of marines raised from the RN was titled the Admiral's Marine Regiment, commanded by the Duke of York. In 1802 they gained the title Royal Marines from King George III to honour their bravery during the French Revolution. The Royal Marines motto is 'By Land or Sea'. They now specialise in amphibious operations, being organised into commandos. A Royal Marine officer afloat always assumes the next rank up, eg, a RM Captain would become a Major.

Master — The title given to the commander of a merchant vessel (*see* Captain). In the days of old, the master was the ship's navigator and the ship's owner was the captain.

Master-at-Arms — This title came from that of the ship's Corporal and was introduced into the Navy during the reign of Charles I. Today the title refers to the Chief Petty Officer responsible for the good order and discipline of the crew. He is often referred to as the ship's policeman.

Master Mariner (M Mar) — A qualification of competency to command a merchant vessel.

Mate — A Merchant Navy title to describe qualified ships' officers (*see* Captain).

Medal — The generic term loosely used to cover all orders, decorations and awards. Strictly, it should only refer to those medals generally issued for campaigns, long service and impeccable character.

Mess — This may come from the Latin word *Mensa,* a table, or more realistically, from Gothic *mes* meaning a dish of food. On board ship the term mess deck refers to the sailors' dining hall. It may also refer to living accommodation aboard ship. There is also the French word *messe* from which it may be derived.

Midshipman — The name was originally given to men and boys stationed amidships who carried messages or, in battle, conveyed ammunition to the gun decks. Before 1815 the rank was associated with ratings. It was in 1813 that the term Midshipman became a rank associated with the sons of gentlemen. The idea was that prospective Naval officers should have a thorough grounding in seaman skills while at the same time understudying the ships' officers. The slang term given to a Midshipman in those early days was that of a 'Snotty', which referred to the young boys who on first going to sea were frequently homesick and seasick. Brass buttons were added to the cuff of a Midshipman's jacket to prevent him wiping his nose on it. Today, Midshipman is the most junior rank in the Navy and considered by some to be technically a rate and not a rank at all. The rank is held by those undergoing their first period of training. In the RAF the rank equates to Pilot Officer in standing, but is technically junior to it.

Mortar — The first recorded use of a mortar was by Charles VIII of France when he captured Naples in 1495. Trials with mortars began in England as early as 1579. However, it was Menno van Coehoan, a Dutch military engineer, who in 1674 began developing the more traditional trench mortar. The definition of a mortar is a high elevation ordnance which 'throws' a comparatively light projectile.

Mufti — The term refers to an official class of men in India who interpreted the law; the ship's chaplain, who 'interpreted the divine law', was often called a 'Mufti'. Since the chaplain always wore plain (civilian) clothes as opposed to uniform the word came to mean someone dressed in civilian clothes.

Ordinary Seaman — The most junior non-commissioned rating in the RN, one rate below Leading Seaman. In the RAF the rate (rank) equates to Leading Aircraftman.

Ordnance — A collective noun for guns or military stores.

Other Rank (OR) — A term which replaced 'rank and file' to denote soldiers below commissioned rank.

Petard — A petard was an old type of mine invented by the Huguenots in 1579 and used by Henry IV at the Battle of Cahors in 1580. From this weapon comes the saying 'Hoist with his own Petard', used by Shakespeare in *Hamlet*.

Petty Officer (PO) — A rating of the seaman branch between Leading Seaman and Chief Petty Officer. In the RAF the rank equates to Sergeant, as it does in the Army.

Pipe — This term refers to an order or information passed either by use of the Boatswain's Call or by making short warnings followed by the spoken word. Example orders might be: 'Pipe dinner', 'Pipe ease to lifelines'.

Pebble Monkey — A popular slang term used in the RAF to describe young RAF Regiment officers (*see* Rock Ape).

Plonk — This word dates from the First World War and is a corruption and mispronouncement of the French word 'blanc' as in 'vin blanc'.

Pilot Officer — Most junior commissioned officer in the RAF, equivalent to a Second Lieutenant (*see* also Lieutenant).

Pistol — A hand-held weapon that feeds cartridges from a box magazine rather than a revolving chamber. The origin of the pistol is a little obscure but it appears to have come into favour in Henry VIII's time, having been brought from Italy.

Pitched Battle — This is nothing to do with the Naval pitch or indeed pouring boiling oil over the uninvited guest scaling a castle. Rather, the term is related to pitching tents or campsites. Traditionally in mediaeval times, battles were held at pre-arranged spots and at a pre-arranged time with each massing before the other (part of the bluff and counter-bluff). Thus, from pitched camps the boys went off for a pitched battle.

Poop — This is a part of the ship from which soldiers fought before the introduction of big guns. It was a development of the ancient after castles (*see* Forecastle) constructed as a raised deck towards the rear of the ship from which sailing ships were steered and commanded, and under which the ship's officers were accommodated.

Private — The early interpretation was 'Private man' meaning a man who was responsible only for himself. Up to the end of the 17th century a soldier was described as a 'private centinel', 'one of a hundred', which was the normal strength of a company. In the RAF the rank equates to Aircraftman.

Prune — Pilot Officer Prune was a mythical aircrew figure (pilot) created during the Second World War as an example of everything a pilot should not be. His exploits became famous as a way of expressing to aircrews the need for flight safety. From time to time there have been movements to resurrect this character in the RAF flight safety magazine *Air Clues*. His modern-day counterpart is a further mythical creation called Wing Commander Spry, who unlike Prune knows all the answers; his moustache bears a striking likeness to that of a Prune.

Pusser — A slang RN term referring to the ship's paymaster and still applied to officers of the supply and secretarial specialisation. The term is derived from the word purser, and is in common usage by the RN and RM to mean Naval equipment. It can also mean of good quality.

Quarter Deck — This was originally defined as the upper deck between the mainmast and the poop where the officers' quarters were located. Naval etiquette requires all persons to salute when coming on the quarter deck. The starboard side of the ship in port and the weather side at sea are reserved for the use of ship's officers, and ceremonial duties are performed there. The term may also be used to refer to a division of seamen responsible for the rear part of a ship.

Quarter Master General (QMG) — The member of the Army Board who is responsible for all quartering.

Rate — The grade below the rank of officer granted by Captains according to qualification and seniority. The ratings start at Junior Seaman, which equates to Aircraftman in the RAF, and rises to Fleet Chief Petty Officer, which equates to the RAF's Warrant Officer.

Rating — A seaman (non-commissioned) holding a rate.

Regiment — A title which has no tactical significance. The word comes from the Latin *regimen,* meaning a rule of system of order. The size and organization of a regiment may vary considerably. In foreign armies it is a tactical formation equivalent to a British brigade.

Rock Ape — A slang term used by the RAF to describe members of the RAF Regiment. The origin dates back to a brief period during the Second World War when members of this exemplary corps were responsible for the care and welfare of the Gibraltar Apes. Any resemblance between the apes and the members of this corps is purely coincidental!

Rubber — The strip of wood, sometimes called a transom, found on the outside of a ship running from stem to stern level with or just below the

gunwale, to protect and strengthen the side of the boat.

Run the Gauntlet — This is nothing to do with 'throwing down the Gauntlet' as in a challenge, but is a corruption from the Swedish word 'gatlopp' which meant a running lane. In the Swedish Army one of the field punishments was for the offender to run between two lines of men who carried sticks or rope ends. The idea was to knock hell out of the offender before he reached the end of the lane, and thus had nothing to do with gloves or Knightlyness at all.

Sam Browne — The leather belt with cross straps worn by Army officers on ceremonial occasions. The belt was invented by General Sir Samuel Browne, VC in 1860. He had lost an arm and required a more convenient method of carrying a sword and revolver for his encounters on the Indian North-West Frontier. It came into general Army use between 1870 and 1880 and is now also worn by Warrant Officers class I.

Sapper (Spr) — The rank given to a Royal Engineer Private soldier. The word is from the French *sapeur.* The Royal Sappers and Miners were formed in 1772 to build gun emplacements and ammunition storage facilities. The primary duty of the Royal Engineer Corps today is to provide technical engineering support to infantry and armoured forces alike, from mine laying to bridge building to airfield construction. Special squadrons of Royal Engineers are attached to the Harrier force and RAF stations in Germany.

Scran — Royal Navy and Royal Marine term often used to describe a meal. A scran bag was a locker where a sailor could store his few cherished possessions.

Sergeant (Sgt) — A senior non-commissioned officer, derived from the Latin *serviens,* which means serving, via the French *sergent.* The rank equates to Sergeant in the RAF and is marked by three chevrons worn on the sleeve. There are no Sergeants in the Household Cavalry. The equivalent to a Sergeant-Major is Corporal-Major. In the RN the rank equates to Petty Officer.

Show a Leg — A Naval expression dating from the time ladies were allowed on board to provide home comforts to the sailors. When a ship was under threat from attack the Boatswain would chase around the decks to wake up the sailors from their hammocks. So as not to disturb the ladies he would cry 'show a leg', thus being able to determine the sex of the hammock occupier.

Sideburns — From the American General Ambrose Everett Burnside (1824-81) who was renowned for his incompetence; he also wore side whiskers. His incompetence was summarised as putting the cart before the horse, hence sideburns.

Slush Fund — This term has nothing to do with British Leyland and owes its origin to the Royal Navy. Cooks would render down the fat and tallow from carcases which they would then sell to the Purser. From this the Purser (pronounced pusser) would make 'pussers candles' which he would then sell back to the sailors. The fat was known simply as slush and hence the 'slush fund'.

Snowdrop — Slang term used to describe an RAF policeman, taken from the white cap cover worn by RAF policeman on their service dress peaked cap; is not a derogatory term.

Splice the main brace — A traditional naval phrase authorising an extra issue of spirit or grog to all entitled, including officers.

Subaltern — A title given to an officer below the rank of Captain. The title comes from the French word *subalterne,* meaning inferior to or subordinate.

Tank (Armoured) — Tank is not an acronym or a word of any deep meaning. When the first prototype tanks were produced under the direction of Sir Ernest Swinton they were moved in secret to the front line and labelled 'Bulk Water Carriers', referred to those in the know as 'wink wink', 'nod, nod', tanks. The name simply stuck. The German Panzer does not mean tank, but armoured.

Tattoo —Originally the beat of a drum or bugle call sounded at 2200 hrs. To 'tap to' was the signal for soldiers to leave the alehouse and return to barracks. The title is now used to mean a display.

Tommy (as in soldier) — In 1815 the first account or pay books were issued to soldiers. The specimen form issued to show how to fill in the personal details described one Thomas Atkins — hence 'Tommy' as a general name for a British soldier.

Trap — An expression used by sailors and Marines meaning a quest for female companionship, as in 'to trap a blonde for the night'.

Trapper — An RAF description meaning an examiner — for example, flying instructors responsible for certificating other instructors and later ensuring that instructors maintain the required standards. It has more recently been used to describe members of the directing staff at training stations.

Troop — The literal meaning is a collection of people, and comes from the French *troupe.*

Wardroom — The term given by the RN to the Officers' Mess. In the early days there was a compartment aboard large ships called the wardrobe, which was used to store valuable articles taken from captured ships. There were normally officers' quarters near by. When the wardrobe was empty, the room was used by the officers as a lounge, and possibly also for meals. In time the need for a wardrobe ceased, and the new name wardroom evolved.

Warrant Officer — An officer who holds a warrant rather than a commission. The warrant is conferred by the Sovereign. There are two classes of warrant; class I equates to an RAF Warrant Officer and class II between Flight Sergeant and Warrant Officer. A Warrant Officer class I might be a Regimental Sergeant Major, Master Gunner or similar. A Warrant Officer class II would be a Company Sergeant Major.

Wazzer — This term, which may be shortened to Waz, is a complimentary term meaning of a good standard, even exemplary. Its usage is confined to the Navy and Marines, with occasional use in the Army. The RAF understanding is not polite, and describes a field activity forced on the individual through lack of facilities.

Wing —A collective RAF term describing two or more squadrons, equivalent in the Army to a battalion formation.

Yeomanry — Originally volunteer part-time cavalry who were part of the Territorial Army. The Yeomanry units that survive today are armoured or artillery regiments within the TA.

Bibliography

The following books were researched in the writing of this book:

A History of the Regiments and Uniforms of the British Army, Major R. M. Barnes (Seeley Service and Co: London) 1962

For Valour: The Air VCs, Chaz Bowyer (William Kimber and Co Ltd: London) 1978

Military Customs, Major T. J. Edwards (Gale & Polden Ltd: Aldershot) 1950

Orders, Medals and Decorations of Britain and Europe, Paul Hieronymussen (Blandford Press: Poole, Dorset) 1967

Military Origins, Major Lawrence Gordon (Kaye and Ward: London) 1971

Ribbons and Medals, Captain H. Tapprell Dorling RN (George Philip and Son Ltd: London) 1963

Badges and Insignia of the British Armed Services, W. E. May, W. Y. Carman, J. Tanner (Adam and Charles Black: London) 1974

Officers Mess Life and Customs in the Regiments, Lt Col R. J. Dickinson (Midas Books: Tunbridge Wells) 1973

Jane's Dictionary of Military Terms, P. H. C. Hayward (Macdonald and Jane's: London) 1975

We Joined the Navy, Robert Burgess & Ronald Blackburn (Charles Black & Co: London)

Jane's Dictionary of Naval Terms, J. Palmer (Macdonald and Jane's: London) 1975

Customs and Traditions of the Royal Navy, Cdr A. B. Campbell (Gate and Polden: Aldershot) 1956

Customs and Traditions of the Royal Air Force, Peter Hering (Gale and Polden: Aldershot) 1961

Debrett's Correct Form, Patrick Montague-Smith (Kelly's Directories: London) 1970

Debrett's Etiquette and Modern Manners, Elsie Burch Donald (Debrett's Peerage Ltd: London) 1981

Customs of the Services, A. H. Stradling (Gale and Polden Ltd: Aldershot) 1966

Action Stations 1, Michael J. F. Bowyer (Patrick Stephens Ltd: Cambridge) 1979

AP 3236 – Works of the Second World War (The Air Ministry/HMSO: London) 1956

Action Stations 4, Bruce Barrymore Halpenny (Patrick Stephens Ltd: Cambridge) 1982

The Squadrons of the RAF, James J. Halley (Air Britain Publications: Tonbridge, Kent) 1980

Royal Air Force Squadron Badges, Peter C. Smith (Balfour: St. Ives, Huntington) 1974

AP 1358 – Dress Regulations for the RAF, MOD (HMSO: London) 1981

AP 818 – Drill and Ceremonial in the RAF, MOD (HMSO: London) 1961

History of the Indian Air Force, Air Marshal M. S. Chaturvedi (Vikas Publishing House PVT Ltd: India) 1978

Attack Warning Red, Derek Wood (Macdonald and Jane's: London) 1976

RNZAF A Short History, Geoffrey Bentley (A. H. & A. W. Reed, Wellington: New Zealand) 1969

History of The Royal Canadian Air Force, Christopher Shores (Arms & Armour Press: USA)

Rhodesia & the RAF (Hortons Ltd: Johannesburg) February 1945

RCAF Squadrons and Aircraft, S. Kostenuk and J. Griffen

Index